# CAESAR TO CHARLEMAGNE:

## THE BEGINNINGS OF FRANCE

*by the same author:*

THE BIRTH OF WESTERN ECONOMY
(1961)

# ROBERT LATOUCHE

# Caesar to Charlemagne

## the beginnings of France

*Translated by*
JENNIFER NICHOLSON

WITH 195 ILLUSTRATIONS
AND 7 MAPS

LONDON: PHOENIX HOUSE

BARNES & NOBLE, Inc. NY, NY 1968
BOOKSELLERS · PUBLISHERS · SINCE 1873

11969

SBN: 460 07728 7

# CONTENTS

# CONTENTS

CONTENTS

# ILLUSTRATIONS

Acknowledgement where not otherwise specifically made is due to the National Library of France. The abbreviation M.A.N. stands for *Musée d'Antiquités Nationale, Saint-Germain-en-Laye.*

xi

*page*

# MAPS

---

# PREFACE TO THE
# ENGLISH EDITION

THE work which follows was originally published in French under the title *Gaulois et Francs*. My object in writing it was to record the origins of the Kingdom of France in the period between Caesar's conquest of Gaul and the dissolution of Charlemagne's empire in 843. To do this I collected the most important original texts, and supplemented my translation of them (they were all written in Latin) by a commentary designed to meet the requirements of the wide public for whom the book was intended.

The book attracted attention in England, and I am grateful to Mr Anthony Dent for suggesting its publication in English by Phoenix House. In return I felt it would be appropriate that in the English edition some space should be devoted to Great Britain. The three chapters which have been added to the original work, short as they are, will show what striking parallels exist between the history of our two nations, in spite of divergences, for which there is usually a geographical explanation.

In the first of the new chapters I remind my readers that Gaul was conquered by the Roman armies, but that Caesar, who landed in Britain on two occasions in the course of his campaigns, had to leave the difficult task of British integration into the Roman Empire to his successors; in fact the Claudian conquest of Britain was never completed, and one of the most striking proofs of the Roman failure is that the conquerors were never able to impose their language on the natives, though on the other side of the Channel the Gaulish tongue was ousted by Vulgar Latin.

Britain, like Gaul, suffered the invasions of the Germanic peoples from the third century onwards, and there is another parallel between the conquest of Gaul by the Franks and that of Britain by the Anglo-Saxons. Tne second of my new chapters deals with the Anglo-Saxon conquest, and some of the legends which have grown up round it.

There is common ground again in the Christianization of the two countries, and this too is worth study. As in Gaul, the native population was the first to find grace, and St Patrick, the apostle of Ireland, can be compared with St Martin of Tours. But the Anglo-Saxons clung fiercely to their pagan traditions, and were less ready than the Franks to listen to the persuasions of their missionaries. It was not until the end of the sixth century, and the mission of that energetic pope St Gregory the Great, that they accepted Christianity. On both sides of the Channel the final triumph of Christianization was the baptism of a king. We can read in detail in the works of the Venerable Bede of the conversion of Edwin, King of Kent; it parallels the conversion of Clovis, recorded by Gregory of Tours in his *History of the Franks*.

# INTRODUCTION

THE kingdom of France was born in 843 with the Treaty of Verdun, and strictly speaking Charles the Bald was the first of the French kings. I have stressed this in an earlier book on mediaeval France, in which I took that date as my starting-point. The choice I made then was perfectly legitimate; and yet we cannot ignore the fact that it is the past which dictates the present. When we see a baby in the cradle, it is instinctive to turn from our study of him to his parents, to try to trace resemblances and discover what has shaped the childish features.

The historian is apt to do the same. In his study of the infant France, he is tempted to go back through the centuries, seeking out in the past whatever it was that moulded her features. But the task is difficult indeed, for there are very few documents, either in writing or in the the plastic arts, to show the successive stages by which Gaul became France. Through all the centuries before the Roman conquest the ancestors of modern France are dumb, and we can only echo the great historian Ferdinand Lot: 'How happy we should be to possess just one page of the language our ancestors spoke! How reverently we should pore over every word! But that is a satisfaction we shall never know.' (*49*: p. 96.)

The discoveries of prehistoric archaeology to some extent make up for this silence; the many Palaeolithic and Neolithic sites of ancient Gaul which have been discovered and excavated take us back to a distant past, and are proof that the region was inhabited in very early times.

The appearance of the Celts, the true ancestors of the French, was a great historical event which unfortunately is still obscure. Its date, the circumstances in which Gaul was occupied by the Celts, their origin and provenance, are all problems which await satisfactory solution and will perhaps never find it. When did they come—about 1000 B.C., or not until four or five hundred years later? Where did they come from? No one knows. Did they come as conquerors, driving out the people they found settled in Gaul, or did they mingle peacefully with them? This second hypothesis is perhaps the more likely, but some historians go further still and think that the Celts were one of the Neolithic races already inhabiting Gaul.

But here I shall leave the prehistorian to probe into the mysteries of the past, and simply begin this collection of texts at the time when Gaul became Roman. Caesar is my first author, and the introduction to this history will be the passages he wrote on Vercingetorix, the defender of Gaul's independence. A strange paradox, but one to which we must resign ourselves, for Caesar's *Gallic Wars* are almost our only source of information on the first of France's national heroes.

Gaul was gradually Romanized in the course of the two centuries which followed Caesar's victory. Despite her Celtic past, she was destined to take her place as part of the bloc of Latin countries, even though she never surrendered her own fundamental character. We shall follow this evolution step by step; it was not without incident.

Then Gaul was Christianized; but the conversion which began in the second half of the second century A.D. was a slow process, and lasted until the fifth century. The Barbarians arrived just as it was ending, and their conquest of Gaul, sometimes accomplished by force and sometimes by infiltration, was made the easier by the growing weakness of a power which no longer wore the halo of sanctity conferred on it by emperor-worship.

The barbarian settlements were many and diverse, as a series of different Germanic peoples sought to establish themselves in Gaul. In the mid fifth century it looked as though the Visigoths were destined to become masters of Gaul. Things turned out differently; the future lay with the Salic Franks, with no better reason than chance and the luck of a clever soldier to account for Clovis's success. It may be added, though, that his rapid triumph was helped on by his well-timed conversion to Catholicism, which won him the support of the influential Gallo-Roman episcopate. From the time of Clovis, Roman Gaul was Frankish Gaul, soon to become France.

Though Clovis was a great king, or at least though his reign is one of the landmarks in the history of France, the Merovingian dynasty he founded is not remembered for its virtues. For the most part his descendants were either profligates or ambitious vulgarians. Seen through the eyes of the great chronicler of the sixth century, Gregory of Tours, who never attempted to disguise the defects of his contemporaries, the Merovingian period has little to commend it. All we need do for the moment is to note how the idea of the common weal had almost entirely disappeared. The old Roman concept of the *respublica* seemed to have perished.

The prestige of the 'kingdom of the Franks' was restored under the first Carolingians, who sought to justify their usurpation by coronation ceremonies designed to confer a religious character on kingship. Charlemagne stands out among them all, shedding incomparable lustre on the Frankish monarchy at the end of the eighth century. But although the essential elements which were to make up France were already to hand, there was as yet no kingdom of France; there was only a vast, ill-defined agglomeration still in process of expansion, especially to eastward—so much so that in the end, under Charlemagne, it comprised almost the whole of western and central Europe. The hexagon of territory which was to be known as France, with Paris and the Île de France at its centre, took shape only in the mid ninth century, and then imperfectly, when the Frankish empire was divided among the grandsons of Charlemagne; but by that time, after long and patient human effort, the kingdom of France would be ready to become a reality.

# REFERENCES

English translations are given, where available, of works of which
the French text was quoted in the original text of *Gaulois et
Francs*. The sources quoted have been arranged alphabetically
and numbered; each quotation is ascribed in the text by the
number of the work in the following list.

1. *Actus Pontificum Cenomannis in urbe degentium*, Le Mans, 1901.
2. Alcuin, in *Mon. Germ. hist. epistolarum*, iv, ed. E. Dümmler, Berlin, 1895.
3. Ammianus Marcellinus, *The Roman History*, trans. C. D. Yonge (Bohn's Classical Library), London, 1862.
4. *Annales regni Francorum*, ed. F. Kurze, Hannover, 1895.
5. Aurelius Victor, *De Caesaribus*, ed. F. Pichlmayr, Leipzig, 1911.
6. Ausonius, *Works*, trans. Hugh G. Evelyn White (Loeb Classical Library), 2 vols., London, 1919–21.
7. Babut, E. C., *Saint Martin de Tours*, Paris, 1913.
8. Baehrens, G., ed. *XII Panegyrici Latini*, Leipzig, 1874.
9. Bede, *Ecclesiastical History of England*, ed. J. A. Giles (Bohn's Antiquarian Library), London, 1881.
10. Blanchet, A., *Les Enceintes Romaines de la Gaule*, Paris, 1907.
11. Boniface, St, *Opera*, in *Patrologia Latina*, lxxxix, ed. J. P. Migne, Paris, 1863.
12. Caesar, *The Gallic War*, trans. H. J. Edwards (Loeb Classical Library), London, 1917.
13. ——, *War Commentaries*, trans. John Warrington (Everyman's Library), London, 1953.
14. Caesarius, St, in *Histoire de Nice*, Nice, 1951.
15. Chlodovald, St, *Vita sancti Chlodovaldi*, ed. B. Krusch, in *Mon. Germ. hist. script. rerum Merov.*, ii, Hannover, 1888.
16. *Concilia aevi merovingici*, ed. F. Maasen, in *Mon. Germ.*, *Concilia*, i, Hannover, 1893.

17. Coulanges, Fustel de, *La Gaule romaine*, Paris, 1891.
18. Dio Cassius, *Roman History*, trans. Earnest Cary (Loeb Classical Library), 9 vols., London, 1914–27.
19. Donnadieu, A., *La Pompéi de la Provence, Fréjus*, Paris, 1927.
20. Dottin, G., *Manuel pour servir a l'étude de l'antiquité celtique*, Paris, 1915.
21. Einhard, *Life of the Emperor Karl the Great*, trans. William Glaister, London, 1877.
22. Eucherius, *Libellus de Laude Eremi*, in *Patrologia Latina*, l, ed. J. P. Migne, Paris, 1846.
23. Eusebius of Caesarea, *Church History*, trans. A. C. McGiffert, 1890 (*Nicene and Post-Nicene Fathers*, I).
24. Fabia, P., *La Table claudienne de Lyon*, Lyons, 1929.
25. Fortunatus, *Opera*, in *Patrologia Latina*, lxxxviii, ed. J. P. Migne, Paris, 1862.
26. Fredegar: *Chronicarum quae dicuntur Fredegarii libri IV*, in *Mon. Germ. hist. script. rerum Merov.*, ii, ed. B. Krusch, Hannover, 1888.
27. Gregory of Tours, *Opera*, in *Mon. Germ. hist. script. rerum Merov.*, i, ed. W. Arndt and B. Krusch, Hannover, 1885.
28. ——, *History of the Franks*, trans. O. M. Dalton, 2 vols., Oxford, 1927.
29. Halphen, L., *Grégoire de Tours, historien de Clovis*, in *Mélanges Ferdinand Lot*, Paris, 1825.
30. Hilary, St, *Opera*, in *Patrologia Latina*, x, ed. J. P. Migne, Paris, 1844.
31. Hist. Aug., *Scriptores Historiae Augustae*, ed. A. Peter, 2 vols., Leipzig, 1865.
32. Honoratus, St, *Sermo de vita s. Hororati*, in *Patrologia Latina*, l, ed. J. P. Migne, Paris, 1846.
33. Jerome, St, *Opera*, in *Patrologia Latina*, xxii, ed. J. P. Migne, Paris, 1864.
34. Jonas, *Vita s. Columbani abbatis*, in *Patrologia Latina*, lxxxvii, ed. J. P. Migne, Paris, 1863.
35. Julian, *Works*, trans. W. C. Wright (Loeb Classical Library), 3 vols., London, 1913–23.
36. Jullian, C., *Inscriptions romaines de Bordeaux*, 2 vols., Bordeaux, 1887.
37. ——, *Histoire de la Gaule*, 8 vols., Paris, 1908–13.
38. Kurth, G., *Clovis*, Brussels, 1923.
39. Latouche, R., *Textes d'histoire médiévale*, Paris, 1951.
40. ——, *Histoire de Nice*, Nice, 1951.
41. Leclercq, Dom, in *Dictionnaire d'archéologie chrétienne*, 2 vols., Paris, 1903–11.
42. Leodegar, St, *Vita s. Leodegarii*, in *Patrologia Latina*, xcvi, ed. J. P. Migne, Paris, 1862.
43. Levi-Provençal, E., *Histoire de l'Espagne musulmane*, Paris, 1950.
44. *Liber historiae Francorum*, in *Mon. Germ. hist. script. rerum Merov.*, ii, ed. B. Krusch, Hannover, 1888.

REFERENCES

45. *Liber Pontificalis*, ed. L. Duchesne, 2 vols., Paris, 1886.

46. Lot, F., *Les Destinées de l'Empire en Occident*, Paris, 1940.

47. ——, *La Fin du monde antique*, Paris, 1951.

48. ——, *Les Invasiones germaniques*, Paris, 1935.

49. ——, *La Gaule*, Paris, 1947.

50. ——, *La Naissance de la France*, Paris, 1948.

51. Lucan, *Pharsalia*, trans. H. T. Riley (Bohn's Classical Library), London, 1853.

52. Maurois, A., *A History of England*, trans. Hamish Miles, London, 1956.

53. Monceaux, P., *Saint Martin*, Paris, 1927.

54. *Monumenta Germ. hist. script. rerum. Merov.*, i, ed. W. Arndt, Hannover, 1884.

55. Nennius, *History of the Britons*, in *Six Old English Chronicles*, ed. J. A. Giles (Bohn's Antiquarian Library), London, 1885.

56. Nibelungs: *The Fall of the Nibelungs*, trans. Margaret Armour (Everyman's Library), London, 1908.

57. Paulus Orosius, *Seven Books of History against the Pagans*, trans. I. W. Raymond, Columbia, 1966.

58. Pflaum, H. G., in *Bibliothèque de l'École des Hautes Études, Sciences philologiques et historiques*, fasc. 293, Paris, 1948.

59. Pliny, *Natural History*, trans. J. Bostock and H. T. Riley (Bohn's Classical Library), 6 vols., London, 1855-7.

60. Plutarch, *Lives*, trans. Dryden, rev. Arthur Hugh Clough (Everyman's Library), 3 vols., London, 1910.

61. Poëte, M., *Une Vie de Cité*, Paris, 1924.

62. Prosper of Aquitaine, *Chronica*, in *Mon. Germ. hist.*, *Auctorum Antiquissimorum*, ix, ed. T. Mommsen, Berlin, 1892.

63. Pseudo-Fredegar, in *Mon. Germ. hist. script. rerum Merov.*, ii, ed. B. Krusch, Hannover, 1888.

64. Ricolfi, H., *Mémorial de Contes*, Nice, 1942.

65. Salvian, *A Treatise of God's government*, London, 1700.

66. Sidonius Apollinaris, *Letters*, trans. O. M. Dalton, 2 vols., Oxford, 1915.

67. ——, *Poems and Letters*, trans. W. B. Anderson, 2 vols., London, 1936.

68. Stein, H., *Date et destinataire de l'Histoire Auguste*, Paris, 1953.

69. Strabo, *Geography*, trans. H. C. Hamilton and W. Falconer (Bohn's Classical Library), 3 vols., London, 1854-7.

70. Sulpicius Severus, *Opera*, ed. Fr. Dübner, Paris, 1890.

71. Tacitus, *Historical Works*, trans. Arthur Murphy (Everyman's Library), 2 vols., London, 1908.

*Part I*

# THE ROMAN CONQUEST

# VERCINGETORIX

THE Roman conquest (58–51 B.C.) is the first decisive event in French history which we can follow in written documents. What were its causes? Chief among them, and a deciding factor in the history of the West for several centuries, was the drive and energy of the Roman people. Once they had seized Spain, at the end of the Punic Wars, they went on to occupy southern Gaul, now to become Gallia Narbonensis, so as to safeguard the route between their two Mediterranean peninsulas. Next their mounting ambition turned to the rest of Gaul, all the more urgently because the invasions of Cimbri and Teutons gave good cause for fear that they would soon have to reckon with Germanic competition there.

An attack on the Helvetii by the Suevi under their ambitious leader Ariovistus gave Caesar the motive, or the pretext, for intervening in Gaul. It is possible that the intention of conquering the whole of Gaul was in his mind from the start; we may well suppose that this was so.

## The Gallic Resistance

The name of Vercingetorix has come to symbolize Gallic resistance to the Romans. He made his appearance comparatively late in the struggle —not until the end of 53 B.C., though Caesar's conquest of Gaul had begun in 58; and only in Book VII of the *Commentaries* does Caesar introduce him to his readers and show him taking a leading part in the general conspiracy which followed the massacre of the Roman citizens of Genabum (Orleans):

'Vercingetorix was a young Arvernian who wielded enormous influence. His father, Celtillus, had exercised a kind of general jurisdiction over the whole of Gaul, and had been murdered by his immediate subjects for attempting to make himself absolute ruler. Vercingetorix mobilized his retainers and was quickly joined by others as soon as his purpose became known. Some of the chiefs, including his uncle Gobbanitio, tried to dissuade him on the grounds that his enterprise was far too risky. Driven from Gergovia, he did not lose heart, but went through the countryside gathering a band of beggars and outcasts. Thenceforward he succeeded in winning over every Arvernian he met. Calling upon them to take arms in defence of Gallic liberty, he soon mustered a powerful force and expelled his opponents in their turn. He was now proclaimed king by his followers, and sent ambassadors all

1. Gaulish warrior. Terra cotta statuette, broken at the legs; note earrings, oval buckler and pleated tunic. Roman.

2. Gold coin of the Veneti (Armorica).

3. Gold stater of the Bituriges Cubi.

4. Helmeted head of Vercingetorix. Arvernian coin.

5. Heads of Roman soldiers, from a bas-relief found at Saintes.

over the country urging the tribes to stand by him in the approaching conflict. Before long he had won support in districts as far apart as Sens, Paris, Poitiers, Cahors, Tours, Evreux, Limoges, Angers and the whole Atlantic seaboard. Armed with this power, he demanded hostages from all his allied states, ordered each of them to furnish a specified number of troops without delay, and gave directions for the manufacture of a fixed quota of arms by a certain date, with special attention to cavalry requirements. Thorough in everything, he backed his authority with a savage discipline that would tolerate no wavering; more serious cases were punished with torture and the stake, while those guilty in a less degree were sent home without their ears, or perhaps with one eye gouged out, to serve as a warning to others of the stern penalties a delinquent might expect.' (*13*: pp. 117–18.)

Caesar adds that this terrorism contributed in no small measure to the recruitment of an army; but we must not forget that this is an enemy's judgment, and the rebels may be credited with other and nobler motives.

5

6. Battle between Romans and barbarians. Bronze sword–belt, Roman.

Caesar himself speaks several times of the love of freedom which inspired Vercingetorix. It was this desire of the Gauls to preserve their independence, this kind of instinctive patriotism, which in the end—and despite civil war and the dissensions of rival factions—succeeded in banding together most of the cities of Gaul against Rome, their common enemy.

The greatness of Vercingetorix was that he had the prestige and authority he needed to impose his will regardless of the dissensions all about him. That he was popular with the common people, even though he was nobly born, shows that he knew how to handle the mob.

## The Siege of Avaricum

But though Vercingetorix was a popular leader, he was also an able tactician who knew how to adapt himself to his circumstances. His first reverses in the struggle against Caesar convinced him that he must change his tactics, and we are told how he expounded the method he was thinking of adopting in a sort of council of war at the beginning of the siege of Avaricum (Bourges):

'Their first endeavour [he said] must be to deprive the Romans of forage and other supplies—an easy matter, considering the Gauls were strong in cavalry, and also had the season in their favour; there was no grass to cut, so the enemy would have to disperse over the countryside to get hay from the farms, and these small isolated parties could be mopped up one by one. Second, all rights of private ownership must be sacrificed in the common interest; villages and farms must be burned everywhere along the Roman line of march, and on each side of it as far as their foragers could possibly reach. The Gauls [he added] were abundantly supplied with such necessities, and could draw on the resources of the local tribes. The Romans, on the other hand, were faced with sure starvation, which they could avoid only by going dangerously far from camp in search of food, and it would then be immaterial whether they were killed outright or simply deprived of their transport,

7. Julius Caesar. Denarius of P. Clodius, 41 B.C.

8. Vercingetorix in captivity (?). Denarius of L. Hostilius Saserna, c.48 B.C.

9. Roman legionary. Tombstone.

the loss of which must, in any case, render their campaign impossible. Finally, all towns would have to be burned unless they were clearly impregnable on account of their natural strength or their fortifications.

'These measures, he acknowledged, might be thought unfair and even terribly cruel; but he urged his hearers to remember that the alternative was infinitely worse: slavery for their wives and children, death for themselves—the universal fate of conquered peoples.' (*13*: pp. 121–2.)

These are the words which Caesar puts into the mouth of Vercingetorix. They have often been quoted by modern historians, though not without reserves on their authenticity. The most tolerant view is that even if Caesar's version of the harangue is not word for word what Vercingetorix said, it is on the whole an accurate report, for Caesar was kept informed of everything that went on in the enemy's councils of war; garrulity and jealousy were common failings of the Gallic chieftains, and it would be easy enough to find one who would give him an exact account of the proceedings. But our attitude may perhaps be rather more sceptical, for we know only too well that for the ancients history was not a science but simply a branch of the art of oratory. It did not matter whether a speech had been delivered or not; so long as it was credible, no writer need feel any hesitation about incorporating it in his narrative. Whatever the truth of the matter, it seems probable that Vercingetorix changed his tactics to meet the needs of the situation; but his systematic refusal to join pitched battle laid him open to bitter criticism, even to accusations of treachery. His abandonment of Avaricum gave his critics an excuse for the most damaging attacks; but, if we are to believe Caesar, he was well able to justify himself:

'The Romans, he said, had not won by courage in the open field, but by cunning and expert knowledge of siege craft, with which the Gauls had not much acquaintance. It was, in any case, foolish to expect unvarying success in war: his hearers could bear witness that he had never really liked the idea of defending Bourges, and this setback was due to their having lent unreasoning support to an impracticable scheme of the Bituriges. However, he promised before long to repair the damage with yet greater victories: he was, he said, doing his utmost to win over the tribes that had so far held aloof, and once a really united Gallic league was formed the whole world could not stand against it. Such a league, he assured them, was already on the way to becoming a reality.' (*13*: pp. 128–9.)

8

## Gallic Victories

Whether or not Vercingetorix really delivered this allocution, the months which followed were the most glorious of his career. The revolt spread to all quarters of Gaul, the most spectacular defection being that of the Aeduani, who until then had been the loyal allies of the Romans. Vercingetorix scored a notable success at the siege of Gergovia, where he put his tactics of caution into practice and forced Caesar to raise the siege after suffering a bloody defeat.

But the victory was not crowned by further successes. Perhaps Vercingetorix let the change in his fortunes go to his head. Perhaps the arrival of reinforcements from a number of cities gave him a false idea of his army's power in attack. Perhaps rumours that Caesar was pulling out from independent Gaul encouraged him to abandon his strategy of caution and stake everything on one throw. We cannot be sure; but Caesar and his staff seem to have realized that Vercingetorix's usual coolness and caution were deserting him.

## The Disaster at Alesia

'Vercingetorix formed three camps about nine miles to the south-west. He summoned a meeting of his cavalry commanders and told them the hour of victory was at hand: the Romans were pulling out of Gaul and making for the province. This withdrawal, he argued, might leave Gaul free for the moment, but it would never guarantee lasting peace and security, for they would only return in greater strength and prolong the war indefinitely. He had therefore decided to make a flank attack on the Roman transport column.'

The proposal and the battle orders issued with it were enthusiastically received:

'The men clamoured for a solemn oath forbidding any one who had not ridden at least twice through the Roman lines access to his house and family.' (*13*: pp. 145–6.)

This outburst of enthusiasm was followed by tragic disillusionment; the Gallic cavalry was routed, and after this decisive defeat Vercingetorix could not hold his ground with his infantry alone. He was forced to retreat. He took refuge at Alesia, and there his army perished. The *oppidum* of Alesia was long ago identified, crowning a height of some 1,300 feet. The height is the Mount-Auxois, and the memory of the

10. Air view of the plateau of Alise-Sainte-Reine, the site of Alesia. The Roman theatre can be seen in the middle of the photograph.

Gallic stronghold lives on in the name of the present-day village of Alise-Sainte-Reine (*arrondissement* of Montbard, Côte d'Or) which dominates it. Excavations begun under Napoleon III and still in progress have removed all possible doubt that this is the historic site.

The events of the siege are well known; the circumvallation works of Caesar's army, the vain attempts of Vercingetorix to break out of the investment, the hurried mobilization of a relief army by the Gallic cities, then the final defeat of the Gauls in a bold counter-attack led by Labienus, the best of Caesar's commanders:

'The trenches and rampart had failed against the Gallic assault; fortunately, however, Labienus had been able to concentrate eleven battalions from the redoubts in his sector, and he now sent to warn me of his next move. I hurried forward to be present at this engagement.

'The enemy recognized my scarlet cloak, and then saw my combined force moving down the slopes. . . . As they joined battle both sides raised a cheer which was taken up by the soldiers on the rampart and along the whole line of fortifications. The legionaries dispensed with pikes, and had got to work with their swords when the Gauls suddenly beheld our mounted squadrons in their rear as fresh battalions of infantry closed in from the south. They broke and fled, but were intercepted by the cavalry and mown down. Sedulius, chief magistrate and commander of the Lemovices, was killed; Vercassivellaunus was taken prisoner in the rout; and I was presented with seventy-four Gallic standards. Very few of that great army got back safely to camp. . . . Were it not for the fact that our men were tired out after a long day's work, in the line or in reserve, the entire enemy force might well have been annihilated.' (*13*: p. 156.)

## Vercingetorix Surrenders

It was an irretrievable disaster; Vercingetorix at once took stock of the situation and accepted its tragic consequences.

'On the following day Vercingetorix addressed a meeting of the chiefs,

11. Arvernian stater, bearing name of Vercingetorix.

12. Bronze boar from the Neuvy-en-Sullias hoard.

and explained that he had embarked upon this war not for private ends, but in his country's cause. "Now", he said, "I must bow to the decrees of Fate." He then invited the assembly to palliate the wrath of Rome in whatever way they chose, either by putting him to death or by delivering him up alive. A deputation having referred the matter to me, they were ordered to surrender their weapons together with their leading men; and seated on the entrenchments before my camp, I received the capitulation of Alesia. The chieftains were marched out, Vercingetorix was handed over, and all their arms were stacked.' (*13*: p. 157.)

Almost at once legend began to embroider the theme. As early as the first century A.D., Plutarch amused himself by dramatizing the scene which Caesar had given in such bare outline.

'Vercingetorix [he tells us in his *Lives*], who was the chief spring of all the war, putting his best armour on, and adorning his horse, rode out of the gates, and made a turn about Caesar as he was sitting, then quitting his horse, threw off his armour, and remained quietly sitting at Caesar's feet until he was led away to be reserved for the triumph.' (*60*: vol. ii, p. 551.)

It was not until six years later that this triumph took place (June 46 B.C.). Vercingetorix was led through Rome in the triumphal procession, and was then strangled in the temple of Jupiter Capitolinus. The agony of Gaul's national hero had been protracted indeed. The historian Dio Cassius says that he had looked for a more generous spirit in his conqueror:

'Now Vercingetorix might have escaped, for he had not been captured and was not wounded; but he hoped, since he had once been on friendly terms with Caesar, that he might obtain pardon from him.' (*18*: vol. iii, p. 469.)

From all these sources we get very little idea of Vercingetorix as a man. We have no record of his physical appearance, although when a number of coins struck in his name came to light some scholars thought that the ringleted head which appeared on the obverse of most of them was an idealized portrait of the hero. But the moneyers of Gaul were only clumsily imitating the Greeks of Marseilles; they were trying to reproduce the head of a pagan god, not to portray their country's leaders. As for the character of Vercingetorix, our only informant is Caesar, who knew him well. It is an unfortunate fact that the man who is regarded nowadays as the incarnation of Gallic patriotism, whose name is familiar to every schoolboy in twentieth-century France, was completely over-looked by earlier generations in the land of his birth. The Middle Ages knew nothing of him; in the light of the Graeco-Roman culture of Renaissance and seventeenth-century France, he could only be regarded as the personification of barbarianism. He was ignored throughout the French Revolution and the First Empire. Only after Napoleon III had begun his excavations to throw light on the Gallic Wars did the fame of Vercingetorix begin to spread. Not until 1863 was his statue erected on the plateau of Alise-Sainte-Reine.

# 2

# CAESAR'S VIEW OF
# THE GAULS

IN MANY respects, then, Vercingetorix is still a legendary figure for us. But our ignorance of independent Gaul and her inhabitants is even more deplorable. What exactly was Gaul? There is little enough for our imagination to build on. What was the bond that held together the sixty or so tribes which inhabited Gaul, tribes with individualities so pronounced that their names have survived down to our own days? Here we come up against the illiteracy of the Gauls; not from them can we learn the secret of their patriotism—a patriotism which, in spite of intertribal feuds and bitter rivalries between the cities, roused almost the entire nation in revolt against Rome. Nor have the Gauls left us any record of their institutions; here again we have to turn to Caesar for the background of what is still a very incomplete picture.

## The Various Tribes of Gaul

'Gaul [says Caesar at the beginning of his *Commentaries*], consists of three distinct regions, inhabited respectively by the Belgae, the Aquitani and a people who call themselves Celts, but are known to us as Galli. The boundary between these latter and the Aquitani is the River Garonne, the Marne and Seine forming the Gallo-Belgic frontier. Variations in custom, language and law distinguish these three peoples, of whom the sturdiest are the Belgae. They are remote from the Roman Province, they have infrequent trade contacts with its high culture and

BATAVI

GERMANIA

BRITANNIA

MENAPII

MORINI        NERVII        EBURONES
                            Aduatuca
ATREBATES     Bagacum

AMBIANI   B E L G I U M        TREVERI

Samarabriva   VEROMANDUI
Rotomagus         REMI          MEDIOMATRICI
         BELLOVACI  Duricortora
                                   Divodurum
LEXOVII                            Argentoratum
AULERCI   Lucotocia                LEUCI
EBUROVICES        MELDI

         PARISII

                CARNUTES    Sequana
Condate                              LINGONES
         AULERCI                           Vesontio
         CENOMANI  Genabum   SENONES        SEQUANI
VENETES                                          HELVETII
                            Alesia               Aventicum
NAMNETES ANDECAVI
                TURONES Avaricum          Arar
Portus Namnetum                   Bibracte
         C E L T I       C     A
PICTONES        BITURIGES CUBI  AEDUI

                                Elaver
         Mediolanum                      ALLOBROGES
         Santonum                  Lugdunum      CEUTRONES
SANTONES  LEMOVICES  Gergovia  Vienna
         Iculisma        ARVERNI          ROMANA   GALLIA CISALPINA
         Vesuna                   Valentia
Burdigala  PETROCORII                    Rhodanus
                CADURCI    GABALI
Garumna     Divona               VOCONTII
                            Arausio
         RUTENI              Avenio
TARBELLI         VOLCAE      Nemausus   Aquae Sextiae
AQUITANIA  TECTOSAGES  PROVINCIA Arelate   SALLUVII  Forum Julii
CONVENAE          VOLCAE ARECOMICI  Massalia
                      Narbo Martius

HISPANIA
TARRACONENSIS

0    50   100   150   200 km

MAP I   INDEPENDENT GAUL

15

refinement, and thus remain unaffected by influences which tend to effeminate character.'[1] (*13*: p. 1.)

Note the allusion to the Province. It is a reminder that in 58 B.C., when Caesar embarked on the conquest of Gaul, the southern part of France—the regions corresponding to Provence, Dauphiné and Savoy as well as Languedoc—had been an apanage of Rome for three-quarters of a century, had been made into a province and was to a great extent latinized.

Caesar's interest in Gaul went considerably further than this brief geographical sketch. He was naturally curious, and well aware that a sound knowledge of his adversaries' life and institutions was greatly to his advantage; he therefore did not think it irrelevant to interrupt the account of his campaigns, in the middle of Book VI of his *Commentaries*, with a short description of Gaulish customs. Thanks to his many sources of information, this is a very valuable document.

He turned his attention first to the political institutions of the Gauls, and what struck him most were the dissensions he found not only in Gaul as a whole, but in every tribe, almost in every household. Everywhere, he says, there were two opposing factions. He made skilful use of these dissensions, courting the Aeduani, for instance, to ensure that the hegemony should pass from the hands of the Sequani, whom he considered dangerous enemies. He was an expert psychologist and his skill in playing off one rival tribe against another was one of the secrets, perhaps the most effective, of his ultimate victory.

He was interested too in the social organization of Gaul:

'Throughout Gaul only two classes of men are of any real consequence —the Druids and the baronage. The common people are treated as little better than slaves: they never venture to act on their own initiative, and have no voice in public affairs. Most of them, burdened with debt, crushed by heavy taxation, or groaning under the hand of more powerful men, enter the service of the privileged classes, who exercise over them the rights enjoyed by a master over his slaves.'

## The Druids

'The Druids are a priestly caste. They regulate public and private sacrifices and decide religious questions. The people hold them in great

[1] *See* Map I, p. 15.

respect, for they are the judges of practically all intertribal as well as personal disputes. They decide all criminal cases, including murder, and all disputes relating to boundaries or inheritance, awarding damages and passing sentence. Any individual or tribe refusing to abide by their decision is banned from taking part in public sacrifices—the heaviest of all their punishments. . . .

'The Druids hold office under the supreme jurisdiction of an arch-priest who is succeeded on his death by the next senior. If there be several of equal rank, the succession is determined by the votes of their colleagues, or sometimes even by armed force. A chapter is held on a fixed date each year at a sanctuary not far from Chartres, which is reckoned the centre of Gaul; and litigants from all over the country meet there for final judgment upon their disputes.

'The druidical doctrine is commonly supposed to have reached Gaul from its original home in Britain, and it is a fact that to this day men going on for higher studies usually cross to Britain for the purpose. The Druids are exempt from military service and do not pay the same taxes as the rest of the people. Such privileges attract a crowd of students, some of whom offer themselves for instruction while others are sent by their parents or relatives. It is said that these young men have to memorize endless verses, and that some of them spend as long as twenty years at their books; for although the Druids employ Greek characters for most of their secular business, such as public and private accounts, they consider it irreverent to commit their lore to writing. I suspect, however, that a double motive underlies this practice—unwillingness to publicize their teaching, and a desire to prevent students relying upon the written word at the expense of memory training; for recourse to text-books almost invariably tends to discourage learning by heart and to dull the powers of memory.

'Their central dogma is the immortality and transmigration of the soul, a doctrine which they regard as the finest incentive to courage since it inspires contempt of death. But they also hold frequent discussions on astronomy, physics and theology, in all which subjects their pupils receive instruction.'

## Gaulish Religion, Divinities and Rites

Caesar underlines the importance of the Druids in the Gallic social structure, and he also stresses one of the chief reasons for their influence, the superstition of the Gauls:

'The Gallic tribes as a whole are slaves of superstition: consequently

13    14    15

persons suffering from serious disease and those engaged in warfare or
other dangerous undertakings offer, or vow to offer, human sacrifices,
at which the Druids officiate. . . . Some of the tribes make colossal
wicker-work figures, the limbs of which are filled with living men: these
images are then set alight and the victims perish in a sea of flame.'

Caesar seems to have highlighted these instances of cruelty with the
express, and perhaps somewhat unscrupulous, intention of showing the
barbarity of the Gauls. There is an ulterior political motive too in his
list of the Gallic divinities:

'Their principal god is Mercury. . . . After Mercury come Apollo,
Mars, Jupiter and Minerva.' (*13*: pp. 103–5.)

Here Caesar is using Latin names to disguise Celtic divinities, with
the object of merging the Gallic pantheon in the Roman. Fortunately we
have other and more trustworthy sources of information on the theogony
of ancient France, in particular inscriptions and sculptures. But we have
literary texts too, chief among them some well-known lines from
Lucan's *Pharsalia*. In Book I of this difficult and turgid poem Caesar
has crossed the Rubicon and is preparing to invade Italy. All his forces
are being mobilized for the struggle, and he recalls the legions on
garrison duty in Gaul. And now, cries the poet, the Gauls are free once
more:

'And thou, Ligurian . . . those, too, by whom the relentless Teutates
is appeased by direful bloodshed, and Hesus, dreadful with his merciless

18

16

17

18

altars; and the shrine of Taranis, not more humane than that of Scythian Diana. . . .' (*51* : lines 442–6.)

Making extensive use of prosopopoeia, he goes on to tell of the bards free once more to chant their hymns, of Druids renewing the bloody sacrifices that war had interrupted. These few lines, into which Lucan tossed perhaps haphazard the names of three Gaulish deities, have had an unexpected and entirely undeserved success. They have been dutifully repeated in all the history books, until the three sonorous names are graven on the memory of every French schoolchild: Hesus, Teutates, Taranis.

## Mistletoe and the New Year Rites

But not all the rites of the Gaulish religion were bathed in blood, and we owe to the curiosity of Pliny the Elder, a writer who is less widely read than he deserves, an account of a Druid ceremony in a peaceful sylvan setting, the gathering of the mistletoe. Here is the passage from his encyclopaedic *Natural History*:

'Upon this occasion we must not omit to mention the admiration that is lavished upon this plant by the Gauls. The Druids—for that is the name they give to their magicians—hold nothing more sacred than the mistletoe and the tree that bears it, supposing always that tree to be the robur.[1] It is the notion with them that everything that grows on that tree has been sent immediately from heaven, and that the mistletoe upon it is a proof that the tree has been selected by God himself as an object of his especial favour. The mistletoe, however, is but rarely found upon the robur; and when found, is gathered with rites replete with religious awe. This is done more particularly on the fifth day of the moon, the day which is the beginning of their months and years, as also of their ages, which, with them, are but thirty years. This day they select because the moon, though not yet in the middle of her course, has already considerable power and influence; and they call her by a name which signifies, in their language, the "all-healing". Having made all due preparation for the sacrifice and a banquet beneath the trees, they bring thither two white bulls, the horns of which are bound then for the first time. Clad in a white robe the priest ascends the tree, and cuts the mistletoe with a golden sickle, which is received by others in a white cloak.' (59: vol. iii, pp. 435–6.)

---

[1] Pliny makes a distinction between the *robur*, a large low-growing oak, and the ordinary oak, or *quercus*.

20

## 3

# STRABO THE GREEK
# ON GAUL

CAESAR was too much of a pragmatist to linger over the kind of detail that simply pandered to his readers' curiosity. But there are other ancient writers who provide us with more explicit accounts. The Greek Strabo (58 B.C.—A.D. 25) has left us, in his *Geography*, a very accurate picture of Gaul; his description of its people is still a classic, and he took great pains to bring out the economic aspects of the countries under discussion. Notice that he was writing in the time of Augustus, when Gallia Comata,[1] conquered half a century earlier, was just beginning to be romanized.

## *The Country*

'The whole of the Narbonnaise [says Strabo] produces the same fruits as Italy. As we advance towards the north, and the mountains of the Cevennes, the plantations of the olive and fig disappear, but the others remain. Likewise the vine, as you proceed northwards, does not easily mature its fruit. The entire of the remaining country produces in abundance corn, millet, acorns and mast of all kinds. No part of it lies waste except that which is taken up in marshes and woods, and even this is inhabited. The cause of this, however, is rather a dense population

---

[1] 'Long-haired' Gaul—independent Gaul, as opposed to Cisalpine Gaul.

than the industry of the inhabitants. For the women there are both very prolific, and excellent nurses, while the men devote themselves rather to war than husbandry. However, their arms being now laid aside, they are compelled to engage in agriculture.' (*69*: vol. i, p. 266.)

We may detect a faint note of disparagement in this panegyric, and it is indeed further tempered by some serious criticisms—traditional criticisms which went on being repeated long after the Gauls had become the French:

## The Gauls, *Ancestors of the French*

'To their simplicity and vehemence, the Gauls join much folly, arrogance and love of ornament. They wear golden collars round their necks, and bracelets on their arms and wrists, and those who are of any dignity have garments dyed and worked with gold. This lightness of character makes them intolerable when they conquer, and throws them into consternation when worsted.' (*69*: vol. i, p. 294.)

Even in Strabo's time this portrait of the Gallic mentality may well have become a commonplace; and we can find more that deserves our attention in his minute and careful description of the costume, arms, food and manner of life of the Gauls:

'The Gauls wear the sagum [a coarse mantle], let their hair grow, and wear short breeches. Instead of tunics they wear a slashed garment with sleeves descending a little below the hips. The wool [of their sheep] is coarse, but long; from it they weave the thick saga called laines. . . . The equipment [of the Gauls] is in keeping with the size of their bodies; they have a long sword hanging at their right side, a long shield, and lances in proportion, together with a madaris somewhat resembling a javelin; some of them also use bows and slings; they have also a piece of wood resembling a pilum, which they hurl not out of a thong, but from their hand, and to a farther distance than an arrow. They principally make use of it in shooting birds. To the present day most of them lie on the ground, and take their meals seated on straw. They subsist principally on milk and all kinds of flesh, especially that of swine, which they eat both fresh and salted. Their swine live in the fields, and surpass in height, strength and swiftness. To persons unaccustomed to approach them they are almost as dangerous as wolves. The people . . . have sheep and swine in such abundance that they supply saga and salted pork in plenty, not only to Rome, but to most parts of Italy.' (*69*: vol. i, p. 293.)

## Marseilles and Gallia Narbonensis

But Strabo did more than paint a picture of Gaul as a whole; he puts on record his own observations on the different regions which he had visited himself. Here are a few of his impressions.

He turned his attention first to Gallia Narbonensis, where the coastal area had been hellenized for over six hundred years; this was no doubt the first region he visited:

'The configuration of this country [he writes] resembles a parallelogram, the western side of which is traced by the Pyrenees, the north by the Cevennes; as for the other two sides, the south is bounded by the sea between the Pyrenees and Marseilles, and the east partly by the Alps and partly by a line drawn perpendicularly from these mountains to the foot of the Cevennes.'

He ends his account of the boundaries of the province by noting:

'To the southern side of this parallelogram we must add the seacoast inhabited by the Massilienses and Salyes, as far as the country of the Ligurians, the confines of Italy, and the River Var.'

He turns next to a description of Marseilles, the ancient Hellenic colony founded by the Phocaeans in the sixth century B.C.:

'Marseilles, founded by the Phocaeans, is built in a stony region. Its

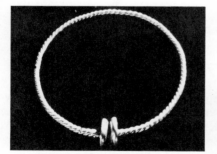

20. Solid gold torc, 3rd to 1st century B.C.

19. Bronze chain and ornament. Gallo-Roman period.

21. Tombstone in the form of a house, 1st to 2nd century.

23. Relief of Artemis, from Marseilles; 6th century B.C.

22. (left), Gaulish warrior from Mondragon. Gallo-Roman.

24. (right), Altar of Rome and Augustus at Lyons. Drawing of a medal reproducing the obverse of a Tiberian coin.

harbour lies beneath a rock, which is shaped like a theatre and looks towards the south. It is well surrounded with walls, as well as the whole city, which is of considerable size. Within the citadel are placed the Ephesium and the temple of the Delphian Apollo. This latter temple is common to all the Ionians; the Ephesium is the temple consecrated to Diana of Ephesus. They say that when the Phocaeans were about to quit their country, an oracle commanded them to take from Diana of Ephesus a conductor for their voyage. On arriving at Ephesus they therefore inquired how they might be able to obtain from the goddess what was enjoined them. The goddess appeared in a dream to Aristarcha, one of the most honourable women of the city, and commanded her to accompany the Phocaeans, and to take with her a plan of the temple and statues. These things being performed, and the colony being settled, the Phocaeans built a temple, and evinced their great respect for Aristarcha by making her priestess.'

This legend, and many others like it, was a constant reminder to the citizens of Marseilles of their origin and the bonds that linked their city with Greece. Strabo's account is proof that even after Caesar's conquest they still remembered the old ties. In any case, Marseilles in the first century was a focal point of Hellenism:

'All who profess to be men of taste turn to the study of elocution and philosophy. Thus this city for some little time back has become a school for the barbarians, and has communicated to the Galatae such a taste for Greek literature, that they even draw contracts on the Grecian model. While at the present day it so entices the noblest of the Romans, that those desirous of studying resort thither in preference to Athens.' (69: vol. i, pp. 267–71.)

Though Strabo was particularly interested in Marseilles, he did not neglect the other Mediterranean cities of Gallia Narbonensis:

'Narbonne is situated above the outlets of the Aude and the lake of Narbonne. It is the principal commercial city of this coast. On the Rhone is Arelate [Arles], a city and emporium of considerable traffic.' (69: vol. i, pp. 271–2.)

Strabo was an acute observer, no less interested in the behaviour of the people than in the physical aspect of their country; and he noted how rapidly romanization had progressed in Gallia Narbonensis at the time of his visit:

'The name of Cavari has so obtained, that all the barbarians inhabiting near [in the lower Rhone valley] now go by that designation; nay, even those who are no longer barbarians, but follow the Roman customs, both in their speech and mode of life, and some of those even who have adopted the Roman policy.'

Archaeology confirms Strabo's evidence of romanization, for it was at the beginning of the first century A.D. that the cities of Gallia Narbonensis began to erect the monuments that were to be their glory. Among the most prosperous towns the geographer mentions Nemausus [Nimes], still today one of the richest in Roman monuments:

'Nemausus is the metropolis of the Arecomisci; though far inferior to Narbonne both as to its commerce, and the number of foreigners attracted thither, it surpasses that city in the number of its citizens; for it has under its domain four and twenty different villages all well inhabited, and by the same people, who pay tribute; it likewise enjoys the rights of the Latin towns,[1] so that in Nemausus you meet with Roman citizens who have obtained the honours of the aedile and quaestorship, wherefore this nation is not subject to the orders issued by the praetors from Rome. The city is situated on the road from Iberia to Italy; this road is very good in the summer, but muddy and over-flowed by the rivers during winter and spring.' (69: vol. i, pp. 278–9.)

## Aquitania

After Gallia Narbonensis, Strabo continues his tour of Gaul with Aquitania, on which he gives us brief but accurate information:

'The Petrocorii [in Périgueux] and Bituriges-Cubi [in Berry] possess excellent ironworks, the Cadurci [in Quercy] linen-factories, and the Ruteni [in Rouergue] silver-mines: the Gabales [in Gévaudan] likewise possess silver-mines.'

Aquitania had gold-mines too:

'These people [the Tarbelli] possess the richest gold-mines; masses of gold as big as the fist can contain, and requiring hardly any purifying, being found in diggings scarcely beneath the surface of the earth, the remainder consisting of dust and lumps, which likewise require but little working.' (69: vol. i, pp. 283–4.)

## Lugdunensis

Lugdunensis held Strabo's attention longer. The old region of Celtica had been renamed Lugdunensis because after the Roman conquest Lugdunum (Lyons) had become the capital of the Province. Indeed, the Roman colony which the proconsul Munatius Plancus had founded in 43 B.C. had become a very important city, a capital in every sense, by the time Strabo knew of, and no doubt visited, it:

'Lugdunum itself, situated on a hill, at the confluence of the Saone

[1] In early times the people of Latium enjoyed a legal status intermediate between full Roman citizenship and the status of non-Romans or travellers. Later the 'rights of the Latin towns' were extended to certain colonies outside Italy.

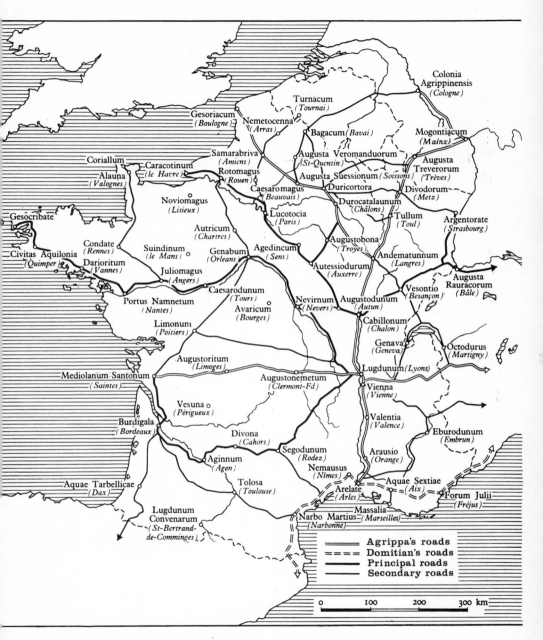

MAP 2   ROMAN ROADS IN GAUL

25. Two-wheeled cart, from a funerary monument; mid-2nd century.

26. Eastern Gaul, from Cologne to Antibes. Fragment of the Peutinger Table.

and the Rhone, belongs to the Romans. It is the most populous city after Narbonne. It carries on a great commerce, and the Roman prefects here coin gold and silver money. Before this city, at the confluence of the rivers, is situated the temple dedicated by all the Galatae in common to Caesar Augustus. The altar is splendid, and has inscribed on it the names of sixty people, and images of them, one for each, and also another great altar.' (69: vol. i, p. 286.)

Not content with turning Lyons into the political, economic and religious capital of Gaul, the Romans made the colony the hub of the Gallic road system, linking Lyons with the most important points in the different provinces. Strabo gives us a clear picture of the general plan which Agrippa worked out when he was legate of the Three Gauls (22–21 B.C.):

'Lugdunum is situated in the midst of the country, something as an Acropolis, both on account of the confluence of the rivers, and of its being equally near to all parts. It was on this account that Agrippa cut all the roads from this [as a centre], one running through the mountains of the Cevennes to the Santones and Aquitaine, another towards the Rhine; a third towards the ocean by the country of the Bellovaci and Ambiani, and a fourth towards the Narbonnaise and the coast of Marseilles. The traveller, also, leaving Lugdunum and the country above on his left, may pass over the Pennine Alps themselves.'

## The Road System

Albert Grenier has succeeded in tracing these five roads on the map, using the valuable information in the *Tabula Peutingeriana* and the *Itinerarium Antonini* to supplement Strabo. (*See* Map 2, p. 27.)

The fourth road, through Gallia Narbonensis, is easily identified: it followed the left bank of the Rhone and led to Arles by way of Vienne, Valence, Orange and Avignon. For most of its distance it followed the line taken by the modern Route Nationale 7.

The road through Aquitania is more difficult to trace; it seems to have run by Fleurs (Loire) and Clermont-Ferrand, and then by Vichy and Limoges to Saintes, whose importance in Roman times is attested by its ancient ruins.

As for the ocean road, it ended in fact at the Channel port of Boulogne, while the Rhone road went through Langres and down the valley of the

Meuse to Mainz and Cologne, the future capitals of the two provinces of Germany.

The last of the roads in Strabo's list was designed to link Gaul with Italy, and we know from another passage in the *Geography* that the mountains were usually crossed by way of the two St Bernard passes:

'One of the passages over the mountains from Italy into Transalpine and northern Keltica is that which passes through the country of the Salassi, and leads to Lugdunum. This [route] is divided into two ways, one practicable for carriages, but longer, which crosses the country of the Ceutrones [Little St Bernard], the other steep and narrow, but shorter [Great St Bernard]; this crosses the Pennine [Alps].' (*69*: vol. i, pp. 309–10.)

The towns strung out along this second route were, from Lyons outward, Bourgoin, Aoste (Isère), Seyssel, Geneva, Vévey on the Lake of Geneva, and Martigny; while the longer road over the Little St Bernard went by Lémenc (Chambéry) and along the upper valley of the Isère. After crossing the passes the two roads joined in Italy, at Aosta, named after its founder Augustus.

## Paris

The Romans lavished all their favours on Lyons, and by comparison Paris cut a poor figure in the first century; Strabo barely mentions the future capital of France in a list of the cities of Lugdunensis and Belgica:

'The Parisii dwell along the River Seine, and inhabit an island formed by the river; their city is Lucotocia. The Meldi [inhabitants of Meaux] and Lexovii [inhabitants of Lisieux] border on the ocean. The most considerable, however, of all these nations are the Remi. Duricortora [Reims], their metropolis, is well populated, and is the residence of the Roman prefects.' (*69*: vol. i, p. 290.)

This last comment is worth noticing. The glorious Roman past of Reims was to be her chief and unchallenged claim to greatness. She did not surrender it even when she became a religious capital; it was there that Clovis, the first Christian king, received baptism, and there later that his prelates claimed the privilege of crowning the kings of France. The old Gallo-Roman city has kept her greatness down to our own days

# 4

# THE NEW DESTINY
# OF GAUL

## *The Benefits of Conquest*

After Caesar's conquest, Gaul became Roman. This was perhaps the most radical change in the whole history of France. The Gauls spoke a Celtic dialect; gradually Vulgar Latin took its place, and the conquerors implanted their own civilization, building towns, creating a road system, bringing with them Roman law and Roman administration.

Present-day historians have studied the metamorphosis of Gaul in great detail, poring over it to see what she gained and what she lost by romanization. It is a fascinating study, the study of the soul of a nation. How far did Rome's imposition of an alien culture do violence to Gaul and hamper the full development of her personality? Would France have had a greater future if her people had remained Celtic instead of becoming a neo-Latin nation?

For many centuries this was a question no one would have dreamed of asking; only classical culture was worthy of a people who prided themselves on being civilized. But the nineteenth century saw an upsurge of nationalist spirit in all European countries, and attention was focused on the problem; and in our own days the apparent decadence of Graeco-Latin civilization has given it new and dramatic relevance.

Should we then condemn the Roman conquest because it prevented the old Celtic nation from developing its full potentialities? The historian may well be tempted to raise the question again, but it is bound to remain hypothetical; and though every now and then the Roman yoke seems to have weighed so heavily on the Gauls that they were eager to

28. Marble head of a man, from Saintes.

27. Youth wearing tunic and sandals;
Gallo-Roman bronze.

throw it off, there is no evidence that they spent much time regretting their past.

This is hardly surprising, for, as the French historian Fustel de Coulanges has pointed out, 'there is no comparison between Gaul under Roman rule and Poland under Russian domination, or Ireland under the harsh administration of England.' (*17*: p. 71.) Another French writer, Camille Jullian, a historian who has never been prejudiced in favour of Rome, has emphasized the pointlessness of this kind of comparison. As he says, we cannot apply our modern concept of international relations to those which existed between imperial Rome and her subject peoples.

'The Roman Empire [he wrote] was something unique, something without parallel in history. The world had become the territory of a city, and Rome the homeland of all mankind. The municipal system had made the whole world one; it had fashioned a marvellous city, the eternal city encompassing all others within her walls.' (*37*: vol. iv, p. 260.)

It was because Roman imperialism thus embraced the world that any resistance on the part of the peoples Rome conquered was doomed to failure, and rebellion rare and sporadic. It was not easy to resist the temptation to become part of an organization so vast that it ruled the world, and the possession of Roman citizenship was a proud boast indeed. As Ferdinand Lot has said in his recent history of Gaul: 'Rome wrought an inward transformation in our ancestors simply and solely through the spell of her language and letters, of her art and her laws'; it was inevitable that they should accept her leadership. But, as he points out, Rome could not transform them completely. 'What never changed was their character. It is not only modern historians who have been struck by the characteristics, laudable or otherwise, which the French share with their ancestors the Gauls.' (*49*: p. 240.)

## Successive Stages of Romanization

It is common experience that those who live through some great event are very seldom aware that their world is the stage for a vast transformation scene and they themselves are the actors in the drama. The historiography of the first century was no exception to the rule; it does not throw any clear light on the stages by which Gaul was romanized, and the most we can expect is an occasional fugitive gleam.

Caesar's conquest was followed by three-quarters of a century of peace in Gaul. This gave Augustus the opportunity to organize the defence of the Rhine frontier against the Germans, who were proving turbulent neighbours. His reign was marked by a complete reform of the administration, in which Gaul was included. Gallia Narbonensis became a senatorial province, and the old Gallia Comata was divided into three imperial provinces: Belgica, Celtica (renamed Lugdunensis), and Aquitania, whose boundaries were now extended beyond the Garonne to the Loire.

## The Troubles of the Year 21

Under Tiberius a spirit of restlessness seized Gaul, and Tacitus devotes a good deal of space in his *Annals* to a revolt which broke out in A.D. 21:

'In the course of the same year a rebellion broke out among the cities of Gaul, occasioned by the load of debt that oppressed the common people. The principal leaders of the revolt were Julius Florus and

Julius Sacrovir; the former a man of weight among the Treveri, and the latter among the Aeduans. They were both of illustrious birth. Their ancestors had deserved well of the Romans and, for their services, received the freedom of the city, at a time when that privilege was rare, and the reward of merit only. By these incendiaries secret meetings were held; the fierce and daring were drawn into the league together with such as languished in poverty, or, being conscious of their crimes, had nothing left but to grow desperate in guilt. Florus undertook to kindle the flame of rebellion in Belgia; and Sacrovir to rouse the neighbouring Gauls. The plan thus settled, they caballed in private, held frequent meetings, and left no topic untouched that could inflame the minds of the people. "Tributes", they said, "were levied with un-abating rigour; usurious interest oppressed the poor, and their haughty masters continued to lord it over them with pride and arrogance. By the murder of Germanicus, disaffection was diffused among the legions, and the opportunity to strike the blow for liberty was now arrived. Reflect on the numbers we can bring into the field; remember the impoverished state of Italy. At Rome every warlike principle is ex-tinguished. The strength of their armies is mouldered away. They have

29. Caricature, possibly of a Roman by a Gaul, cut in marble, from the villa at Mont-maurin, near Toulouse.

no national strength, but depend altogether on foreign nations to fight their battles.''

'A general spirit of revolt prevailed in every part of Gaul. Scarce a city was free from commotion. The flame blazed out among the Andecavians and the people of Tours.' (*71*: vol. i, p. 155.)

Tacitus was writing nearly a century after the rising, and it is significant that he gives so detailed an account; the revolt had obviously made a considerable impression in Rome. It had spread with remarkable swiftness. Though Florus and Sacrovir had fomented the revolt in eastern Gaul, one in the Trèves district and the other in Autun, it irrupted first in Anjou and Touraine—that is, in western Gaul.

The immediate causes of the rebellion do not emerge clearly from the summary Tacitus gives us of the rebel leaders' arguments. But we may suppose that the death of Germanicus, a popular commander and much loved by his troops, was followed by unrest in the Roman army of occupation in Gaul. This spread to the civilian population, who were suffering heavy taxation under Tiberius, and a popular uprising began under cover of the confusion in the army.

30. Wrestler and dancer; Gallo-Roman bronzes.

Tacitus claims that the revolt of the Andes and Turoni was quickly suppressed.

## *Sacrovir and the Autun Rising*

'The Aeduan commotions were not so easily quelled. The state was rich and powerful, and the force necessary to subdue the insurrection lay at a considerable distance. Sacrovir strained every nerve to support his cause. He seized the city of Augustodunum, the capital of the Aeduans, and took into his custody the flower of the young nobility, who resorted thither from all parts of Gaul, as to a school of science and liberal education. By detaining those pledges, he hoped to attach to his interest their parents and relations. He supplied the young men with arms, which had been prepared with secrecy by his directions. His numbers amounted to less than forty thousand, a fifth part of which were armed after the manner of the legions; the rest carried hunting-poles, knives,

31. Dueller, Gallo-Roman bronze.

32. Small toilet-jar from Rheims, silver-plated copper.

33. Detail of 32. Scenes from a gladiatorial school. Practice fight between HEROS and AUDAX; on the left, the instructor with his switch.

and other instruments of the chase. He had, besides, pressed into his service a body of slaves reared up to the trade of gladiators, and, according to the custom of the country, clad with an entire plate of iron. In the language of Gaul they were called *Crupellarians*. Their armour was impenetrable to the stroke of the enemy, but at the same time rendered the men too unwieldy for the attack. The adjoining provinces had not taken up arms; but a number of individuals caught the infection, and joined the rebel army.' (71 : vol. i, pp. 156–7.)

There are a number of curious points to note here. Less than a hundred years after the conquest, the Romans had established schools at Autun which were obviously prospering, if several thousand young men were attending them; but it seems that they were hotbeds of sedition, for though Tacitus confuses the issue by his use of the word *pignus*, Sacrovir would not have armed forty thousand men at Autun if he had had any doubts where their sympathies lay.

The news of the revolt alarmed public opinion in Rome, and the rumours that ran through the city exaggerated the gravity of the situation.

'A report prevailed at Rome [says Tacitus] that not only the Aeduans and the Treviri, but several other cities of Gaul, to the number of sixty-four, had thrown off the yoke. Germany, it was added, had joined the league; and Spain was wavering. The rumour, as usually happens, was magnified by the credulity of the populace. Good men felt for their country: the greater part, detesting the present system, and wishing for nothing so much as a change, enjoyed the confusion and triumphed in the common danger. Invective did not spare Tiberius. . . . Amidst these murmurs of discontent, Tiberius appeared with an unruffled temper, never once changing his look, his place of abode or his habits of life.' (*71*: vol. i, p. 157.)

## *Tiberius Quells the Revolt*

Tacitus implies that, if Tiberius kept his head, it was because he had it on good authority that the danger was slight, much less serious than it was rumoured to be. He was perfectly right, to judge by the ease with which the Roman legate Silius disarmed Sacrovir and his makeshift army:

'Silius marched at the head of two legions into the territory of the Sequanians. . . . He laid waste the country, and proceeded, by rapid marches, to Augustodunum. At the distance of twelve miles from Augustodunum, Sacrovir appeared in force. His line of battle was formed on the open plain. The gladiators, in complete armour, were stationed in the centre, his cohorts in the two wings, and his half-armed multitude in the rear. He was himself mounted on a superb horse, attended by a number of chiefs. He rode through the ranks, haranguing his men: he called to mind the glory of their ancestors, their brave exploits against the Romans, and the eternal honour of succeeding in the cause of liberty. A defeat, he said, would bring with it infamy, and chains, and bondage.

'The speech was short, and the soldiers heard it without emotion. The legions advanced in regular order. A band of raw recruits, lately levied in the towns of Gaul, could not sustain a sight so terrible. By the Romans victory was already anticipated. To exhort them was unnecessary, yet Silius thought proper to inflame their ardour. "The disgrace", he said, "would be great, if the victorious legions, who had conquered in Germany, were now to consider the Gauls as an equal enemy. The rebels of Tours have been chastised by a single cohort; a detachment of cavalry crushed the insurgents at Trèves; and a handful of this very army gave the Sequanians a total overthrow. The Aeduans are now before you; not an army, but an effeminate race, abounding in wealth and enervated by luxury. Charge with valour, and to pursue the runaways will be your only trouble." This speech was received with a general shout. The rebels were soon hemmed in by the cavalry; the front of their line gave way at the first onset of the infantry, and the wings were put to flight. The men in iron armour still kept their ranks. No impression could be made by swords and javelins. The Romans had recourse to their hatchets and pickaxes. With these, as if battering a wall, they fell upon the enormous load and crushed both men and armour. Some attacked with clubs and pitchforks. The unwieldy and defenceless enemy lay on the ground, an inanimate mass, without an effort to rise. Sacrovir threw himself into the town of Augustodunum, but in a short time, fearing to be given up a prisoner, withdrew, with his most faithful adherents, to a villa in the neighbourhood, where he put an end to his life. His followers, having first set fire to the place, turned their swords against themselves, and perished in one general carnage.

'Tiberius, at length, thought fit to write to the Senate on the subject of these commotions. In one and the same letter he gave an account of the war begun and ended. He neither magnified nor disguised the truth, but in plain terms ascribed the whole success to the valour of his officers, and the wisdom of his counsellors. Why he did not go in person, or send his son Drusus, the same letter explained: "The extent and majesty of the Empire claimed his utmost care. It was not for the dignity of the prince, on the revolt of one or two cities, to relinquish the seat of government." ' (*71*: vol. i, pp. 158-9.)

Sacrovir's revolt against Tiberius, when for a brief moment the spirit of Gaul woke from its sleep, seems to have made a considerable impression, to judge by the lengthy account that Tacitus gives of it. But we should perhaps add that it is hardly likely that the triumphal arch at Orange was erected to commemorate the suppression of the revolt, as is sometimes said. Indeed, as Camille Jullian pertinently remarks, 'Tiberius was anxious to make light of the episode, and he would not have countenanced any such demonstration.' (*37*: vol. iv, p. 160, note.)

# FIRST INTERLUDE IN BRITAIN

## The Roman Expansion from Gaul into Britain

Roman imperialism, which led successively to the conquest of Iberia and Gaul, was not brought to a halt on the shores of the western ocean. To their knowledge, the Isle of Britain had been circumnavigated by such bold mariners as Pytheas, and the Romans intended to add it to their Empire.

The first stage in this conquest was undertaken by Julius Caesar during the progress of his campaign in Gaul. The first expedition to Britain had happened in the late summer of 55 B.C., and this is the reason he gives for it:

'Only a small part of the summer remained favourable [he says in Book IV of his *Commentaries*]. Now although in these latitudes, due to the fact that Gaul lies open towards the north, the winters are early and severe, he was determined to set sail for Britain because he bore in mind that, in almost every action which we had fought in Gaul, the enemy had been reinforced by men and materials of British origin. He also bore in mind that, even if there was not enough time left in this campaigning season to finish off the war, it would nevertheless prove very useful to have made a landing in the island, if only to reconnoitre the strength of the local manpower, the harbours and the lines of communication; about these last matters the Gauls themselves appeared badly informed for, except for some merchants, none of them had made so bold as to journey there, and even the merchants were only familiar with the coast-line facing the north coast of Gaul.'

The first expedition, therefore, was too hurriedly mounted to produce satisfactory results, and lasted only during the full moon of the autumnal equinox (the 'harvest moon' of British agricultural tradition). An equinoctial gale in the Channel caused severe losses to the expeditionary fleet and the troops, once landed, fell into an ambush laid by the natives.

This rebuff, which Caesar tried to minimize, was a salutary lesson to him. The campaign of the following year, 54 B.C., was prepared with minute care and undertaken by troops who had been quartered in Gaul the preceding winter: 600 load-carrying vessels and 28 warships were fitted out (approximately 1,100 years later the expeditionary force led by William the Conqueror required 700 ships). Caesar, in his *Commentaries*, congratulates both those who planned the enterprise and the soldiers who carried it out, and he adds that he outlined his plans and ordered a concentration at what he calls Portus Itius, which is probably Boulogne, because he had learned that this was the easiest point of departure for the crossing to Britain, which was only thirty Roman miles.

He himself embarked there with five legions and 2,000 cavalry. This is his account of the crossing:

'We weighed anchor at sunset and set sail on a light south-westerly breeze; when the wind fell off towards midnight we could no longer hold on our course, from which we were carried further by the current, so that at first light we observed the coast of Britain to port. Then, as the tide began to set the other way, and rowing with the current, we came within sight of that part of the island which, it had been observed the previous summer, offered the best landing point.'

This is supposed to mean that the landing took place near Sandown Castle to the north of Deal, about the middle of the day. The first operation consisted of a night march and brought Caesar a dozen Roman miles inland, face to face with the enemy which had taken up their position in a woodland fortress which they had very cleverly improvised, using felled trees as obstacles; but the soldiers of the Seventh Legion stormed it by adopting the formation known as 'the tortoise', and they put the garrison to flight. However, Caesar forbade pursuit because he wished to devote the rest of the day to consolidating his own position. This prudence was justified, because this initial success was followed by frustrating events which compromised ultimate success. The following

41

morning, cavalry patrols guarding the original bridge-head reported that a violent storm had driven nearly all the ships on to the lee shore and many had been wrecked. Hearing this, Caesar returned to the bridge-head to find forty ships a total loss and, in order to avoid further casualties of this nature, he had the remaining vessels drawn up on shore and enclosed by a fortification of earthworks. Then, returning to the point which his troops had reached inland, he found them facing a British force under the orders of the renowned chief, Cassivellaunus, whose lands were situated on the left bank of the Thames. Nevertheless, the supreme command here in Kent had been entrusted to him by consent of the Britons.

Now began a hard campaign. The heavily armed Roman infantry learnt at their cost the danger of pursuing an enemy who slipped away nimbly only to fall on their adversaries again when least expected. Once he had learned to allow for these characteristic British tactics, Caesar led his army up to the Thames and across it.

Caesar's policy was clever; it depended on exploiting the internal quarrels of the native tribes and thus weakening the most powerful elements, in this case, the Trinovantes (of Essex) whose chief, Mandrubracius, could never forget that his father had been killed by Cassivellaunus. His example proved infectious and many other tribes sent plenipotentiaries to the Roman commander and placed themselves at his mercy.

'From them [says Caesar], I learnt that we were not far from the chief stronghold of Cassivellaunus, the approaches to which, however, are blocked by forest and swamps. . . . We marched towards it with the legions. The place proved to be remarkably well sited and skilfully improved by works of fortification: however, a converging attack from both flanks was decided upon. After a short resistance, the enemy were unable to withstand the onslaught of our men and fled by the back entrance to the fortress. Inside it we discovered large quantities of live-stock, and many fugitives were captured and killed.'

This victory had a decisive effect, although Cassivellaunus made another attempt to attack the fleet base. This attack failed and the British chief was constrained to surrender. Caesar, seeing that the summer was already advanced, did not follow up the advantages which he had gained, but contented himself by taking hostages and fixing an annual tribute on the British kings which the Roman Senate and people never actually collected.

To tell the truth, the net result of these campaigning seasons was perhaps to give the Romans a clearer idea of what the isle of Britain and its inhabitants were like and it is in Caesar's *Commentary on the Gallic War* that we find the oldest and most exact description of the isle of Britain in the whole of classical literature:

'The interior of the island is populated by tribes who, according to oral tradition, are the aboriginal inhabitants, whereas the coastal region has been settled by people who came over from Belgica to rob and make war and who, after the campaign, settled down to till the land. The population density is high and the houses near enough the same as those in Gaul. They keep large quantities of cattle. Copper and gold coinage are in circulation besides iron currency bars of uniform weight. Tin is found in the centre of the island and there are deposits of iron ore in the coastal regions, but in very small quantities, and all the copper that they use is imported. There are trees of every species exactly as in Gaul, except for the pine tree and the beech. The inhabitants have a taboo against eating hare or chicken or goose, but they keep the two last-named for sport and pleasure. The climate is more temperate than that of Gaul, the frosts being less severe.

The island is shaped like a triangle of which one side faces Gaul. At one of the angles of this side is the district of Kent, where almost all the ships coming from Gaul land; it looks towards the east. The other angle lower down looks south. The whole coastline on this side extends for some 500 Roman miles. The second coastline is turned toward Spain and the west and off it lies the island of Hibernia, which, according to estimates, is only half the size of Britain, but the sea passage between these two islands is as long as that which separates Britain from Gaul. Half way over there is an island called Mona.'[1]

Caesar adds that the total length of this second coastline of the triangle is of the order of 700 Roman miles. As for the third side, he says it is exposed to the north wind but has no land facing it except at the southern end, which faces Germany. Its estimated length of 500 Roman miles made up a total perimeter of 2,000 miles.

[1] This evidently means Man, but there is some confusion between Mona, which was properly the name for Anglesey and is represented in modern Welsh by *Mon*, and Monebia, the Isle of Man (called in Modern Welsh *Manau*). Only the latter can properly be described as half way between Britain and Ireland.

The last observations on Britain by Caesar concern the Kingdom of Kent: 'Of all the Britons, the most civilized by far are those who inhabit Kent, the wholly coastal district whose culture resembles that of Gaul.'

Once Caesar was dead, Britain was forgotten for a whole century, as André Maurois says in *A History of England*. Nevertheless, there was not a total lapse of memory, because the merchants continued to come over from Gaul. But the Roman government showed no interest, or no effective interest, in Britain until the time of the Emperor Claudius. Now, however, the methodical conquest of the island was undertaken and its progress is fairly well known to us, thanks to the evidence of Tacitus. This historian was married to the daughter of Julius Agricola, who for six years (78–84) was governor of Britain and whose biography Tacitus composed. If occasionally *De vita et moribus Julii Agricola* sounds like a panegyric, we can make sufficient reservations about these perhaps excessive eulogies to recognize that it is a most valuable work constructed on the basis of ample documentation and evidence.

It was in the year 43 that the Emperor Claudius sent into Britain a total force of four legions, together with auxiliary infantry and cavalry, to the total number of 50,000 men. Vespasian was associated with the operation and Tacitus tells us that this was the foundation of his fortune. The historian adds that the first Roman of consular rank promoted to the government of Britain was Aulus Plautius, and he was succeeded by Ostorius Scapula; both of them were remarkable as military men and little by little the nearest part of the island was converted into a province, in addition to which a colony of veterans was founded (at Colchester).

Tacitus then gives a list of the *legati* who had preceded Agricola as governors, and he goes into some detail about a revolt which had broken out under one of them, Suetonius Paulinus by name. He was a man of consular rank and had gone on an expedition to Anglesey, which was the religious centre of Druidism and a hotbed of nationalist agitators. Emboldened by the absence of the governor, the Britons began to discuss the evils of slavery and they worked themselves up into a state of indignation by mutual exhortation.

We need not repeat what Tacitus presents as the inflammatory British oratory because, no doubt, he invented it for aesthetic purposes.

'These speeches [he writes] were the prelude to a general revolt' the gravity of which he describes with some relish:

'Supporting each other on these and similar complaints, they rose up in a body under the leadership of Boadicea, a woman of royal stock, for they make no distinction of sex in their successions to the throne. Having attacked the Roman soldiers, who were spread about in forts, and reduced the garrisons, they overran the colony of veterans which they considered the source of their humiliation, and their victorious anger allowed them to practise every sort of barbarous cruelty on their prisoners. If Paulinus, on receiving the report of this revolt, had not come rapidly to the rescue, Britain would have been lost.'

The situation was restored, but Tacitus adds that the unrest which reigned in Britain was not dispelled and was mainly due to the fact that certain governors were of a pitiless hardness, whereas others, on the contrary, had been too soft.

Such was the condition of Britain when Julius Agricola crossed the Channel. His first task was the reconquest of Anglesey. Then, being well aware of the state of feeling in the country which he had been called on to govern and being of the opinion that very little is to be gained by warfare alone, he made great efforts to extinguish the cause of bitterness among the population by attacking the abuses which were present in the government of the province.

Among the reforms mentioned by Tacitus, the following appear to us the most important:

'In order to accustom them to the enjoyment of pleasures and to induce them to taste the benefits of peace and tranquillity, Augustus persuaded the Britons, who were thinly dispersed over the country, illiterate and consequently warlike, to build temples, market places and town houses, works which he subsidized from public funds. He praised those who were active in this matter and scolded the idle, preferring emulation as an incentive rather than compulsion. Furthermore, he had the sons of the chiefs instructed in the liberal arts and professed a great belief in the natural genius and ability of the Britons rather than in the skills that they had acquired by imitation of the Gauls. This was so successful that people who but recently had affected to despise the Roman language now made great efforts to be fluent in it. Another consequence was that Roman dress enjoyed great prestige and the toga became fashionable.'

Reading here between the lines and taking these remarks in conjunction with the evidence of archaeology and linguistics, we must conclude that romanization not only began later but proceeded more slowly in Britain than in Gaul, and that it was never really completed. As a French historian has noted, London grew great in the time of the Romans because they laid out roads from north to south so as to pass through it on the crossing of the Thames. But the greater part of the country and the mass of the population were not deeply transformed by Roman rule. The most significant proof of this is that the Celtic language remained the common speech of the island, whereas in Gaul it was swept away by Vulgar Latin which was spoken by all classes and which became French later on.

It should be added that despite the campaigns of successive *legati* in charge of Britain and, in particular, despite those of Agricola which Tacitus has chronicled, the Romans never achieved the total conquest of the island. They refrained from mastering the extreme north, which was populated by fierce tribes known as Caledones and subsequently as Picts, who time and again raided the more southerly parts of the island to rob and pillage.

The Emperor Hadrian put in hand defences against these disturbing adversaries when he visited the island between A.D. 122 and 124 by planning the construction of a fortified frontier approximately sixty-five miles long from the Solway Firth on the Irish Sea to the mouth of the Tyne on the North Sea. Farther north, in the reign of the Emperor Antoninus and the governorship of Urbicus, a second defensive work less than forty miles long was built between Bridgeness on the Firth and West Kilpatrick on the Clyde, but the defensive value of this second fortification proved negligible. When Septimus Severus came to Britain at the end of his reign (he died there in 211) he confined himself to rebuilding and consolidating the *vallum Hadriani*, which remained thereafter the frontier of direct Roman government in Britain.

*Part II*

# THE ROMAN PEACE

# 5

# THE EMPEROR CLAUDIUS
# AND THE GAULS

THE Gaulish revolt of A.D. 21 was a serious warning from which the Romans were quick to learn. The immediate successors of Tiberius, in particular Claudius, who had been born at Lyons, adopted a policy of conciliation which was largely responsible for the assimilation of Gaul.

The great public works programme was begun under these emperors. But it was the reign of Claudius that saw the disappearance of the old Gallic institutions such as the office of the *vergobrets*, the chief magistrates of some of the tribes.[1] Suetonius congratulates Claudius too on finally putting an end to the cruel sacrificial rites of the Druids, whereas Augustus had merely forbidden them to Roman citizens.

## Claudius and his Policy of Integration

Even clearer evidence of Claudius's policy for Gaul is to be found in the speech to the Senate in Rome, delivered during his censorship, in which he urged that the chief men of the cities of Gallia Comata should be admitted to the ranks of Roman senatorial magistrates. Augustus and Tiberius had already conceded the privilege to Gallia Narbonensis. Why should it not be extended to the federation of the Three Gauls? That was the theme of his speech. It was received with great enthusiasm by

[1] Among the Aedui, the Lexovii and the Santones, the supreme magistrate bore the title of vergo-bretos. Vergo in the Celtic tongue meant 'judgment', bretos 'effective'. (*20*: p. 66.)

49

the Gauls, and as a mark of gratitude they caused it to be inscribed on a bronze tablet, to be affixed to the wall of the temple of Augustus which had been built by the Three Gauls on the slopes of the Croix-Rousse hill at Lyons. For many hundreds of years the tablet lay buried, until it was dug up in 1524 by workers making a garden in the area, and bought by the town of Lyons in 1529. Today it is preserved in the municipal museum at the Palais des Arts.

The inscription, a fragment of which is missing, has been frequently published, translated and discussed. That it is not a masterpiece of eloquence will be clear from the extract given below.

Claudius begins by recapitulating, without real or even apparent reason, the political changes that have taken place in the Roman state since the time of Romulus. Then he comes to the point:

'Indeed it was something entirely new when my maternal great-uncle, the god Augustus, and Tiberius Caesar, my paternal uncle, decided to admit to the Curia [the Senate of Rome] the flower of the

34. 'It is now time, Tiberius Caesar Germanicus . . .' Fragment of the Claudinian Table, engraved bronze, affixed to a wall of the Temple of Augustus at Lyons.

35. Head of an unknown man. Limestone, 2nd century.

colonies and municipalities, that is, the flower of their honest and well-to-do men. What, you will say, is not an Italian senator to be preferred to a provincial? Later, when I come to ask you to approve that part of my censorship, I will tell you my opinion on that question, and bring facts to support it. But as for the provincials themselves, I think that as long as they are an ornament to the Senate, they should not be rejected.

'Look at the very honourable and powerful colony of the people of Vienne: how long has it not furnished the Curia with senators?'

Here the emperor loses the thread of his speech. He pays tribute to a member of this colony, Lucius Vestinus, with whom he was on friendly terms, and then alludes to someone he calls a brigand, but does not name. Then he comes back to his argument:

'It is now time, Tiberius Caesar Germanicus [he admonishes himself], for you to discover to the conscript fathers the purpose of your argument; for now you have reached the outermost limits of Gallia Narbonensis.[1]

'All these distinguished young men I see before me, we cannot regret that they are senators, any more than I regret that my friend Persicus, a man of great nobility, reads in the list of his ancestors the name of an Allobrogian. If you agree with me, what would you more but that I should point to the soil beyond the frontiers of Narbonensis, which already sends us senators, since we do not regret having men of our order from Lugdunum. . . .

'And now I must plead openly the cause of Gallia Comata. If it be

[1] Vienne was in Narbonensis, but lay close to the frontier of Lugdunensis.

51

objected that the Gauls harassed the late and divine Julius in ten years of war, let us put into the other side of the scales their loyalty that has remained constant for a hundred years, and the obedience that has more than stood the test of many conjunctures that were indeed critical for us. When my father Drusus was subduing Germany, he had a sure peace in his rear, guaranteed by their calmness.' (24: pp. 62–5.)

The speech is no masterpiece of composition, and the main thread is often lost among the frequent digressions. But the chief interest of the Lyons tablet is that it provides an authentic report of the emperor's speech, and the clearest possible indication of his attitude to Gaul.

## Two Renderings of Claudius's Speech

Even without the fortunate accident which led to the discovery of the original text of Claudius's speech, we should still know something about it; such was its success that Tacitus reproduced it in the *Annals*. But the version we have from him, though a polished piece of work, is misleading. A comparison of the two texts is revealing, and an excellent illustration of the methods used by a historian of the ancient world. With him literary considerations carried more weight than scrupulous accuracy. He rewrote any speech that he thought ill-composed, without always respecting the orator's meaning. This accusation has been brought against a good many Roman historians, Livy in particular; but Tacitus, as we shall see, was as unscrupulous as any of them:

'Attus Clausius, by birth a Sabine, from whom I derive my pedigree [says Claudius], was admitted, on one and the same day, to the freedom of Rome, and the patrician rank. Can I do better than adopt that rule of ancient wisdom? It is for the interest of the commonwealth that merit, wherever found, should be transplanted to Rome and made our own. Need I observe that to Alba we are indebted for the Julii, to Camerium for the Coruncani and to Tusculum for the Portii? Without searching the records of antiquity, we know that the nobles of Etruria, of Lucania, and, in short, of all Italy, have been incorporated with the Roman Senate. The Alps, in the course of time, were made the boundaries of the city; and by that extension of our privileges, not simply individuals, but whole nations, were naturalized at once and blended with the Roman name. In a period of profound peace the people beyond Po were admitted to their freedom. Under colour of planting colonies we spread our legions over the face of the globe; and, by drawing into our civil union the flower of the several provinces, we recruited the strength of the mother country. The Balbi came from Spain, and others of equal eminence from the Narbon Gaul: of that accession to our numbers have we reason to repent? . . . The Spartans and the Athenians, without all question, acquired great renown in arms. To what shall we attribute their decline and total ruin? To what, but the injudicious policy of considering the vanquished as aliens to their country? The conduct of Romulus, the founder of Rome, was the very reverse: with wisdom equal to his valour, he made those fellow citizens at night, who, in the morning, were his enemies in the field. . . .

'But the Senones waged war against us: and were the Volscians and the Aequi always our friends?[1] The Gauls, we are told, well nigh overturned the capitol;[2] and did not the Tuscans oblige us to deliver hostages? Did not the Samnites compel a Roman army to pass under the yoke? Review the wars that Rome had upon her hands, and that with the Gauls will be found the shortest.[3] From that time, a lasting and an honourable peace prevailed. Let them now, intermixed with the Roman people, united by ties of affinity, by arts, and congenial manners, be one people with us. Let them bring their wealth to Rome, rather than hoard it up for their own separate use. The institutions of our ancestors, which we so much and so justly revere at present, were, at one time, a novelty in the constitution. The magistrates were, at first, patricians only; the plebeians opened their way to honours; and the Latins, in a short time, followed their example. In good time we embraced all Italy. The measure which I now defend by examples will, at a future day, be another precedent.' (71: vol. i, pp. 306–7.)

The emperor's speech as reported in the *Annals* is a coherent statement of the policy of assimilation (or, in modern terms integration) which Rome adopted for the countries she conquered. But Tacitus lays himself open to serious charges. He rewrote the speech at the beginning of the second century, more than half a century after it had been delivered, at a time when the Empire was at peace and fully conscious of its universal role. The version of Tacitus has a nobility and serenity more characteristic of the Flavians or Antonines than of the last emperors of the Julio-Claudian dynasty fifty years earlier. Tacitus has produced not only a distortion, but an anachronism.

[1] The Senones were a Gaulish tribe living in the region of Sens; the Volscians and Aequi were tribes of ancient Italy, subdued by the Romans in the Samnite wars.

[2] In the sack of Rome, *c.* 388 B.C.

[3] The Gallic war lasted only eight years. The three Samnite wars went on from 312 to 290 B.C.

# 6

# CHECKMATE TO ROME:
# THE CRISIS OF A.D. 69-70

THE repercussions of the crisis which followed Nero's death in A.D. 68 were felt in Gaul, as in the rest of the Empire. Tacitus had a special interest in Gaul and Germany, and he has left a detailed account of the unrest and confusion in the two countries. The threat of dissolution already hung over the Empire, as it did, even more menacingly, in the third century.

## *Mariccus Leads the Peasants' Revolt*

The troubles began with the rebellion of Vindex, a senator and governor of Lugdunensis; but, as Ferdinand Lot says, this was not a national rising. Then came the revolt of Mariccus, briefly and almost regretfully reported by Tacitus in the *History*, and this has a rustic flavour about it. Mariccus was a visionary, one of the Boian tribe which originally came from the Danubian plains and had been settled by Caesar among the Aeduani. He called on the peasantry of the region to take arms against Rome, and his rebellion is worth noting because ancient historians seldom felt that popular movements were of much interest:

'Amidst the dangers that involved the first men of the age, it may be thought beneath the dignity of history to relate the wild adventures of one Mariccus, a Boian by birth, and sprung from the dregs of the people. This man, however mean his condition, had the presumption to mix his name with men who fought for the empire of the world. In a fit of enthusiasm, pretending to have preternatural lights, he called himself the tutelar deity of Gaul and, in the character of a god, dared to defy the Roman arms. He played the imposter so well that he was able to muster eight thousand men. At the head of that deluded multitude he made an attempt on the adjacent villages of the Aeduans. The people of that nation were not to be deluded. They armed the flower of their youth and, with a reinforcement from the Roman cohorts, attacked the fanatics, and put the whole body to the rout. Mariccus was taken prisoner and soon after given to the wild beasts. The populace, astonished to see that he was not immediately torn to pieces, believed him to be sacred and inviolable. Vitellius ordered him to be executed under his own eye; and that catastrophe cured the people of their bigotry.' (71: vol. ii, p. 117.)

## Civilis and the Conspiracy of Gaul

The rebellion of Civilis was less easily suppressed, and the considerable space which Tacitus devotes to it in the *History* is indication of its seriousness. Civilis was a Batavian of royal blood, in command of a cohort of German auxiliaries, who incited his tribe to mutiny on the pretext that he was supporting Vespasian's claim to the Empire. But Tacitus says that his real aim was to make himself king over all the Transalpine tribes. He recruited an army from his fellow countrymen in the Rhine district, and then sought Gaulish help to stiffen the rebellion, even though the Gauls were mistrustful of their German neighbours. But the burning of the Capitol at Rome by the Illyrian legions after the assassination of Vitellius acted like magic on the Gauls, and they plunged headlong into revolt. The rising soon became general, and spread to a large part of the Roman Empire.

'Above all, the destruction of the Capitol announced the approaching fate of the Roman empire [says Tacitus]. The Druids . . . taught that, when Rome was formerly sacked by the Gauls, the mansion of Jupiter being left entire, the commonwealth survived that dreadful shock; but the calamity of fire, which had lately happened, was a denunciation from heaven, in consequence of which, power and dominion were to circulate round the world, and the nations on their side of the Alps were in their turn to become masters of the world. A report prevailed, at the same time, that the chieftains of Gaul, who had been employed by Otho against Vitellius, bound themselves by solemn league, if the civil dissensions of

36. Roman cavalryman of the second *ala Flaviana*.

37. Denarius of Civilis (reverse), A.D. 70. Two clasped hands holding a bunch of ears of corn and a standard surmounted by a boar.

Rome continued, to watch their opportunity, and, by one brave effort, recover their natural independence.'

## The Beginning of the Struggle

The assassination of Hordeonius Flaccus, the legate of upper Germany, was the signal for open rebellion.

'Before the murder of Hordeonius Flaccus [says Tacitus], this confederacy was a profound secret. That tragic event no sooner happened, than a negotiation took place between Civilis and Classicus, who commanded a squadron of Treverian horse, and was, at that time, a leading chief among the Gauls, in fame and wealth surpassing the rest of his countrymen. He derived his origin from a royal line. . . . His plot was strengthened by the accession of Julius Tutor and Julius Sabinus; the former a Treverian; the latter, one of the Lingones. . . .[1] The conspirators . . . held a general meeting in the Agrippinian colony [Cologne] . . . declaring with vehemence "that Rome was brought, by the madness of her own intestine divisions, to the brink of ruin; her armies were cut to pieces; Italy was laid waste and the city taken by storm. In other parts of the Empire the legions have different wars upon their hands; what then remains but to take possession of the Alps? Secure the passes over those mountains, and Gaul will not only recover her liberty, but establish an independent empire. She may then deliberate where to fix the extent and boundaries of her own dominions". This great and daring project was approved as soon as heard.' (*71*: vol. ii, pp. 256-7.)

The rebels lost no time in acting on these proposals, and there followed what Jullian calls 'the strange scene of the proclamation of independence'. The prelude to this was the massacre of the legate Vocula, whose attempts to keep the legions loyal to Rome were completely unsuccessful. Tacitus reports the speech he made to his troops; they would not listen, and Tacitus goes on:

'Vocula retired, with his own hand determined to deliver himself from a seditious army. His slaves and freedmen interposed, but their officious care reserved him for a harsher fate. Classicus dispatched his assassin, by name Aemilius Longinus, a deserter from the first legion. That ruffian struck the fatal blow. Herennius and Numisius, who had each the command of a legion, were secured in chains. Classicus, a short time afterwards, entered the camp, with the pomp and apparel of a Roman commander; and though he brought with him a mind prompt and daring, he made no attempt to harangue the men, content with repeating the words of the oath. The soldiers swore fidelity to the empire of the Gauls.' (*71*: vol. ii, p. 260.)

Simultaneously with the Gallic insurrection, the Germans under the Batavian Civilis were in full revolt. Tacitus' work on Germany is proof of his interest in the country and his knowledge of it; and in his account of the rebellion he takes obvious pleasure in highlighting typical details, in particular the curious part played by the prophetess Veleda:

[1] The Treveri inhabited Trèves, the Lingones Langres.

'Civilis, when he first took up arms against the Romans, bound himself by a solemn vow, according to the custom of those barbarous nations, to cherish the growth of his hair, which was now waving about his shoulders, dishevelled, long and red. Thinking himself absolved by the slaughter of the legions, he cut it short for the first time during the war. He is said to have given his infant son some Roman prisoners, as a mark to be levelled at with little darts and arrows, for the diversion of a child. It is worthy of notice that, in the height of his zeal for the empire of Gaul, he neither swore fidelity himself nor required that act of submission from the Batavians. He relied on the valour of the Germans; and should it be necessary to contend for the sovereign power, he considered his own abilities, and his fame in arms, as a decided superiority. Mummius Lupercus, the commander of a legion, was sent, among a number of ample presents, to Veleda, a prophetess of the Bructerian nation. She ruled over a large tract of territory. Her name was held in veneration throughout Germany. The superstition of the country ascribed to numbers of women a preternatural insight into future events; and, in consequence of that persuasion, many have been revered as goddesses. Veleda at that time was the oracle of Germany. She had foretold the success of her countrymen and the destruction of the legions. Her fame, in consequence of that prediction, rose to the highest pitch. Lupercus was murdered on the road.' (*71*: vol. ii, p. 262.)

Chateaubriand conferred on Veleda a fame she would never otherwise have achieved by giving her a leading role in his novel *Les Martyrs*. But he completely transformed her, and turned the Bructerian tribal prophetess of Vespasian's days into a Druid priestess of the time of Diocletian, conducting her sacrifices against the romantic backcloth of the Armorican coast; the only common factor is her name.

## Cerialis Defends the Roman Peace

Meanwhile the natural antagonism between Gauls and Germans, and dissensions within Gaul, were paralysing the rebellion; and the news that a strong Roman army was advancing brought the Gauls to a more reasonable and moderate frame of mind. The Gallic cities met in conference at Reims. Tacitus, in his summary of the debate, lays special stress on the speech of Julius Auspex, one of the chief citizens of the city of the Remi, emphasizing the power of Rome and the advantages of the Pax Romana.

Cerialis, the legate of Vespasian who had just been proclaimed

38. Roman horse-trapping; ornament for breast-strap.

emperor, found his task made even easier by the defeat of the Gaulish chieftain Tutor by a troop of auxiliaries, and the rout of the Treveri. Cerialis was a newcomer to Gaul, but, as Jullian says, he soon showed himself to be 'a prudent general, a fine orator and a shrewd politician'. Going first to Mainz, he had no difficulty in extinguishing the last flicker of revolt there, and a few days later proceeded, almost without opposition, to Trèves, where he set up his headquarters. He then summoned the Treveri and the Lingones, the only Gallic tribes who had persisted in rebellion, and addressed them in a speech which Tacitus reports thus in his *History*:

'Eloquence is not my province: it is a talent which I never cultivated. Arms have been my profession; in the field of battle I have given you proof of Roman valour. But words, and what you call eloquence, are in your estimation superior gifts, of power to change the colours of good and evil. It is not by the nature of things that you form your judgment: the speech of a seditious incendiary has more weight and influence. But a few plain words may prove a seasonable antidote. I shall, therefore, explain myself to you on certain points which, now the war is over, it will be more in your interest to hear than in mine to enforce. When the Roman generals at the head of their armies entered your territories and the other provinces of Gaul, they were neither led by their own ambition nor the lust for conquest. They were invited by your ancestors, at that time torn by intestine divisions, and driven to the brink of ruin. You had called the Germans to your aid, and those barbarians proved the worst of tyrants: they enslaved, without distinction, those who invited them, and those who resisted. The battles which Rome has fought with the Teutones and the Cimbrians need not be mentioned. Her wars in

59

Germany, and the toil and vigour of her legions, with the various events that followed, are all sufficiently known. If the legions seized the banks of the Rhine, can the defence of Italy be deemed the motive? The protection of Gaul was the object, and another Ariovistus may not aspire to reign over you. And do you now imagine that Civilis, or the Batavians, or the nations beyond the Rhine have that affection for you and your welfare which your forefathers never experienced from their ancestors? The same motives that first incited the Germans to cross the Rhine will ever subsist: ambition, avarice and the love of new settlements will be perpetual incentives. The Germans will be ready at all times to change their swampy fens and barren deserts for your fertile plains and fruitful valleys. On your own soil they wish to lord it over you. They come to ravage your land, and liberty is the pretext. But the rights of men, and other specious names, are the language of all who want to usurp dominion over others.

'Your country, till you put yourselves under our protection, was at all times harassed with wars and oppressed by tyrants. Rome has been often insulted, often provoked, by the unruly spirit of the Gauls; and what has been the use of her victories? She required no more at your hands than what was necessary for the aid of a government that defends and protects you. To maintain the tranquillity of nations, arms are necessary; soldiers must be kept in pay; and, without a tribute from the provinces, how are supplies to be raised? In common with the citizens of Rome you enjoy every benefit. Our legions are often commanded by you; you are governors of your own provinces, and even of others subject to the Empire. All posts of honour are open to you: nothing is precluded. Does a virtuous prince rule at Rome; though placed at a distance, you feel the mildness of his government. Does a tyrant rule with an iron rod, his weight is felt by those immediately within his reach. Natural evils, such as incessant rains and barren seasons, you are forced to bear; political evils, such as the avarice and prodigality of princes, should in like manner be endured. As long as there are men there will be vices. But vice is not without interruption. Better times succeed, and the virtue of a good prince atones for antecedent evils. But perhaps you expect from Tutor and Classicus a mild and equitable reign. Under their auspices armies must be raised to repel the Germans and the Britons; and this, you fancy, will be done with lighter taxes than you pay at present. Overturn the Roman power (may the gods avert so dire a calamity!) and what think you will be the consequence? The nations will rise in arms and the world will be a theatre of war. During a space of eight hundred years the mighty fabric of the Empire has been raised by the valour of the legions and a series of victories; nor can the fabric be rent from its foundation without burying all who prevail against it in one general ruin. In that scene of wild commotion Gaul will be the sufferer. You have gold and riches: those great incentives of ambition, and the prime cause of war. Peace is in your interest. Cherish it, therefore, and honour the city of Rome: a city that protects her subjects and is ever ready to receive the conquered upon equal terms with her own inhabitants. Take warning from your own experience; you have known the smiles and frowns of fortune. It will now be yours to show that you have the wisdom to prefer to a revolt, which may involve you all in ruin, a pacific temper, and a due regard to your own internal happiness.' (*71* : vol. ii, pp. 272–4.)

Tacitus has forged this harangue to the rebel Gauls, just as he forged the address of the Emperor Claudius to the Senate. In both speeches we can detect the pride of a Roman of Trajan's time, a pride based on the conviction that Rome has received from the gods, by the unprecedented favour of fortune, the mission of keeping peace throughout the world. But the speech of Cerialis is even more improbable than that of Claudius. Tacitus's rewriting of a speech which Claudius did indeed deliver before the Senate is reprehensible enough, but the harangue he puts into the mouth of Cerialis is sheer imagination; we can hardly believe that a legate, however scholarly his tastes, could have, or indeed would have, composed an oration so well documented and so persuasive for the ears of a totally uneducated audience. Let us accept this speech for what it is: an exercise in eloquence by a writer who never missed an opportunity of exalting Rome, even at the risk of distorting historical truth.

# 7

# INSCRIPTIONS AND THEIR
# VALUE TO HISTORY

ALTHOUGH Cerialis's speech was never delivered in the form which Tacitus gives it, it deserves notice because it reflects the attitude of the most intelligent thinkers of the Antonine age; it mirrors the pride of a Roman of the second century A.D. in the Pax Romana which reigned throughout the world.

For Ferdinand Lot the speech is in a way symbolic. It shut the door on the past. Gaul made no further attempt to break away from the Empire, at least for nearly a century. The full integration of her people in the Empire now seemed an accomplished fact. Silence falls until the final disruption of the Empire, when the voice of Gaul is heard once more.

The monuments erected in early imperial times (temples, theatres, amphitheatres, triumphal arches, aqueducts), as well as roads and ports, bear silent witness to the prosperity of Gaul. But they are not the only evidence; thousands of inscriptions have survived, and from them we can learn something of life in Gaul, even though their wording is conventional and so to some extent insincere. Here are a few examples.

## The Imperial Cult

Emperor-worship, a remarkably effective instrument of romanization, was soon established. In every city an altar was set up and dedicated to the emperor. But the adoption of emperor-worship did not necessarily

39. Solid gold patera found at Rennes; A.D. 210. Border of Imperial Roman coins, central medallion representing Bacchus' challenge to Hercules.

40. Mercury. Bronze from
Chanceaux (Côte-d'Or).

mean that the traditional cults were abandoned; sometimes they existed side by side, and one and the same altar served to satisfy both official regulations and popular piety, as in this inscription from an altar found at Bordeaux:

AUGUSTO SACRUM
ET GENIO CIVITATIS
BIT [*urigum*] VIV [*iscorum*]

Sacred to Augustus
and the genius of the city
of Bordeaux.
(*36*: vol. 1, p. 44.)

41. Hammer-god (Taranis). Bronze found at Orpierre (Hautes-Alpes).

The imperial government organized the cult of the emperor with great ingenuity, appointing a flamen in every provincial capital to preside over the ceremonies, and with great political wisdom choosing him from among the local aristocracy. The office of flamen commanded great respect and was much sought after, and there are many funerary inscriptions to show the esteem in which it was held. A typical example comes from Cimiez, now a district in the town of Nice, which was the capital of the Alpes Maritimes under the early Empire:

'To the sacred memory of C. Subrius Secundinus, flamen and patron of the province, a model of piety, eloquence and moral character, C. Subrius Severianus, his brother, grievously unprepared for his untimely death. He lived forty-two years, four months and a few days. He would have been fortunate had he been granted longer life, but jealous fate refused it. O unhappy mortals! They who would not live, live on, and they who should live, die, the victims of cruel destiny.' (*40*: p. 7.)

## Religious Syncretism

But though emperor-worship spread throughout Gaul, the old divinities still had their votaries and altars were still dedicated to them. The most touching examples are to be found in country districts, like this inscription carved on an old pagan altar which is still preserved in a chapel of the penitents in the mountains behind Nice. Its top had been

hollowed out, and it was taken into use as a holy-water stoup, perhaps owing its preservation to this change of function:

| | |
|---|---|
| SEGOMON | To Segomon |
| CUNTINO | of Contes |
| VIC [*ani*] CUN [*tini*] | the villagers of Contes |
| P[*osuerunt*] | have erected this altar. |
| | (*64*: p. 35.) |

The inscription, brief as it is, tells us a great deal: it shows us the inhabitants of the village of Contes, nowadays a small country town in the Alpes Maritimes, clubbing together for an altar in honour of Segomon, a Gallic divinity who was a sort of Celtic Mars.

Gradually the traditional gods of Gaul were merged with the Roman pantheon. The conquerors encouraged this syncretism (to use a term in

42. Mercury wearing travelling-cap and holding a purse. Bronze from Puy-de Dôme.

43. Mounted god (Jupiter) with fish-tailed monster, from Neschers (Puy-de-Dôme).

44. Abundantia holding a cornucopia; a child at her side. From Agey (Côte-d'Or).

67

45. Minerva, originally holding a spear. Bronze from Lons-le-Saunier.

vogue among the historians of religions); as we saw in Chapter 2, this was the policy of Rome as early as Caesar's time.

The Gauls seem to have held Mercury, the god of trade, in special veneration. One example will suffice. A little altar, on which the god was represented naked but for a cloak flung over his left shoulder, was discovered in the foundations of the Roman wall of Bordeaux. The inscription records that its donor was from Limoges, perhaps a merchant trading with Bordeaux:

MERC [*urio*] VIDUCO CIVIS LEMOVIC [*us*]
V [*otum*] S [*olvit*] L [*ibens*] M [*erito*]
To Mercury, Viduco, a citizen of Limoges,
discharges his vow of his free will and in gratitude.
(*36*: vol. i, p. 44.)

The Gauls were not content to assimilate their national gods with the gods of the Romans. They welcomed with open arms divinities from other lands, particularly those from the east who found their way into Gaul with the army. One of the most popular of these was Cybele, the Great Mother, a Phrygian goddess, in whose honour bulls were sacrificed, and the faithful sprinkled with their blood. This ceremony sometimes had an official character, for from time to time bulls were sacrificed for the health of the emperor. Here is a curious inscription from Fréjus (perhaps incomplete, since the donor's name is missing), which records

47. Hygeia found at Cimiez (Alpes Maritimes).

46. Mercury with caduceus, on one side of the lec'h (carved menhir) from Kervadel (Finistère).

the sacrifice of a bull for the health of Antoninus Pius, emperor from 138 to 161:

| | |
|---|---|
| PRO SAL [*ute*] | For the health |
| ANTONIN [i] | of Antoninus |
| TAUROBOLI | a bull has been sacrificed |
| UM FECIT | |
| [*Matri*] D [*eum*] M [*agnae*] | in honour of the Great Mother of the gods |
| I [*daeae*] | of Ida (that is, Phrygian; Mt Ida was in Phrygia). |
| | (*19*: p. 135.) |

The most effective contribution to the Romanization of Gaul was made by the regional and local institutions set up by the emperors. While each provincial capital had an assembly which supervised the administration of the imperial government, the cities administered themselves, having a senate of decurions recruited from the local inhabitants, as well as municipal magistrates, duumvirs, aediles and quaestors. Local activities flourished in Roman Gaul under the early Empire, as is shown by the large number of gilds of artisans and merchants recorded in inscriptions.

Inscriptions of all kinds, religious, honorific or funerary, provide a rich harvest of names and titles; but they are so concise that it takes a real effort of imagination to discern the human reality behind the conventional formula. We must make the most of the all too rare inscriptions which have broken with the traditional brevity.

## *The Thorigny Marble: the Career of a Magistrate*

Of these more informative texts, one of the most remarkable ever discovered within the boundaries of ancient Gaul is the Thorigny inscription, published by H. G. Pflaum (*58*). It is on the base of a statue in red marble, found in the sixteenth century in the village of Vieux near Caen. It was taken to Thorigny by the count of Matignon, and in 1814 handed over to the museum at St Lô, where it was badly damaged when the town was bombed on 6th June 1944.

The statue itself has disappeared; it was carved in A.D. 238, and represented Titus Sennius Sollemnis, a citizen of Vieux, which is now a small country town in the Department of Calvados, but was then the capital of the Viducassi.

Sollemnis had had a brilliant career. He began as a municipal magistrate and, thanks to his own merits, and also perhaps to influential patrons, became high priest of Rome and Augustus at the assembly of the Three Provinces which met every year at Lyons; he was then military tribune in Numidia and Britain, and ended his career as assessor to the iron-workings. It is difficult to estimate the importance of this post, but we should probably not be far out in equating it with the directorship of a great nationalized enterprise in our own times.

The career of Sollemnis is summarized on the front face of the monument, which reminds us that, even if he enjoyed a high salary, he was capable of spending it generously on occasion:

'To Titus Sennius Sollemnis, son of Sollemninus, four times duumvir without decision by lot, augur, invested with all honours in his own city: at the same time, being high priest at the altar of Rome and Augustus, he

48. Mother-goddesses, protectors of the harvest. Votive monument, early third century.

presented all kinds of public shows; there were gladiatorial combats to the number of thirty-two, of which eight, in the space of four days, were fights to the death.

'He completed the baths which Sollemninus had bequeathed for the benefit of his fellow countrymen, after laying their foundations; and he left a legacy for their upkeep in perpetuity.

'Sollemnis was the friend and client of Tiberius Claudius Paulinus, legate of Augustus with praetorian powers in the province of Lugdunensis. Afterwards, when Paulinus became legate with praetorian powers in Britain, he joined his staff at the Sixth Legion's headquarters.'

The inscription goes on to say that Sollemnis was the client of another high-ranking magistrate, Aedinius Julianus, and then on the suite of the military tribune of the Third Legion in Numidia; and it ends:

'To the assessor to the iron-workings, the first to whom the three provinces of Gaul have ever erected a monument in his own town. The place has been given by the order of the decurions of the free city of the Viducassi.

'Erected on the seventeenth day of the January kalends, in the consulship of Pius and Proculus.' [16th December 238.]

49. Sacrifice of bull. Low relief, found near Vaison.

50. Altar dedicated to the ears of Cybele. Glanum excavations.
51. Officiating priest, wearing toga. Bronze statuette found at Lyons.
52. Servant of the goddess Attys holding a casket. Bronze appliqué figure.

Not content with this dedication, the 'committee' which erected the monument went on to record, on the two sides of the base, letters testifying to the merits of Sollemnis from the two high-ranking magistrates who were his patrons.

The more flattering of these testimonials comes from the praetorian prefect Aedinius Julianus:

'When I was chief magistrate in the province of Lugdunensis, I recognized the merits of many worthy men, among them the high priest Sollemnis, a native of the city of the Viducassi, whom I came to love for his high principles and upright life. I must add that, when certain men tried to level an accusation in council, ostensibly with the consent of the provinces, against my predecessor Claudius Paulinus, thinking that his treatment of their merits gave them ground for grievance against him, my friend Sollemnis opposed their purpose . . . and for that reason the accusation was dropped; and so my affection and esteem for him grew even greater. . . .'

73

53. Birth of Venus. Silver patera handle, 2nd century, from Bondonneau (Drôme).

The second letter is a curious document. It comes from the propraetor Claudius Paulinus, whose name occurs in the first letter and whom Sollemnis had championed at the council of Gaul. It lists the presents offered to Sollemnis, as well as the salary he was to draw when he accompanied Paulinus to Britain as tribune:

'Though your deserts are greater, yet I would have you cheerfully accept these small offerings as due to your office: a cloak from Canusium, a tunic from Laodicaea, a gold brooch inset with jewels, two mantles, a British tunic and a sealskin. Your warrant as tribune I will send shortly, when a vacancy arises. Meanwhile accept the pay due to your office, that is, twenty-five thousand sesterces in gold. By the favour of the gods and the sacred majesty of the emperor, you shall obtain in due course a return more worthy of the merits of your goodwill towards me. In all friendship.'

It is hardly likely that any monument to an officer of the law erected in our own day would include any mention of the emoluments of his office or the presents in kind he was given. Times have changed. But we can learn a good deal from this monument about a career in the magistracy; and we may note that in the early days of the Roman Empire, as at many other times, the patronage of the influential was by no means without its uses for advancement.

74

*Part III*

# THE THIRD AND FOURTH CENTURIES

# 8

# THE DISASTROUS THIRD CENTURY

THE Thorigny marble brings us to the third century. The Pax Romana is foundering; the accession of the Severans in 193 ushered in a period of disorders at home and perils abroad which was to lead to the Later Roman Empire. H. G. Pflaum says in his penetrating commentary on the Thorigny inscriptions that they may be seen as a reflection of the political crisis of the early third century, when the privileged classes of senators and equites were threatened by mounting pressure from the new class of parvenus. He suggests that the Thorigny marble may have been erected by their partisans, in honour of an honest man who kept faith with his friends.

Whether this was so or not, third-century Gaul was ravaged by revolutions and invasions. Behind the accounts of historians such as the authors of the *Historia Augusta*, unreliable as they are, we can occasionally glimpse these upheavals. But to fill in the gaps in his documentation the modern student of history has to call in the help of the numismatist and the archaeologist. We are indeed hard to please; we treat with suspicion the great Latin historians, Caesar and Tacitus, and accuse them of distorting the facts; but without them we are lost, reduced to begging from door to door for scraps of information which can never be anything but inadequate and uncertain, however ingenious a use we make of them.

The end of the reign of Alexander Severus (235) coincided with an upsurge of the German barbarians and mounting pressure on the Rhine. We find new peoples making their appearance, or perhaps only new names for barbarian peoples.

## First Appearance of the Franks

After the Alemanni, the Franks make their first entry into history in the middle of the third century. This important moment is recorded by the biographer of the Emperor Aurelian in the *Historia Augusta*.[1] Talking of Aurelian as a young man (he was born in 214), he says:

'Aurelian was tribune of the Sixth Legion (Gallicana) at Mainz when the Franks attempted to overrun the whole of Gaul. He shattered their attack, killing seven hundred of them and selling three hundred prisoners as slaves. And so this refrain was made about him:

We have killed a thousand Franks and a thousand Sarmatians once and again.
Now we are looking for a thousand Persians.' (*31*: vol. ii, p. 141.)[2]

## The Usurper Postumus

With the increasing threat of invasion by the Germans, with anarchy reigning in the Empire as the armies proclaimed and then assassinated one emperor after another, and the general unrest in all quarters of the globe, it became abundantly clear that the task of governing this immense Empire had become too great for any one man. The hard fact was recognized when the tetrarchy was set up at the end of the century. The need to have a man on the spot who wielded full powers was felt in Gaul as early as the middle of the third century, when a military leader called Postumus, whom the Roman Emperor Gallienus had left with his son, as the boy's adviser, on the Rhine, usurped the imperial power, but without any intention of overthrowing the sovereignty of Rome. One of the authors of the *Historia Augusta* wrote a short biography of

[1] The title *Historia Augusta* has been given to a collection of biographies of emperors, covering the 166 years between the accession of Hadrian (117) and the death of Carus and his sons (283). A recent student of this curious and important (but somewhat misleading) work, Henri Stein, thinks that it was written in the mid fourth century. Six authors, whose names have come down to us, seem to have collaborated in it.

[2] A similar refrain (*cantilena*) had already been written for Aurelian after a victory over the Sarmatians.

78

54. Bronze coin of Postumus,
reverse. Four standards, surrounded
by the legend 'FIDES
EXERCITUS.'

55. The emperor Postumus.
Obverse of an aureus, third
century.

Postumus, or more accurately a panegyric inspired by a rather too
obvious dislike of the unhappy Gallienus, then emperor in Rome:

'Postumus was so courageous in war, so steadfast in peace, so dignified
in his whole life, that when Gallienus left his son Saloninus in Gaul he
entrusted the boy to Postumus, to watch over his character and way of
life and organize the imperial administration. But later, as many assert
(though it is not in keeping with his character), he broke faith, killed
Saloninus and seized supreme power. Others say (and this is more
probable) that the Gauls had a violent hatred of Gallienus and could not
bear the boy to rule over them; so they proclaimed emperor the man
who wielded the imperial power which had been entrusted to him, and
sent soldiers to kill the youth. After the assassination Postumus was
gladly accepted by all the army and the whole of Gaul, and for seven
years[1] so conducted himself that he restored all Gaul; meanwhile
Gallienus gave himself up to riotous living and gormandizing, and wore
himself out in a passionate love affair with a barbarian woman. Gallienus,
however, made war on Postumus, and was wounded by an arrow.
Indeed all the people of Gaul had great love for Postumus, because he
had driven back all the German tribes and had restored the Roman
Empire to all its former security. But even while he was reigning so
worthily, he was assassinated at the instigation of Lollianus, by reason of
that habit of mind of the Gauls which makes them always eager for
change.' (31: vol. ii, pp. 92–3.)

Numismatic evidence supports this eulogy of Postumus. It is well
known that in troublous times individuals tend to collect and conceal
reserves of precious metal. The first barbarian invasions produced this
reaction among the Gallic peoples towards the end of the third century,

[1] It is difficult to determine how long Postumus reigned, and this estimate has been
challenged; F. Lot (49: p. 332) thinks that he ruled for ten years, from 257 to 267.

56. Head of a man, stone, second to
third century.

and many coins with the effigy of Postumus have been discovered in
hoards buried at that time. They bear characteristic legends, many
referring to Postumus as the saviour of Gaul and to his reign as a time
of felicity.

## The Short-lived Empire of Gaul

Once Postumus had disappeared from the scene, the Gallic Empire he
had founded followed the deplorable example of Rome. Emperor
followed emperor in quick succession; first Lollianus, who had in-
stigated the assassination of Postumus, then Marius the blacksmith,
then Victorinus; finally a peace-loving senator, Tetricus, was raised to
the supreme power by Victorina or Victoria, the mother of Victorinus;
she was a contemporary and emulator of the famous princess of Palmyra,
Zenobia. Tetricus made his submission to the emperor, and thus ended a
regime which had lasted no more than fifteen years (258–73), and to
which modern historians have given the grandiose title of the Empire of
Gaul.[1] The biographer of Postumus has left us a picturesque, if fictitious,
portrait of Marius the blacksmith, who reigned for three short days:

[1] F. Lot (49: p. 322) dismisses this title as absurd. 'Postumus was not a Gaul, and
would have been horrorstruck at the idea of setting up a state separated from Rome.'

57. Large compass and blacksmith's tongs.
Gallo-Roman tools.

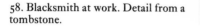

58. Blacksmith at work. Detail from a
tombstone.

'After Victorinus, Lollianus[1] and Postumus had been assassinated, Marius reigned for only three days; it is said that he had been a black-smith. I do not know what more information is needed about him, unless that it was the shortness of his reign that makes him noteworthy. For he is like the consul surrogate[2] who held his consulship for six hours one afternoon, whom Cicero aspersed with the jibe: "We have had a consul so stern and severe that during his term of office no one dined nor supped nor slept;" and of Marius it can be said that he was made emperor one day, was seen to reign the next and was assassinated the third day. He was energetic in his life, and had risen to the supreme power through the various ranks of the army. Many called him Marmurius,[3] and some Veturius,[4] since he had been a blacksmith. But we have already said too much about him, and we need only add that no one had more strength in his hands, whether in striking or pushing; he seemed to have sinews instead of veins in his fingers. It is said that he could push back a moving cart with his forefinger, and knock down the strongest men with one finger, and that they felt as much pain from it as if they had been hit by a piece of wood or iron. Many things he could reduce to powder by crushing them between two

[1] Other historians call him Laelianus.
[2] Caninius Rebilus, surrogate of Quintus Fabius Maximus, a consul who died on his last day of office.
[3] The name of a legendary Etruscan blacksmith.
[4] Possibly Vecturius, though this word could more easily mean a wagoner.

MAP 3
GAUL AT THE END OF THE FOURTH
CENTURY DIVIDED INTO TWO DIOCESES
*(see page 91)*

Diocese of the Gauls:

*1* L = Lugdunensis Prima, metropolis Lyons
*2* L =      —      Secunda,   —   Rouen
*3* L =      —      Tertia,    —   Tours
*4* L =      —      Quarta,    —   Sens
*1* B = Belgica Prima, metropolis Trèves
*2* B =    —    Secunda,   —   Reims
*1* G = Germanica Prima, metropolis Mainz
*2* G =     —     Secunda,   —   Cologne
    Maxima Sequanorum, metropolis Besançon
Alpes Graiae et Poeninae, metropolis Moûtiers


Diocese of Vienne:


Viennensis, metropolis Vienne

*1* N = Narbonensis Prima, metropolis Narbonne
*2* N =      —      Secunda,   —   Aix
    Alpes Maritimae, metropolis Embrun
*1* A = Aquitania Prima, metropolis Bourges
*2* A =     —     Secunda,   —   Bordeaux
    Novempopulana, metropolis Eauze


*Names of metropolises are underlined on the map.*

82

fingers. He was killed by a soldier who had once worked in his forge, but whom he had treated with contempt either when he had command in the army or when he seized the supreme power. The story goes that his assassin said as he killed him: "This is the sword you forged with your own hands." It is said that his first speech to the army was in these terms: "I know, comrades, that I may be taunted with my former trade, of which you are all witnesses. But let people say what they will. Better to go on working iron than to be ruined by wine and flowers and women and taverns, like Gallienus, who is unworthy of his father and his noble birth. Let people taunt me with being a blacksmith, so long as foreign nations admit, after the disasters we inflict on them, that I know how to handle iron. And finally, let all the territories of the Alemanni

60. Peasant wearing the cucullus, a coarse woollen garment with hood.

59. Pacatianus, lieutenant of Septimius Severus. Detail of bronze statue from Vienne (Isère).

and the Germans and the other tribes round about them think that the Roman people is a race of iron, and especially fear the iron in us. And I would wish you for your part to think that you have crowned a man who never knew how to handle anything except iron. And this I say because I know that that monster of profligacy can reproach me with nothing save that I once forged swords and arms." ' (*31*: vol. ii, pp. 96–7.)

This curious biography is symbolic of its times. The stress it lays on the brutality of the blacksmith is clear proof that the atmosphere prevailing at the end of the ill-starred third century was very different from that of Trajan's or Antoninus Pius's time. Fear reigned supreme, and in an ill-governed empire the sword was the only protection against the barbarian lurking on the Rhine frontier.

Aurelius Victor,[1] another biographer of the emperors, and a conscientious collector of facts, stigmatizes one of the vices which were spreading like a gangrene through the administration of the Empire and reducing it to impotence: the corruption of the government clerks. Through all the ages, including our own, government bureaucracy has never lacked critics; but in the third century fraudulence seems to have flourished as never before or since:

'Two days after Marius had been murdered, the choice fell on Victorinus, who was Postumus' equal in knowledge of war, but a man of unrestrained depravity. At first he curbed his passions, but after he had reigned for two years, and when he had violated a great many women, he seduced the wife of Attitianus, and she revealed his villainy to her husband; the soldiers were secretly incited to revolt, and Victorinus was killed in an uprising. The factions of the clerks, of whom Attitianus was one, were so powerful in the army that the crime was perpetrated on their insistence. They are, and were especially at that time, a worthless class of men, corrupt, crafty, seditious and grasping, committing and concealing frauds as if by instinct. As victuallers to the army, they are naturally hostile to those who ply useful trades and to the fortunes of those who till the soil. They are skilled in choosing the right moment to bribe those at whose expense, and by whose foolishness, they have enriched themselves.' (*5*: p. 110.)

This stern judgment should be noted. Behind it we can glimpse the misery of the country people exploited by the clerks who bought

[1] Author of several historical works, the most important being the *Liber de Caesaribus*, apparently written in 360. This consists of a series of biographies of the emperors from Augustus to Julian.

supplies for the army, and can guess at innumerable shady transactions and unvoiced resentments—a sombre background to the picture of the third century, which is saddening even today.

## The Barbarian Threat to Gaul

The biographer of Postumus claims that he halted the German invasions; but the check was only temporary, and a few years later, on the death of the Emperor Aurelian, the storm of invasion broke in redoubled violence. Vopiscus, one of the authors of the *Historia Augusta*, who wrote the life of Probus, has given us details of the invasion and of the victorious counter-offensive of his hero, whom he considers, perhaps over-enthusiastically, to have been the greatest and most famous of all emperors:

61. Two German prisoners, chained together by neck. Carved stone.

## Counter-attack by Probus

'After this Probus led a great army into Gaul, which was in a state of confusion since the murder of Postumus, and had been seized by the Germans after the death of Aurelian. His campaign was so successful that he retook sixty cities from the barbarians, which were among the noblest in Gaul, and all the booty which had brought the invaders not only wealth but renown as well. And while they ranged confidently along our frontiers and even right through Gaul, he slaughtered almost 400,000 of them who had occupied Roman territory and drove the survivors back beyond the Neckar and Elbe. He captured as much booty from the barbarians as they had taken from the Romans; and he built fortified Roman towns on barbarian soil and garrisoned them. He gave fields, granaries, houses and provisions to all those living beyond the Rhine whom he had settled there as his outposts. Fighting went on ceaselessly, and every day barbarians' heads were brought to him, for each of which he paid one gold piece; until the day nine petty kings from different tribes came and fell at his feet. He demanded hostages in the first place, and these were immediately produced; and then corn, and finally cattle and sheep. . . . Further, he received 16,000 recruits, whom he dispersed among the different provinces, incorporating them in groups of fifty or sixty in the units of the regular army or the frontier forces; for he said that it must be felt, and not seen, when Romans were reinforced by barbarians.' (*31*: vol. ii, p. 196.)[1]

## Organization of Defences

Doubts have been cast on the accuracy of this account and the seriousness of the barbarian invasion of 276. But one fact should be noted, which seems proof of its veracity. The end of the third century is a crucial date in the history of Gaulish towns. Constantly threatened by invasion, reduced to poverty, often razed to the ground, they walled themselves in with a girdle of stone.

In most cases town walls were built as hasty defences against the barbarian onslaught, and their builders used whatever materials came

---

[1] 'As for the figure of 400,000 barbarians massacred by Probus,' says Lot (*49*: p. 327), 'this is pure invention.' He goes on to call the *Historia Augusta* 'a hotchpotch of anachronisms, errors and misrepresentations'. Not all modern historians would describe it so damningly. If the reader gains nothing more from the arguments on both sides, he will at least realize the difficulty of writing a history of the period based on the comparatively late and certainly tendentious compilations that have come down to us.

62. Town gate and
ramparts. Fragment of
Roman mosaic.

to hand, especially monuments that had fallen into ruin. Towns became fortresses crammed into the smallest possible space, most of them reduced to an area of some twenty or thirty acres.

In some towns, such as Le Mans, there is still plenty of evidence of the line of the town walls; and we have useful pointers, such as the re-use in the foundations of older inscribed stones, as well as coin-hoards, which date them towards the end of the third century.

There are very few towns which can be specifically dated. But in the case of Grenoble we have the text of two inscriptions commemorating the building of the town gates. The first was the Traine gate, demolished in 1591. The inscription ran:

'*Muris Cularonensibus cum interioribus aedificiis providentia sua institutis adque perfectis portam Romanam Joviam vocari jusserunt*—The walls of Cularo, with the buildings within, having been begun and completed by the foresight of Diocletian, it was ordered that the Roman gate be called the Jovian gate.'

(Cularo was the original name of Grenoble, which was renamed Gratianopolis after Gratian, emperor from 375 to 383; it was in his reign that Grenoble became the see of a bishop, and perhaps then too that it became a *civitas*. Jovian—from Jupiter—was the surname usually given to Diocletian.)

The second gate, which survived until 1804, was the Porta Viennensis, so called because it opened on to the Roman road to Vienne. It was dedicated to Diocletian's associate, the Emperor Maximian, who bore the surname Herculean:

'*Portam Viennensem Herculeam vocari jusserunt*—It was ordered that the Vienne gate be called the Herculean gate.' (*10*: p. 150.)

This transformation of the cities had a lasting and serious consequence —the decay of town life. Cities were no longer pleasant places to live in, and the Gallo-Roman aristocracy gradually deserted them for their fine villas in the country, where food was plentiful. This is common experience, after all; we always rediscover the advantages of country life in times of war and unrest.

The third century is a turning-point too in the organization of military defence. The depopulation of the Empire and its people's dislike of military service forced the emperors to recruit volunteers from beyond its frontiers, even from among the barbarians. At first these recruits were dispersed among the various units of the army; but they soon became the essential element in most of them.

History has its surprises. Though the successful campaign of Probus against the Germans was his chief claim to the thanks of his contemporaries, they seem to have been grateful to him mainly because 'he allowed all Germans, Spaniards and Britons to grow vines and make wine.' (*31*: vol. ii, p. 215.)

This is what Aurelius Victor says on the subject:

'After Florianus had with difficulty maintained himself on his throne for a month or two, he was killed by his own troops at Tarsus. After that they proclaimed Probus emperor in Illyria. His extensive knowledge of war and his various methods of training soldiers and inuring young men to hardship made him almost a second Hannibal. And as Hannibal had set the legions to planting olive trees in most parts of Africa, thinking that to keep them unemployed was dangerous both for the state and for the leaders of the army, so, after the barbarian tribes had been wiped out, Probus furnished Gaul and Pannonia and the hill slopes of the Moesians with vineyards.' (*5*: p. 115.)

# 9

# TOWN LIFE UNDER THE LATE EMPIRE

By SETTING up the tetrarchy, the great emperors Diocletian and Constantine prolonged the life of the Empire as it tottered on the brink of dissolution; but their greatest service to Western civilization was the reorganization of its government and administration on a new basis. We may censure their rigorous policy of state control, but their reforms were justified by results, and even the Christian Church acknowledged the soundness of their methods when she adopted the new administrative divisions of the Late Empire as her own.

## Government Reforms

The radical changes effected at the end of the third and the beginning of the fourth centuries were based on these principles. First, the supreme authority was divided among several rulers with the imperial title of Augustus or Caesar; this was the beginning of the separate empires of East and West. Secondly, much bloodshed had shown that the combination of civil and military powers ended in anarchy; Diocletian kept them separate. Finally, if the Empire was to be efficiently administered, a clearly defined hierarchy was essential. Constantine can claim the credit for establishing it. The Empire was divided into two urban prefectures, Rome and Constantinople, and then into four praetorian prefectures covering the rest of the imperial territory. Each praetorian prefecture included a number of dioceses subdivided into provinces. The base of the pyramid was the city.

63. Bust, said to be of Constantine. Gold and cameo, 4th century.

One of the two prefectures was set up in Gaul, with its headquarters first at Trèves and later at Arles. Gaul was further subdivided into two dioceses: the diocese of Trèves or of the Gauls, with ten provinces, and the diocese of Vienne or of the Seven Provinces, which, as its name implies, had only seven. The *Notitia provinciarum et civitatum Galliae*, an official list dating from the early fifth century, gives 112 Gaulish cities, which are shown on Map 3 on p. 82.

This *Notitia* is a valuable document, and has several times been edited. But, like all official documents, it fails to show us the living, moving reality. For a more detailed description of Gaul we must go to Ammianus Marcellinus, an excellent historian who, because his style lacks polish, is less widely read than he ought to be. He was a professional soldier, a member of the privileged corps of officers known in the Later Empire as *Protectores domestici*; he accompanied Julian to Gaul, and his *History* contains a sketch of the country which gives us some idea of Gaul in the mid fourth century.[1]

[1] The classification adopted by Ammianus Marcellinus differs slightly from that of the fifth century *Notitia* on which our map is based.

## The Changing Provinces

'But now the whole extent of the country is portioned out into many provinces. The second (or lower) Germany is the first, if you begin on the western side, fortified by Cologne and Tongres, both cities of great wealth and importance.

'Next comes the first (or high) Germany, in which, besides other municipal towns, there is Mayence, and Worms, and Spiers, and Strasburg, a city celebrated for the defeats sustained by the barbarians in its neighbourhood.

'After these the first Belgic province stretches as far as Metz and Trèves, which city is the splendid abode of the chief governor of the country.

'Next to that comes the second Belgic province, where we find Amiens, a city of conspicuous magnificence, and Chalons [sur Marne] and Rheims.

'In the province of the Sequani, the finest cities are Besançon and Basle. The first Lyonnese province contains Lyons, Chalons [sur

64. Money-changers at their counter.

Seine], Sens, Bourges and Autun, the walls of which are very extensive and of great antiquity.

'In the second Lyonnese province are Tours, and Rouen, Evreux and Troyes. The Grecian [Rhaetian] and Penine Alps have, besides other towns of less note, Avenche, a city which indeed is not deserted, but which was formerly one of no small importance, as even now is proved by its half-ruinous edifices. These are the most important provinces, and most splendid cities of the Galli.

'In Aquitania, which looks towards the Pyrenees, and that part of the ocean which belongs to the Spaniards, the first province is Aquitanica, very rich in large and populous cities; passing over others, I may mention as pre-eminent, Bordeaux, Clermont [Ferrand], Saintes and Poictiers.

'The province called the Nine Nations [*Novempopulana*] is enriched by Ausch and Bazas. In the province of Narbonne, the cities of Narbonne, Euses and Toulouse are the principal places of importance. The Viennese exults in the magnificence of many cities, the chief of which are Vienne itself, and Arles and Valence; to which may be added Marseilles, by the alliance with and power of which we read that Rome itself was more than once supported in moments of danger.

'And near to these cities is also Aix, Nice, Antibes and the islands of Hieres.'

The picture is completed by a curious description of the course of the Rhone:

'Since we have come in the progress of our work to this district, it would be inconsistent and absurd to omit all mention of the Rhone, a river of the greatest celebrity. The Rhone rises in the Penine Alps, from sources of great abundance, and descending with headlong impetuosity into the more champaign districts, it often overruns its banks with its own waters, and then plunges into a lake called Lake Leman, and though it passes through it, yet it never mingles with any foreign waters, but, rushing over the top of those which flow with less rapidity, in its search for an exit, it forces its own way by the violence of its stream.

'And thus passing through that lake without any damage, it runs through Savoy and the district of Franche Comté; and, after a long course, it forms the boundary between the Viennese on its left and the Lyonnese on its right. Then after many windings it receives the Saone, a river which rises in the first Germany, and this latter river here merges its name in the Rhone. At this point is the beginning of the Gauls. And from this spot the distances are measured not by miles but by leagues.

'From this point also the Rhone, being now enriched by other rivers, becomes navigable for large vessels, which are often tossed about in it by gales of wind; and at last, having finished the course which nature has marked out for it, foaming on it joins the Gallic Sea in the wide gulf which they call the Gulf of Lyons, about eighteen miles from Arles.' (*3*: pp. 78–80.)

It would be waste of time to try to list all the contradictions between the picture of the country which Ammianus Marcellinus has rapidly sketched in for us and the official list of provinces; all the more so because the two are not exactly contemporary. But two points seem worth making. First, Ammianus Marcellinus in his survey of the outlying regions of Gaul makes no mention of Armorica; there is no reference to Rennes, or to Nantes, or of course to Cornwall. This may well indicate that the Breton peninsula, undermined by the endemic unrest which contemporary writers mysteriously call the 'Bagaudae', was already breaking away from the Empire.

In contrast to the anarchy prevailing in north-west Gaul, the region round Bordeaux and Toulouse was at the height of its prosperity; of that we shall find abundant and detailed evidence in the poems of Ausonius.

The curiosity of Ammianus Marcellinus was attracted by the mountains too, and his description of the Alps has nothing bookish about it. It was after all written by a man who had himself crossed the Alps, in the depths of the winter of 355, with the young Emperor Julian and his guards:

## *Crossing the Alps*

'This country then of the Gauls was by reason of its lofty mountain ranges perpetually covered with terrible snows, almost unknown to the inhabitants of the rest of the world, except where it borders on the ocean; vast fortresses raised by nature, in the place of art, surrounding it on all sides.

'On the southern side it is washed by the Etruscan and Gallic sea: where it looks towards the north it is separated from the tribes of the barbarians by the River Rhine; where it is placed under the western star it is bounded by the ocean, and the lofty chain of the Pyrenees; where it has an eastern aspect it is bounded by the Cottian Alps. In these mountains King Cottius, after the Gauls had been subdued, lying by himself in their defiles, and relying on the rugged and pathless

94

character of the country, long maintained his independence; though afterwards he abated his pride and was admitted to the friendship of the Emperor Octavianus. And subsequently he constructed immense works to serve as a splendid gift to the emperor, making roads over them, short and convenient for travellers, between other ancient passes of the Alps.

'In these Cottian Alps, which begin at the town of Susa, one vast ridge rises up, scarcely passable by anyone without danger.

'For to travellers who reach it from the side of Gaul it descends with a steepness almost precipitous, being terrible to behold, in consequence of the bulk of its overhanging rocks. In the spring, when the ice is melting, and the snow beginning to give way from the warm spring breezes, if anyone seeks to descend along the mountain, men and beasts and wagons all fall together through the fissures and clefts in the rocks, which yawn in every direction, though previously hidden by the frost. And the only remedy ever found to ward off entire destruction is to have many vehicles bound together with enormous ropes, with men or oxen hanging on behind, to hold them back with great efforts; and so with a crouching step they get down with some degree of safety. And this, as I have said, is what happens in the spring.

'But in winter, the ground being covered over with a smooth crust of ice, and therefore slippery underfoot, the traveller is often plunged headlong; and the valleys which seem to open here and there into wide plains, which are merely a covering of treacherous ice, sometimes swallow up those who try to pass over them. On account of which danger those who are acquainted with the country fix projecting wooden piles over the safest spots, in order that a series of them may conduct the traveller unhurt to his destination; though if these piles get covered with snow and hidden, or thrown down by melting torrents descending from the mountains, then it is difficult for any one to pass, even if natives of the district lead the way.

'But on the summit of this Italian mountain there is a plain, seven miles in extent, reaching as far as the station known by the name of Mars; and after that comes another ridge, still more steep, and hardly possible to be climbed, which stretches on to the summit of Mons Matrona, named so from an event which happened to a noble lady.

'From this point a path, steep indeed, but easily passable, leads to the fortress of Virgantia [Briançon]. . . .

'And although this road which I have been speaking of runs through the centre of the district, and is shorter and more frequented now than any other, yet other roads also were made at much earlier periods, on different occasions.

95

'The first of them, near the Maritime Alps, was made by the Theban Hercules; and he it was who gave to these Alps the name of the Grecian Alps. In the same way he consecrated the citadel and port of Monaecus to keep alive the recollection of his name for ever.' (*3*: pp. 75–6.)

This description of the Alps, by a man who knew them at first hand, would be convincing proof, if any were needed, that a feeling for mountains is modern, an emotion which ancient writers never experienced, sensitive as they were to some of the beauties of nature. For men of the fourth century, the Alps were nothing but an immense barrier, appallingly difficult to cross, and what we romantics think grand and uplifting was for them simply 'terrible to behold'.

## Ups and Downs of Urban Life

It is indeed not often that we see things with the eyes of ancient writers, and when we turn to the cities of Gaul we must not be deceived by the praises which Ammianus Marcellinus lavishes on many of them. Cramped within their encircling walls, airless, dark, with narrow streets and little comfort, fourth-century towns rarely had as many as five thousand inhabitants. As we can see from the account of Ammianus

65. A teacher, terra cotta. Caricature, or student's amulet.

Marcellinus, they were first and foremost strongholds. Town life in Gaul was suffering an eclipse that was to last for several centuries.

Some of the ancient cities were even falling into decay. Lyons, for instance, stricken at the height of her prosperity by the revolt of Albinus against Septimius Severus in 197, and the fire which followed it, was but a shadow of her former self. But other towns were struggling painfully towards recovery. The capital of the Aeduani, Autun, whose schools were renowned, made valiant attempts to restore them after the sack of the town in 269.

Towards the end of the third century the Emperor Constantius Chlorus, governor of Gaul, charged the celebrated rhetorician Eumenius with the restoration of the ruined schools of Autun; the text of the rescript laying this task on him is included in Eumenius' panegyric, 'On the Restoration of the Schools'.

## The Schools of Autun

'Our Gauls [wrote the emperor] deserve that we should wish to develop the natural abilities of their children who are instructed in the arts in the town of Autun, and those young men too who cheerfully took service in our retinue when we, Constantius Caesar, returned from Italy. What other reward then ought we to bestow on them, which fortune can neither give nor snatch from them? Wherefore we have determined to appoint you, in preference to all others, to the charge of the school which death has robbed of its master; for we have knowledge, through our administrative experience, of your eloquence and high moral character. We urge you, therefore, to return to teaching the art of oratory (while retaining all the privileges of your rank), and to cultivate the mind of youth in its eagerness for a better life in that city of Autun which, as you know, we would restore to its former glory; and do not think that the honours you have already acquired are in any way diminished by this office, since the noble profession of teaching embellishes all dignities rather than weakens them. Finally, we wish you to draw a salary of 600,000 sestertii from the resources of the state, so that you may know that our clemency has regard for your merits. Farewell, Eumenius, whom we hold dear.' (8 : pp. 125–8.)

The rhetorician's reply to the rescript is couched in eloquent, if pompous, terms. We shall quote only the passage where he refers to the stipend offered him, and promises to use it for rebuilding the schools:

66. Scene in the schools. Detail of the Brescia casket, ivory, 4th century.

'What then shall be done with the money paid out to me? . . . It is proper, your excellency, that I should accept the 600,000 sestertii, inasmuch as they are attached to my office. But in fact, and as to their use, I make them over to the state, and preferably to the building in which our studies are to be carried on.

'Indeed, if the plunder of war is dedicated to Mars, everything won from the sea to Neptune, harvests to Ceres, if commercial profits are offered to Mercury and the gains from all forms of business are used to honour their tutelary deity, to what should the rewards of teaching properly be devoted if not to the place whence the teacher speaks? Especially since, besides the love of learning which I share with others, I have particular affection for the Maenian schools in remembrance of my ancestors. For although even before I entered adolescence they were no longer frequented by students, yet I am told that one of my forbears taught there. He came from Athens, and had for long been well known in Rome; but he was soon detained in that town by its inhabitants' evident love of learning and their respect for his own work. If I succeed in setting up once more and adorning the place in which the venerable old man, as they tell me, taught for more than eighty years, I shall feel that by following him in his profession I have called him back to life.'

Eumenius interrupts this passage by an appeal for corroboration addressed to one of his audience, Glaucus by name; no doubt Glaucus had been one of the old man's pupils.

What happened to the university of Autun? ('University' is Camille Jullian's term, over-ambitious no doubt, since the teaching given in the schools throughout Roman imperial times corresponded to the fifth-form work of our grammar schools.) There is no telling; but the panegyric on the Autun schools and Ammianus Marcellinus' reference, three-quarters of a century later, to the decaying state of the town's fortifications hardly lead us to believe that Autun enjoyed a renaissance.

## A Winter at Paris in the Fourth Century

Unlike the cities which flourished in the early days of the Roman Empire and declined after the late second century, Paris made her appearance in history under the Later Empire. And she made it modestly enough, for Ausonius, in the collection of poems he calls *The Order of Famous Cities*, says nothing about Lutetia, and Ammianus Marcellinus, who must have accompanied the Emperor Julian thither, omits her altogether from his picture of Gaul. But her position made her a valuable observation post. As the French historian M. Poëte has said, she was 'the fortified city beside the great road leading from the Rhine, whence the barbarians came, to the south which was their objective. It would have been impossible to leave this crossroads undefended, where the river flowing east to west intersects the land route which follows the great natural passage from north to south'. (61: p. 44.) Julian seems to have been the first to realize the strategic value of Lutetia. When the Emperor Constantius gave him the imperial crown and responsibility for the defence of Gaul against the latest offensive by the Germans (in 356), he chose Lutetia for his winter quarters in 357–8 and again the next year, and used her as his army headquarters for his great Gallic campaign.

67. The emperor Julian. Gold medallion, Constantinian.

Lutetia had already expanded beyond the little island in the Seine still called the Île de la Cité, as is shown by the remains of the Roman baths in the boulevard Saint-Michel, and the amphitheatre discovered in 1869 when the rue Monge was being cut; but Julian entrenched himself on the island, no doubt where the Palais now stands. His *Misopogon* gives us his impressions of the city, and we may suppose, reading between the lines, that his choice owed something to considerations of climate as well as to military expediency:

'I happened to be in winter quarters at my beloved Lutetia—for that is how the Celts call the capital of the Parisians. It is a small island lying in the river; a wall entirely surrounds it, and wooden bridges lead to it on both sides. The river seldom rises and falls, but usually is the same depth in the winter as in the summer season, and it provides water which is very clear to the eye and very pleasant for one who wishes to drink. For since the inhabitants live on an island they have to draw their water chiefly from the river. The winter too is rather mild there, perhaps from the warmth of the ocean, which is not more than nine hundred stades distant, and it may be that a slight breeze from the water is

68. Rowing-boat. Detail from funerary monument.

wafted so far; for sea water seems to be warmer than fresh. Whether from this or from some other cause obscure to me, the fact is as I say, that those who live in that place have a warmer winter. And a good kind of vine grows thereabouts, and some persons have even managed to make fig trees grow by covering them in winter with a sort of garment of wheat straw and with things of that sort, such as are used to protect trees from the harm that is done them by the cold air.' (*35*: vol. ii, pp. 429–31.)

Lutetia in the fourth century was still only a little city, a fortress (*castellum*); but from then on her name crops up on every page of French history, from St Denis' conversion of the Gauls to St Geneviève's resistance to the Hun invader Attila; by the time of the Merovingians she had already the look of a capital city.

## Trèves, Outpost on the Rhine

But the most important city of Gaul under the Later Roman Empire, the city which for the time being eclipsed all others, was Trèves (Trier). Here was the usual residence of one of the four princes of the Tetrarchy,

Constantius Chlorus, and in the second half of the fourth century of the Emperor Valentinian I, who established himself there in 367. Trèves is, moreover, the only city of north-eastern Gaul whose Roman monuments can compare with those of the southern Gaulish cities. The most famous is the Porta Nigra, which has been called perhaps the most complete specimen of Roman military architecture in the whole of Gaul.

For at least seven years Trèves guarded the Rhine, and Valentinian, who hardly ever went outside his capital, sent for the rhetorician Ausonius to come and tutor his son Gratian there. Ausonius, who came from Bordeaux, was too much attached to his native city to find the garrison town of Trèves attractive; but as he was living in the imperial palace he could hardly deny Trèves a place in *The Order of Famous Cities*. It is a short platitudinous piece of verse, obviously written to order:

'Long as Gaul, mighty in arms, yearned to be praised, and that royal city of the Treveri, which, though full near the Rhine, reposes unalarmed as if in the bosom of deep profound peace, because she feeds, because she clothes and arms the forces of the Empire. Widely her walls stretch forward over a spreading hill; beside her bounteous Moselle glides past with peaceful stream, carrying the far-brought merchandise of all races of the earth.' (6: vol. i, p. 271.)

For nearly twenty years the proximity of the Germans made the fortune of Trèves, but at the end of the fourth century, when the emperors abandoned the defence of the Rhine against the barbarians, Trèves was sacrificed. The praetorian prefecture was transferred to Arles, and the Rhine frontier lay open to the invaders. The Emperor Theodosius (388–95) has been censured, and no doubt rightly, for this policy of withdrawal; he was the only emperor since the restoration of Aurelian who never crossed the Alps or set foot in Gaul.

## The Cities of the South

Arles was a river-port, as well as a sea-port handling the wealth brought to her from overseas, and in the fourth century she was the most important market of Gaul. Her fortune dates from the Emperor Constantine, who was impressed by her fine position and in 314 convoked there the first council of the churches of Gaul. Not surprisingly, it was Arles that welcomed the central administration when at the end of the century

it was dislodged from Trèves. There are many references to the cosmo-
politan life of Arles, the best known being the preamble to a rescript
of the emperor Honorius, convoking the assembly of Gaul at Arles in
418:

'Such is the favourable situation of this place, such the wealth of her
trade, such the host of those who visit her, that products of whatever
kind may here be most conveniently distributed. No produce which any
province thinks itself fortunate to possess is not brought forth by the
fertile soil of Arles also. All that is best in the opulent East, in perfumed
Arabia, delicate Assyria, fecund Africa or fruitful Gaul, is offered in
abundance, as if all the magnificence of the world originated here.' (*49*:
pp. 405–6.)

Tourist propaganda perhaps, designed to attract as many delegates
as possible to the assembly. But we must not dismiss it too summarily,
for the short poem which Ausonius wrote a few years later on the 'little
Rome of Gaul' corroborates the more pompous praise of the rescript
(*6*: vol. i, p. 277.) He shows us Arles welcoming the trade of the whole
world and, with Narbonne, acting as emporium for the towns of
Aquitania. It may be added that the treasures of the Arles art museums,
whether pagan or Christian, and especially the carved sarcophagi, show
how vast were the fortunes amassed by her citizens; and these fortunes
came chiefly from trade.

But all the same Ausonius preferred Aquitania. In his day it was the
most prosperous and the most peaceful region of all Gaul, and even in the
fifth century Salvian interrupts the impetuous stream of his polemic to
praise her prosperous and pleasant farmlands:

'Every one knows that the *Aquitanes*, and the *Novem-Populi* [Gascony], had the very Marrow of almost all Gaul, and the Breasts of all its Plenty; and not only of Plenty, but of what is sometimes preferr'd before it, of Delight, Pleasure, and Beauty. The whole Country there was so intermixt with Vineyards, and curious flow'ry Meads, chequer'd with various Tillage, planted with Orchards, or the pleasantest Groves, water'd with Fountains, or flow'd between by Rivers, or cover'd all over with Harvests plenty; so that the Possessors and Owners of that Country seem'd not so much to enjoy that Portion of the Soil, as the very Resemblance of Paradise.' (*65*: pp. 201–2.)

Ausonius did not forget Toulouse in his collection of poems; it was there that he had begun his studies at the age of twelve. Brick was already the normal building material:

'Never will I leave unmentioned Toulouse, my nursing mother, who is girt about with a vast circuit of brick-built walls, along whose side the lovely stream of the Garonne glides past, home of uncounted people, lying hard by the barriers of the snowy Pyrenees and the pine-clad Cevennes between the tribes of Aquitania and the Iberian folk. (*6*: vol. i, p. 279.)

But Ausonius kept the best of his inspiration for Bordeaux, his native town. With his lines in praise of her he brought his little collection to an end on a note of spontaneous enthusiasm. His description of Bordeaux will serve as epilogue to our chapter on fourth-century Gaul, and as prologue to a chapter on its author, who was the best qualified, and we may well think the most congenial, of all representatives of Gallic culture in the Later Roman Empire:

'Long have I censured my unduteous silence [says Ausonius] in that of thee, my country, famed for thy wine, thy rivers, thy famous men, the virtue and wit of thy inhabitants and for the senate of thy nobles, I did not tell among the foremost; as though, well knowing thee a little town, I shrank from touching praises undeserved. For this no shame is mine; for mine is neither a barbarous land upon the banks of Rhine, nor icy home on frozen Haemus.[1] Bordeaux is my native soil, where are skies temperate and mild.' (*6*: vol. i, p. 283.)

But it was not only the climate he praised; he boasted of the beauty of the town; streets well laid out, houses regularly plotted, spacious pro-

---

[1] Haemus: the Balkans, which had a reputation in the ancient world for extreme cold.

70. Ox-cart. Mosaic from the Roman villa at Orbe, Switzerland.

menades that did not belie their name, gates directly facing the cross-roads opposite, and the channel of the fine river running right through the town.

The poem ends with a comparison between Rome and Bordeaux, in which the praises of his native town are constantly interrupting the homage he pays to the Eternal City:

'This is my own country, but Rome stands above all countries. I love Bordeaux, Rome I venerate; in this I am a citizen, in both a consul;[1] here is my cradle, there my curule chair.' (6: p. 285.)

[1] Ausonius did indeed hold municipal office in Bordeaux, and had been a consul.

# 10

# A CULTURED GALLIC HOME
# IN THE FOURTH CENTURY

AUSONIUS was born at Bordeaux in 309, and died about 394. He was an inexhaustible writer; but unlike many of the versifiers of the ancient world, who thought that all they had to do was to regale their readers with mythological subjects wrapped up in an intentional obscurity, he did not feel it beneath his dignity to talk about himself, his parents, his wife and children, his teachers and his cook, or to let us into the secrets of his daily life, all with a wealth of detail rarely found in ancient writers. Since his lifetime spanned almost the whole of the fourth century, he is living witness to the century which lay between the ill-starred third century and the great barbarian invasions. There is something symbolic about him. He is typical of the man of culture to be found in any period of French history, but chiefly in the sixteenth century—the humanist who is to all appearance Christian but is still rooted in the classical tradition; Ausonius anticipates his compatriot Montaigne, with a little of Rabelais thrown in. That this type of Frenchman makes his appearance in so characteristic a form as early as the fourth century is surely proof that he represents something fundamental in French culture.

## Self-portrait of a Humanist

Ausonius needs no introduction beyond the little preface (*praefatiuncula*) which he addresses to his reader:

'My father was Ausonius, and I bear the same name. Who I am, and what is my rank, my family, my home and my native land, I have written here, that you might know me, good sir, whoever you may have been, and when you know me, might honour me with a place in your memory. Bazas was my father's native place; my mother was of Aeduan race on her father's side, though her mother came from Aquae Tarbellae; while I myself was born at Bordeaux: four ancient cities contribute to the origin of my family. Thus my connections are widely spread. . . .

'I gave myself up to grammar, and then to rhetoric, wherein I gained sufficient skill. I frequented the courts as well, but preferred to follow the business of teaching, and won some repute as a grammarian; and though my renown was not of so high a degree as to approach that of Aemilius, or Scaurus, or Probus of Beyrût; yet it was high enough to let me look back upon the teachers of my day, men famous in Aquitania, as their equal rather than their inferior.

'Afterwards, when three decades with all their festivals were passed, I left my toils as a provincial teacher, receiving the command to enter the emperor's golden palace. There I taught the young prince grammar, and in due time rhetoric; for, indeed, I have good reason for satisfaction and my boasting rests upon firm ground. Yet I confess that there have been tutors of greater fame, so but 'tis granted that there has been none to a nobler pupil. . . .

'He created me companion and quaestor, and crowned my honours with the prefectship of the provinces of Gaul, Libya and Italy. I became consul, too. . . . Such, then, is Ausonius.' (6: vol. i, pp. 3–7.)

71. 'Through these six and thirty years, unwedded, I have mourned . . .' Funeral scene.

73. Head of a young woman, from Neumagen; second half of the 2nd century.

72. The poet. One panel of diptych, 6th century.

## Sentimental Verses

This autobiography is not without a touch of boastfulness; but the Ausonius revealed in his poems, far from being a genius, is a straight-forward, honest man, by no means a fool, with a streak of malicious humour in him. He was a good son, and in a poem he wrote to be inscribed below the portrait of his dead father he has left us a character sketch which does him credit. (6: vol. i, pp. 3, 41–3.) He tells us that his

108

father was born at Bazas, lived at Bordeaux where he had a respectable career in the profession of medicine ('the only one of all the arts', says Ausonius, 'which produced a god'), and died at the age of ninety. (It is interesting to note the admission that Ausonius puts into his father's mouth: 'For Latin I never had a ready tongue.' This shows that in the old man's youth, that is, at the end of the third and perhaps the beginning of the fourth century, the common tongue was still Gaulish.)

Ausonius seems to have been a good husband as well as a good son. In the collection of poems he called *Parentalia*, which commemorates all the dead members of his family, is a dirge, a 'nenia', to his late wife Attusia Lucana Sabina. The poem is a little pompous, and we need quote only a few lines, from which we learn that Sabina died at the age of twenty-eight and that Ausonius did not marry again:

'In youth I wept for you, robbed of my hopes in early years, and through these six and thirty years, unwedded, I have mourned, and mourn you still. Age has crept over me, but yet I cannot lull my pain. . . .

'Cheerful, modest, staid, famed for high birth as famed for beauty, you were the grief and glory of Ausonius your spouse. For ere you could complete your eight-and-twentieth December, you deserted our two children, the pledges of our love.' (6: vol. i, pp. 71–3.)

He pays a more spontaneous tribute to his wife in this charming epigram, composed during her lifetime:

TO HIS WIFE

'Dear wife, as we have lived, so let us live and keep the names we took when first we wedded: let no day ever make us change in lapse of time; but I will be thy "Lad" still and thou wilt be my "Lass". Though I should outlive Nestor, and thou too shouldst outstrip Deiphobe of Cumae in rivalry of years, let us refuse to know the meaning of ripe age. Better to know Time's worth than count his years.' (6: vol. ii, p. 181.)

Though Ausonius was faithful to his wife's memory, his natural cheerfulness did not desert him in his widowerhood, and several of his epigrams verge on indelicacy. The best are also the shortest, for it cannot be denied that he finds it difficult to avoid coarseness when he lets himself dwell on a suggestive topic. We will quote only one of his little poems, about Laïs, a famous courtesan who lived in Corinth about 400 B.C., and was the mistress of Diogenes and Aristippus. Ausonius imagines her an old woman, and the lines he puts into her mouth breathe a tender melancholy:

ON LAÏS DEDICATING HER MIRROR TO VENUS

'I, Laïs, grown old, to Venus dedicate my mirror: let eternal beauty have the eternal service which befits it. But for me there is no profit in this, for to behold myself such as I am I would not, such as I was I cannot.' (6: vol. ii, p. 195.)

The greatest years of Ausonius' life were spent at the imperial court, first as tutor to Gratian, the son of the Emperor Valentinian I, then as praetorian prefect (369–79). His tutorship earned him a succession of honours, crowned by the consulship. He was vain enough to take pleasure in the society of the great, and he always found those years a little dazzling when he looked back on them. His court life was passed at Trèves, and inspired his famous poem *The Moselle*; it is a graceful piece of writing, but the historian will find more to interest him in other more personal and intimate works.

Ausonius spent his last years near Bordeaux, in the district which he loved so well, and where he had lived most of his life. He was happy in the society he found in academic circles there, and he dedicated a curious collection of reminiscences to the professors of Bordeaux. In it he mentions no fewer than twenty-nine grammarians and rhetoricians, and such a profusion of teachers, each drawing his salary, may well seem surprising when we think that only a century and a half later nothing was left of this flourishing centre of learning.

74. Lady at her toilet. Detail from a sarcophagus.

The twenty-five 'dirges' which Ausonius wrote in honour of the Bordeaux professors are not all brilliantly original. More to our taste than his copybook eulogies of the leading lights among them are his lines on the less exalted teachers (Ausonius was careful to leave no one out):

'Now, as the pious homage of my mournful task shall present each one, I will tell of those who, though of humble birth and rank and merit, instilled into the uncultured minds of the people of Bordeaux the love of letters.

'Let Macrinus be named amongst these: to him I was entrusted first when a boy; and Sucuro, the freedman's son, temperate and well suited to form youthful minds. You too, Concordius, were another such; you who, fleeing your country, took in exchange a chair of little profit in a foreign town. Nor must I leave unmentioned the old man Phoebicius, who, though the keeper of Belenus' temple,[1] got no profit thereby. Yet he, sprung, as rumour goes, from the stock of the Druids of Armorica, obtained a chair at Bordeaux by his son's help. . . .

'I will sing of Ammonius also—for indeed it is a solemn duty to commemorate a grammarian of my own native place—who used to teach raw lads their alphabet; he had scant learning and was of an ungentle nature, and therefore—as was his due—was held in slight repute.

'For Anastasius also shape a mournful lay, my Muse; and you, my dirge, recall that poor grammarian. He was born at Bordeaux, but ambition transferred him to Poictiers. There he lived a poor man, stinted alike in food and dress, and in his old age lost the faint glimmer of renown which his country and his chair had shed on him. Howbeit, I have here paid a tribute to his name, that the tomb should not swallow up his name with his bones.' (6: vol. i, pp. 115–17.)

A strange string of names; but from it we can imagine something of what education was in this corner of Gaul in the days of Ausonius. The Gaulish language was still spoken, and the imperial government was doing all it could to acclimatize Latin, recruiting not only qualified teachers, but pathetic creatures who for a pittance taught children the rudiments of Latin. It is hardly surprising that Ausonius' allusions are often critical.

The professors of Bordeaux may not all have been in the first flight; but they were not all as temperate as Sucuro either, and in his eulogy of

---

[1] Belenus was a Gaulish divinity.

Crispus, who taught him his alphabet, Ausonius has no scruples about repeating what was rumoured of him: 'At times it was thought that you used to prime yourself with wine in order to produce verse rivalling passages of Vergil and of Flaccus.' (*6*: vol. i, p. 131.)

## *The Daily Round*

Ausonius was not an egotist, and was distressed to think that the memory of men he had known might perish; but he was not unmindful of himself, and made good use of any opportunity to remind his readers of his own existence. An odd little poem, *The Daily Round*, tells how he habitually spent his day:

'Hi, boy! Get up! Bring me my slippers and my tunic of lawn: bring all the clothes that you have ready now for my going out. Fetch me spring water to wash my hands and mouth and eyes. Get me the chapel opened, but with no outward display: holy words and guiltless prayers are furniture enough for worship. I do not call for incense to be burnt nor for any slice of honey-cake: hearths of green turf I leave for the altars of vain gods. I must pray to God and to the Son of God Most High, that co-equal Majesty, united in one fellowship with the Holy Spirit.' (*6*: vol. i, p. 15.)

The tone of the prayer that follows is very personal, and a careful study of it suggests that if Ausonius turned to Christianity it was because he saw it as a highly spiritual religion, repudiating the bloody sacrifices which dishonoured pagan cults, and easily reconcilable with the Stoicism practised in his circles. His conversion seems to have brought no anguish in its train, no violent break with the past:

'Give me a heart, O Father [he says in the course of his long prayer], to hold out against all deeds of wrong, and deliver me from the Serpent's deadly venom, sin. Let it suffice that the Serpent did beguile our old mother Eve and involved Adam also in his deceit.

'Prepare a road that I, being freed from the fetters of this frail body, may be led up on high, where in the clear heaven the Milky Way stretches above the wandering clouds of the wind-vexed moon—that road by which the holy men of old departed from the earth; by which Elias, caught up in the chariot, once made his way alive above our lower air; and Enoch, too, who went before his end without change of body.

76. Servant pouring wine.

75. Glass bottle, 4th century.

'Grant me, O Father, the effluence of everlasting light for which I yearn, if I swear not by gods of stone.'[1]

Then he prays that he may learn to live by rules of conduct which are inspired quite as much by the moral teaching of the Stoics as by Christianity:

'Naught may I fear, and naught desire. . . . Let me not do to any that which at the same time I would not have done to me. . . . Let me be moderate in food and dress. . . . In mind and body let me be free from pain. . . . Let me enjoy peace and live quietly, . . . and when the hour of my last day shall come, grant that the conscience of a life well spent suffer me not to fear death, nor yet long for it.'

[1] Ausonius speaks elsewhere of his determination to have no more part in sacrifices of blood.

77. Preparing a meal. Detail from the Igel column, 3rd century.

But Ausonius is no mystic. He is ready to devote a fair ashare of his day to religion, but not to let it absorb him; he is impatient to get back to his preoccupations on earth:

'Now I have prayed enough to God, albeit we sinful men can never entreat Him enough. Boy! Bring me my morning coat. I must exchange my "Hail" and "Farewell" with my friends.'

(These were the customary forms of greeting.) But now there are only four hours to midday, and Sosias the cook must have his orders.

## Invitations

'And now the time for inviting my friends draws on. So, that no fault of mine may make them late for lunch, hurry at your best pace, boy, to the neighbours' houses—you know without my telling who they are— and back with you before these words are done. I have invited five to lunch; for six persons, counting the host, make the right number for a meal: if there be more, it is no meal but a mêlée. Ah, he is off! and I am left to deal with Sosias.'

## Orders to the Cook

'Sosias, I must have lunch. The warm sun is already passed well on into his fourth hour, and on the dial the shadow is moving on towards the fifth stroke. Taste and make sure—for they often play you false—that the seasoned dishes are well soused and taste appetizingly. Turn your

114

bubbling pots in your hands and shake them up: quick, dip your fingers in the hot gravy, and let your moist tongue lick them as it darts in and out.' (6: vol. i, pp. 15–23.)

## The Little Villa Inside and Out

Here ends the account of his day. Ausonius never finished it, and the reader may continue it as he will. We know the background; for when Ausonius left the court and retired to his little corner of Gaul he settled down on an estate near Bordeaux, a family property which he describes in an idyll called 'On his little Patrimony':

'Hail, little patrimony, the realm of my forbears, which my great-grandfather, which my grandfather, which my father tended so carefully, which the last named left to me when he died all too soon, albeit

78. Double ladle from Alesia and ribbed bowl from Saintes.

in a ripe old age. Ah me! I had not wished to be able to possess it so early. 'Tis indeed the natural order when the son succeeds the father; but where there is affection, it is a more pleasing course for both to reign together. Now all the toil and trouble falls on me; of old the pleasure only was my share, the rest was all my father's. . . .

'But now you must know of what size is this estate of mine. . . . I keep in tillage two hundred acres: a hundred more are grown with vines, and half as much is pasture. My woodland is more than twice as much as my pasture, vineyard and tilth together; of husbandmen I have neither too many nor too few. A spring is near my house and a small well, besides the unsullied river, which on its tides bears me by boat from home and back again. I have always fruits in store to last me two whole years: who has short victual by him, he too has famine at hand.

'This my estate lies not far from the town, nor yet hard by the town, to rid me of its crowds while reaping its advantages. And so, whenever satiety moves me to change my seat, I pass from one to the other and enjoy country and town by turns.' (6: vol. i, pp. 33–5.)

With this peaceful scene, untroubled by forebodings of the great invasion of 406, we shall bring our survey of the fourth century to a close. History has many contrasts like this. The euphoria of 1900 was the prelude to the bloody war of 1914, infinitely more devastating than the barbarian onslaught which ushered in the fifth century.

*Part IV*

# CHRISTIANITY COMES
# TO GAUL

# 11

# THE ORIGINS OF CHRISTIANITY: ITS FIRST MARTYRS IN FRANCE

THE cult of Rome and the emperor was an admirable political instrument, but not a religion which could meet the spiritual needs of the Gallo-Romans. The decline of Druidism and the slow death of the old Gaulish divinities left a vacuum which explains the vogue of oriental religions; Mithraism especially had a large following in Gaul from the second century onwards.

In the end the vacuum was filled by Christianity, but the process was slow, as Sulpicius Severus, the biographer of St Martin, noted when he said: *Serius trans Alpes Dei religione suscepta*—'It was long before the religion of God was adopted beyond the Alps.'

It must have been the second half of the second century when Christianity came to Gaul, and our earliest evidence of the existence of Christians there is the moving letter written by the 'most celebrated churches' of Lyons and Vienne in 177, 'relating what was done among them'. Eusebius of Caesarea quotes it in his *Church History. (23: pp. 212–15; 217.)*

'The greatness of the tribulation in this region, and the fury of the heathen against the saints, and the sufferings of the blessed witnesses, we cannot recount accurately, nor indeed could they possibly be recorded. For with all his might the adversary fell upon us.

'He endeavoured in every manner to practise and exercise his servants against the servants of God, not only shutting us out from houses and baths and markets, but forbidding any of us to be seen in any place whatever. But the grace of God led the conflict against him, and delivered the weak, and set them as firm pillars, able through patience to endure all the wrath of the Evil One.'

The essential purpose of the letter is to record their heroic resistance:

'They endured nobly the injuries heaped upon them by the populace; clamours and blows and draggings and robbings and stonings and imprisonments, and all things which an infuriated mob delight in inflicting on enemies and adversaries. Then, being taken to the forum by the chiliarch and the authorities of the city, they were examined in the presence of the whole multitude, and, having confessed, they were imprisoned until the arrival of the governor. When, afterwards, they were brought before him, he treated us with the utmost cruelty.'

80. Bust of Marcus Aurelius, gold, found at Avenches (Switzerland).

79. (facing), Heddernheim relief, early 3rd century. Mithras, supported by two torchbearers, sacrificing a bull; above, signs of the zodiac and four scenes from the life of Mithras.

Not all the members of the Christian community put up a heroic fight. Some were still weak and could not face the prolonged strain. About ten gave in, and their capitulation was a great grief to their fellow Christians. But naturally enough the spokesmen of the churches of Lyons and Vienne dwelt longer on the heroism of the more courageous:

'The whole wrath of the populace, and governor, and soldiers was aroused exceedingly against Sanctus, the deacon from Vienne, and Maturus, a late convert, yet a noble combatant, and against Attalus, a native of Pergamos, where he had always been a pillar and foundation, and Blandina, through whom Christ showed that things which appear mean and obscure and despicable to men are with God of great glory, through love toward him manifested in power, and not boasting in appearance. For while we all trembled, and her earthly mistress, who was herself also one of the witnesses, feared that on account of the weakness of her body, she would be unable to make bold confession, Blandina was filled with such power as to be delivered and raised above those who were torturing her by turns from morning till evening in every manner.'

## Pothinus, Bishop of Lyons

Then the authors tell of the tortures inflicted on the martyrs. Not a single Christian was spared, not even the Bishop of Lyons, Pothinus, whose great age should have roused pity in his executioners:

121

'The blessed Pothinus, who had been entrusted with the bishopric of Lyons, was dragged to the judgment seat. He was more than ninety years of age, and very infirm, scarcely indeed able to breathe because of physical weakness; but he was strengthened by spiritual zeal through his earnest desire for martyrdom. Though his body was worn out by old age and disease, his life was preserved that Christ might triumph in it. When he was brought by the soldiers to the tribunal, accompanied by the civil magistrates and a multitude who shouted against him in every manner as if he were Christ himself, he bore noble witness. Being asked by the governor who was the God of the Christians, he replied, "If thou art worthy, thou shalt know." Then he was dragged away harshly, and received blows of every kind. Those near him struck him with their hands and feet, regardless of his age; and those at a distance hurled at him whatever they could seize; all of them thinking that they would be guilty of great wickedness and impiety if any possible abuse were omitted. For thus they thought to avenge their own deities. Scarcely able to breathe, he was cast into prison and died after two days.'

The Christians who survived the torture met a heroic death in the amphitheatre at Lyons, where they were thrown to the beasts. 'It was proper, therefore,' as the writers of the letter said, 'that the noble athletes, having endured a manifold strife, and conquered grandly,

81. Lion leaping to the attack. Mosaic from the Roman villa at Orbe.

should receive the crown, great and incorruptible.' The story of their last battle is dramatically told. First Maturus is thrown to the beasts, then Sanctus and Attalus, and the letter ends with the martyrdom of Blandina.

## The Last Combat of Blandina

'But the blessed Blandina, last of all, having, as a noble matron, encouraged her children and sent them before her victorious to the King, endured herself all their conflicts and hastened after them, glad and rejoicing in her departure as if called to a marriage supper, rather than cast to wild beasts. And, after the scourging, after the wild beasts, after the roasting seat, she was finally enclosed in a net, and thrown before a bull. And having been tossed about by the animal, but feeling none of the things which were happening to her, on account of her hope and firm hold upon what had been entrusted to her, and her communion with Christ, she also was sacrificed. And the heathen themselves confessed that never among them had a woman endured so many and such terrible tortures.'

This eye-witness account needs no commentary. It is a moving prologue to the history of the Church in France. After it almost complete silence falls for nearly a century. It seems likely that the first Christian community which had come from the east and made its way up the valley of the Rhone did not long survive its cruel ordeal, and we may assume that savage persecution successfully halted, or at least slowed down, the advance of a doctrine which had roused the fierce jealousy of the Roman administration. Only in the course of the third century, with the decline of imperial power, did Christianity begin to gain ground.

## 'Except a corn of wheat . . .'

The heroism of the martyrs makes an unforgettable prologue to the story; but in early days popular piety demanded something more than purely spiritual values. Legend was called in to exalt the prestige of the shrines reputed to possess the bodies of a number of people named in the Gospels—Martha, Mary Magdalene and Lazarus, with their companion Jacobea, sister of the Virgin, and the black slave Sara. It was said that they had sailed to the shores of Provence, and become the first missionaries to Gaul.

We must not judge too harshly these fabrications of popular imagination. Medieval art and modern poetry have found them a rich source of inspiration, and to them we owe the great Romanesque churches of Vézelay and Stes Maries-de-la-Mer, the Gothic cathedral of St Maximin, as well as the eleventh canto of Mistral's poem *Mireille*; but truth makes its own claims, and the historian must respect them. The story of the martyrdom of St Pothinus, St Blandina and their fellow Christians is still one of the greatest pages of French religious history, and the earliest.

82. Fragment of decorated pottery from Tours, showing a martyr, with hands bound and disordered hair, surrounded by palms and dolphins, emblems of resurrection; left, a tripod; right, paws and jaws of a lion.

# THE SPREADING OF
# THE GOSPEL

## *The Autun Inscription*

The moving letter written by the Christians of Lyons and Vienne in 177 is the earliest proof we have of the existence of a Christian community in Gaul. Apart from this, the only—or almost the only—early piece of evidence is a mysterious Greek inscription, found at Autun in 1839, from which we may deduce that the new religion had adherents in the city which its schools had made so famous.

The mystical, somewhat enigmatic nature of the inscription, its allusion to the fish which symbolized Christ, and especially its poetical form, suggest that its author was an educated man, and it seems likely that he was in touch with the Graeco-Asiatic Church of Lyons:

'Divine offspring of the heavenly Fish, let thy heart be strong since among mortals thou hast drunk of the spring of immortality. Beloved, comfort thy soul with the never-failing waters of wisdom which is the giver of riches. Take the honey-sweet food of the Saviour of the saints and eat it with delight, holding the Fish in thy hands.[1] Fill me with the Fish, I pray thee, Lord and Saviour. Light of the dead, may my mother sleep well, I implore thee. Ascandius my father, beloved of my heart, with my sweet mother and my brothers, remember Pectorius in the peace of the Fish.' (*41*: vol. i, col. 3197.)

But there cannot have been many Christians at Autun at that time,

---

[1] Perhaps this may be taken as evidence of communion in two kinds.

83. Glass fish, Gallo-Roman, found at Chalon-sur-Saône.

for when at the end of the third century the Emperor Constantius Chlorus laid on the rhetorician Eumenius the task of restoring the schools at Autun, he did so, as we have seen, in the name of traditional paganism.

## Slow Beginnings of Evangelization

Indeed, the mass conversion of Gaul dates only from 312, when Constantine established religious toleration throughout the Empire. Ausonius, as we have seen, was a Christian, though his father was not. The townspeople became Christian in the course of the fourth century. In country districts the work of evangelization started later and proceeded more slowly, and the reason why the word *pagani* (pagans), which in classical Latin meant 'country dwellers', acquired in Late Latin the meaning which it still has in its English form, was that country people were still loyal to their traditional religions long after the towns had adopted Christianity.

## Seven Missionary Bishops

Not until the second half of the third century was Christianity preached throughout Gaul, where before only a handful of isolated Christian communities had precariously existed. The statement of Sulpicius Severus that Christianity came late to the Transalpine peoples is confirmed by a well-known passage from Gregory of Tours' *History of the Franks*:

'At this time seven men consecrated as bishops were sent into Gaul to

126

preach, as we read in the history of the passion of the holy martyr Saturninus. It is there written: "In the consulate of Decius and Gratus, as is faithfully recorded, the city of Toulouse had already its first and greatest bishop in the holy Saturninus."[1] These are the names of those who were sent: to Tours, Bishop Catinus; to Arles, Bishop Trophimus; to Narbonne, Bishop Paulus; to Toulouse, Bishop Saturninus; to Paris, Bishop Dionysius; to Clermont, Bishop Stremonius; to Limoges, Bishop Martialis. Of these, the blessed Dionysius bishop of Paris, after enduring divers torments for the name of Christ, ended this present life under the sword. Saturninus, when he was certain of his martyrdom, said to two of his priests: "Behold now I am made a scarifice, and the time of my dissolution is at hand. I pray you that until my destined end be accomplished, ye leave me not wholly." But when he had been arrested and was being led to the Capitol, he was dragged thither alone, for these twain forsook him. When therefore he saw that they had abandoned him, he is said to have prayed after this manner: "Lord Jesus Christ, hear me from Thy holy heaven, and grant that to the end

---

[1] St Saturninus, or St Sernin, to whom the famous romanesque church of Toulouse is dedicated.

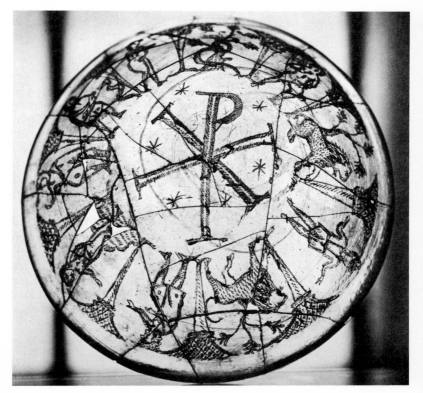

84. Engraved glass bowl from the cemetery at Homblières; early Christian art, 4th century.

of time this Church may never have a citizen of Toulouse for her bishop." And we know that it hath never so befallen in that city until the present time. Saturninus was bound at the heels of a maddened bull and driven headlong from the Capitol, so ending his life. Gatianus, Trophimus, Stremonius, Paul and Martial, after lives passed in the greatest sanctity, during which they won over much people to the Church, and spread the faith of Christ on every hand, passed from the world in the glad confession of their faith. In this wise leaving this earth, the first as martyrs, the rest as confessors, they were all together united in heaven.' (*28*: vol. ii, pp. 20–1.)

Gregory of Tours is a conscientious historian, and his outline of the early history of Christianity in Gaul carries conviction.

## *The Young Diocese of Tours*

Only in the mid third century, then, were the first bishoprics set up in a few of the cities of Gaul.

Gregory of Tours gives us an example from his personal knowledge, his own diocese of Tours. At the end of his *History* he briefly summarizes the lives of all his predecessors. This is what he tells us of the first two bishops of Tours, Gatianus and Litorius. The third was St Martin, consecrated bishop in 371:

'The first bishop, Gatianus, was sent by the Pope of Rome in the first year of the Emperor Decius. There was then living in Tours a multitude of pagans addicted to idolatry, some of whom he converted to the Lord by his preaching. But sometimes he had to conceal himself from the attacks of the powerful, who, if they found him, would often subject him to railing and abuse; for this cause he used secretly to celebrate the holy mystery on the Lord's Day in crypts and hiding-places with the few Christians whom, as I have said, he had converted. He was a very pious and God-fearing man; had he not been such a one, never would he have forsaken his houses, his kinsfolk, and his country for love of the Lord. In this manner he lived of his own choice in the city for fifty years, died in peace, and was buried in the cemetery of the quarter belonging to the Christians. The see then remained vacant for thirty-seven years.

'In the first year of the Emperor Constans, Litorius was consecrated second bishop; he was a citizen of Tours and of great piety. He it was who built the first church erected in the city of Tours, for the Christians were now numerous; for the first basilica, he converted the house of a certain man of senatorial family. In his time the holy Martin began to preach in Gaul. He held the see for thirty-three years and died in peace; he was buried in the aforesaid basilica, which today bears his name.' (*28*: vol. ii, pp. 469–70.)

## *The Golden Legend of St Julian*

These terse biographies inspire confidence by their very simplicity; in striking contrast is the biography of the first bishop of a diocese close to Tours, Le Mans. This biography dates from the ninth century, and the humble truth has had plenty of time to disguise itself. Indeed, the early Christians of Gaul were not content with the assertion that illustrious people from the Gospel story, Lazarus, Martha and Mary Magdalene, had landed upon their shores. Parochial pride led many churches to make themselves out to be very much older than they were, to claim the honour of having been founded by the immediate disciples of the apostles—even by the immediate disciples of Christ. These claims took shape in Carolingian times; that is why the writer of the *Actus Pontificum Cenomannis in urbe degentium* proudly presented the first bishop of Le Mans, St Julian, as one of the seventy disciples sent out by Jesus, even though the diocese cannot have been founded before the fourth century, perhaps not before the fifth. The account he gives is curious, and shows how successfully legend can change the face of history:

'The first bishop in the city of Le Mans was St Julian. He was of noble Roman stock, and learnedly instructed from childhood in the lore of Holy Scripture. He was ordained by the apostles among the seventy disciples, and afterwards was skilfully instructed by the Roman pope Clement, St Peter's successor, in the episcopal ministry. After being canonically ordained by the pope, he was sent to preach at Le Mans, with the priest Turibius and the deacon Pavatius as his companions. . . .

'When under God's guidance he came to the aforesaid city of Le Mans, before entering the city which was still some way off, he sat down in much distress of mind and began to ponder what he should do; for if he entered the city thus, no man would receive him, but rather they would overwhelm him with insults and drive him out, and all would be to no avail. But as he reflected thus and was troubled in mind, he received comfort from God, so that without hesitation he executed the command he had been given. Rising to his feet, he thrust into the ground the staff

85. Sarcophagus from La Gayole, late 2nd century: above, the Good Shepherd and Christ (?); below, Fisherman and woman praying.

he carried, which the blessed Clement had given him at his ordination; and at once a spring of living water burst forth from the ground. . . .

'When the men of that place, both from the city and its suburbs, saw the miracle he had performed in the name of Christ, and a spring flowing where no suspicion of water had been, they marvelled greatly. And looking on the blessed Julian, they began to ask him whence he came, who he was, and for what purpose he was there. And the blessed Julian answered, saying: "I am the envoy of Christ Jesus the Nazarene, who took upon him the human flesh of the Virgin Mary, and suffered and was crucified and buried for the salvation of us all; who on the third day rose again, and afterwards ascended into heaven, whence he shall come on the day of judgment to judge the whole human race and render to each according to his works."

'The people of that place were heathens, and had never before heard Christ preached or named, nor seen a bishop, nor did they know anything of the Christian religion; but rather they adored idols and worshipped demons; and they venerated mountains and trees and stones. But when the inhabitants of the aforesaid place heard the preaching of the blessed Julian, his words were confirmed in them, and became as sweet honey in their hearts, and they gladly heard the teaching of the blessed Julian, and said they would believe in Christ whom he preached.' (*1*: p. 28.)

The clerk of Le Mans adds that the news of the preaching of the blessed Julian, 'the Roman bishop', spread through the city and came to the ears of the official he calls 'the prince of that place', who had the title of 'Defensor'. And here, oddly enough, the chronicler gives himself away, for the title of *Defensor* was given in the Later Roman Empire to magistrates appointed by the Emperor Valentinian I to defend the interests of the native population of the cities against oppression by the great. It is obvious that Julian, said to be a disciple of the apostles, could not have arrived to convert the people of Le Mans until the second half of the fourth century at earliest. Even if St Julian's very existence is not debatable, his connection with the apostles cannot be anything but a pious legend.

The biography of St Julian, then, shows us what a clerk, a man of education, writing in the ninth century, believed about the origins of his church, which he dates without turning a hair to the very century when Jesus Christ lived on earth. Gregory of Tours was more modest in his claims when he wrote about his predecessors. His account takes us back to the third century, and makes no attempt to turn the founder of the diocese into one of the seventy disciples ordained by the apostles, as the *Actus* did for St Julian. Gregory of Tours does not try to disguise the slow, laborious beginnings of the Gospel in Gaul. He tells of no sensational miracles, no wholesale conversions, no generous prince loading the missionary from Rome with gifts; but the reader is left with the impression that his account is a great deal nearer the truth; and that, even if less spectacular, is perhaps more moving.

# 13

# ST HILARY AND HIS THEOLOGY
# AND ST MARTIN AND HIS CLOAK

Two great figures dominate the Church of Gaul in the fourth century—
St Hilary of Poitiers and St Martin of Tours. St Hilary was a theologian,
a doctor of the Church, deeply versed in exegesis of the most subtle kind
and even more deeply in the thorny problems of Christology. St Martin
was a more human figure, first and foremost a missionary, simple and
direct.

## The Athanasius of the West

Hilary was born at the beginning of the fourth century—at Poitiers, says
St Jerome. He had a first-class education. He had already reached
manhood when he was baptized, and his late baptism was the beginning
of a truly Christian life. In 350, or perhaps a few years later, he was
called to be bishop of Poitiers on the death of Bishop Maxentius. One
single thought guided his whole life as bishop: the war against Arianism.
While his contemporary St Martin devoted himself body and soul to
his pastoral mission and to preaching the gospel to the people, St
Hilary applied himself to defending in all its purity the dogma laid
down by the council of Nicaea—the principle of the divinity of Christ,
which the Arians denied.

So he became the 'Athanasius of the West', and his uncompromising
defence of Catholic doctrine quickly developed into a personal conflict
with Constantius, one of the sons of Constantine the Great, who had

become sole emperor after the death of his brothers in 353, and who was himself an Arian. About half-way through 356 Constantius exiled Hilary to Asia Minor, but to no effect; Hilary stuck to his guns, and when the emperor gave way for the sake of peace and quiet and let him return to his diocese in 360, he hurled at his imperial adversary a pamphlet in which, as Camille Jullian says, 'the verve and energy of the speech *In Catilinam* were combined with a sincerity and righteous indignation which Cicero lacked'. (*37*: vol. viii, p. 272.)

Suspicious and warped as Constantius was, he was certainly a less redoubtable adversary than Nero or Decius, the emperors of the 'great persecutions; but Hilary would have preferred, he says, a more violent, even a more cruel, hostility. From Hilary's portrait of the emperor in this pamphlet, the portrait of a superstitious man who was anxious to keep on good terms with the clergy, one feels that what Hilary detested above all in him was his hypocrisy, and what he chiefly censured was his encouragement of divisions within the Church.

## Hilary Longs for the Days of the Persecutors

'Would that thou, Almighty God and Creator of the universe, Father of our one Lord Jesus Christ, hadst given me rather the days of Nero or Decius as the age and time when I must fulfil my ministry of confessing thee and thine only begotten Son! For then, through the mercy

86. Sarcophagus-cover said to be from the tomb of St Abre, daughter of St Hilary. 5th century.

87. The Good Shepherd, carrying a lamb (head missing) on his shoulders. Marble, 4th century.

of our Lord and God thy Son Jesus Christ and the inspiration of the Holy Spirit, I would not have feared the rack, knowing how Isaiah was cut in two; nor dreaded the fire, remembering how the children of the Hebrews sang amidst the flames; nor flinched from the cross and the breaking of my legs, for I would have recalled how the thief was afterwards transported to Paradise; nor trembled at the depths of the sea and the tides of the Black Sea, for thou wouldst have taught me by the example of Jonah and Paul that the faithful still live on in the sea. Such a battle against thy declared enemies would have been happiness for me.'

## The Persecutions of Constantius

'But now we fight against an elusive persecutor, against an enemy who caresses us, against the Antichrist Constantius; who does not scourge the back, but pampers the stomach; does not proscribe us that we may have immortal life, but enriches us that we may die; does not thrust us into prison, where we may be free, but loads us with honours within his palace that we may be slaves; does not torture the body, but makes himself master of the heart; does not behead with the sword, but slays the soul with gold; does not in public threaten with burning, but in private kindles the fires of hell; does not fight, lest he be overcome, but flatters that he may rule over us. He confesses Christ only to deny him; works for unity only to destroy peace; represses heresies in such wise that no Christians may be left; honours priests that he may do away with bishops; builds roofs for the Church that he may destroy her faith. He proclaims thee in words and with his lips, [O Christ]; and does everything, in all ways, that men shall not believe that thou art God, as is the Father.'

## Hilary Clears Himself of the Charge of Slander

'A truce then to this campaign of abuse and suspicion of falsehood. For it behoves the ministers of the truth to utter true words. If we spoke falsehood, our scurrilous words would be a disgrace. But if all that we say is manifestly true, we do not go beyond the bounds of apostolic freedom and moderation when we make these accusations after long silence. But perhaps I shall be thought rash, because I call Constantius Antichrist. If anyone esteems this impudence rather than steadfastness, let him read again what John said to Herod: "It is not lawful for thee" to do this.' (30: col. 580.)

Hilary follows up this reference to the gospel according to St Mark by other quotations from the arsenal of the Bible. We need not repeat them; all they do is to prove that Hilary was never at a loss for arguments to support his cause. Indeed he is very rarely as incisive as in this pamphlet. His other works, theological and exegetical treatises, are less comprehensible to the modern reader. It would ill become us to suggest that they can be boring. But indeed his passion for controversy sometimes leads him into verbalism. One of his biographers has noted that Hilary did his best to put into practice the maxim he formulated and commented on in his treatise on the Trinity: 'A virtuous man is of use only to himself, if he is not a scholar.'

Let us now turn to St Martin, who had no pretensions to scholarship and no very deep knowledge of theology; from him we shall learn that saintliness can be of use to many more than its possessor, even when it does not go hand in hand with scholarship.

prestare uictouam · quā uṭ fubacuī
fineſ fanguinie hoſtib; nemo moreret̄ ·

88. 'Life and miracles of St Martin': manuscript executed at Tours about 1100 (also 89 and 90). St Martin asks for his discharge and leaves the army.

## Good St Martin

St Martin was, and still is, the most popular of the saints of Gaul. More than four thousand French churches are dedicated to him, and every French department could produce a whole list of places called St Martin, with the common variants Dammartin and Donmartin. Martin is nearly as common a surname in France as Smith in England. And the saint has found his way into everyday life. St Martin's Day, 11th November, had ceased to be a public holiday before 1918, when Armistice Day took over the date; but in many regions of France Martinmass is still the

time when towns-people move house and country people pay the rent
for their fields. The fine spell that often comes at the beginning of
November is a St Martin's summer. Since the loving-kindness of St
Martin, like that of St Francis of Assisi, extended to all living creatures,
the French have, with a certain lack of respect, adopted 'martin' as the
common name for some animals—donkeys and bears, as well as king-
fishers. All these usages are eloquent proof of the benign influence of
the saint and the lasting value of his work.

The writer Sulpicius Severus, who was a contemporary of St Martin
and knew him personally, has perpetuated his memory in his *Life* of the
saint; and not only in that, but in the *Dialogues* which complete the
biography and contain a number of anecdotes of great interest. E. C.
Babut, in his book on St Martin, has made serious criticisms of Sulpicius
Severus; but the portrait of the saint preserved for posterity in the *Life*
and *Dialogues* seems to have been a good likeness. We are free to make
our own reservations about the miracles which Sulpicius Severus, with
the credulous faith of his times, attributes to his hero; but the portrait
of the saint himself, the anecdotes about him and his sayings have the
unmistakable ring of sincerity.

89. St Martin gives a part of his cloak to a beggar, and the next night dreams that he sees Christ wrapped in it.

90. St Martin has taken poison and prays God to save him.

## The Soldier's Cloak

St Martin was born in Pannonia of pagan parents. His father was a military tribune; he intended his son to be a soldier, and Martin began his career in the army. But he was already a Christian in spirit, and it was while he was on garrison duty at Amiens that he performed one of his most famous acts of charity:

'Once, when he was wearing nothing but his arms and a plain soldier's cloak, in the depths of a winter more than usually severe, so that the intensity of the cold had killed many people, he met at the gate of the city of Amiens a naked beggar, who implored the passers-by to have pity on him; but all passed him by in his misery. The man of God understood that the beggar was reserved for him, since no other showed him any pity. But what could he do? He had nothing but the cloak in which he was wrapped, for he had already given away the rest in a similar need. So drawing the sword with which he was armed, he divided his cloak down the middle, gave one part to the beggar, and wrapped himself again in what remained. Meanwhile some of the bystanders laughed, because he looked grotesque in his mutilated cloak. But many others, who had more sense, lamented that they had not done likewise, when, having more, they could have clothed the beggar without stripping themselves.' (*70*: pp. 7–8.)

Martin was then eighteen. The next night he dreamed that he saw Jesus wrapped in the piece of cloak he had given to the beggar, and distinctly heard him say: 'Martin, though still a catechumen, covered me with this garment.' Encouraged by the vision, he at once sought baptism, and two years later applied for his discharge from the army. On his release he went to join St Hilary, who was known far and wide as a man of rock-like faith. Hilary of Poitiers kept Martin with him, and ordained him exorcist in his church. But Martin's saintliness soon made him a popular figure, and though he did not live in Poitiers, but some way out of the town at the monastery of Ligugé which he is said to have founded, the people sought him out there and begged him to accept the vacant bishopric of Tours.

91. Haloed saint (?St Martin) standing in prayer between sun and moon. Terra cotta brick found at Tours. 5th or 6th century.

92. Ancient glass vessel, perhaps an ampulla brought back by St Martin from a pilgrimage to Agaunum. Church of Candes (Indre-et-Loire).

## The Election at Tours

'About the same time he was begged to accept the episcopate of the church of Tours; but as he could not easily be uprooted from his monastery, a certain Rusticus, one of the inhabitants, pretending that his wife was ill, flung himself down at the saint's knees and succeeded in bringing him out. A crowd of citizens had already been posted along his route, and he was led under escort to the city. Wonderful to see, an extraordinary multitude had assembled, not only from the town but from neighbouring cities too, to cast their vote. They all had but one will, one desire, one opinion—that Martin was the most worthy to be bishop; and that the church of such a priest would be fortunate indeed. But a few, and some bishops among them, who had been summoned to consecrate him bishop, impiously opposed his election, saying that he was a contemptible person, unworthy to be made a bishop, a man of despicable appearance, dirty in his dress and unkempt. . . . But they could not do other than what the people, by God's will, compelled them to do.' (70: pp. 16–17.)

## A Simple, Unpretentious Life

St Martin disliked all ostentation, and when he became bishop he continued to live simply and unpretentiously. One of his most devoted disciples, Gallus, supplied his friend Sulpicius Severus with details of his simplicity of life:

141

'Even in church, no one has ever seen him sitting in the bishop's throne, whereas, as God is my witness, I have seen, and not without shame, a certain bishop sitting in a raised seat, a high throne like the judgment-seat of a king, and Martin sitting on a rustic stool, such as are used by slaves, which we country Gauls call *tripeccia*, but you scholars (and certainly you, Sulpicius Severus, who come from Greece) call tripods.' (70: p. 65.)

But a man in the saint's high position could not avoid the society of the great, even of the imperial family. It gave him no pleasure. He even refused several times to eat with the Emperor Maximus who, although he had usurped the imperial power, led an exemplary life in private. In the end St Martin gave way, and, what was even more remarkable, put up with the presence at the meal of the empress, who held him in the highest respect:

'At last she asked her husband's help to constrain Martin to accept that she alone should serve his meal, the servants having nothing to do with it; and the saint could not continue his obstinate resistance. The pious preparations were made by the queen's own hands. She herself laid a cover over a little stool, drew up a table, and poured water over his hands; she brought dishes which she had cooked herself; and while Martin ate, she stood apart, as servants are taught to do, motionless and as if rooted to the ground, showing throughout the correctness of an attendant and the humility of a servant. She herself mixed the wine when he would drink and handed him the cup. After the meal she removed the broken bread and gathered up the crumbs.'

It is a pleasant story; and it is typical of Martin's teaching to his clerks, which Gallus, who told it to Sulpicius Severus, formulated thus in one of the intimate conversations so happily preserved in the *Dialogues*: 'So heed the lesson: let a matron serve you, not command you.' (70: pp. 74–6.)

Martin's precepts may have been austere, but his commentaries on them did not lack humour; for example, when he compared the life of a religious with that of a soldier to convince a hermit that it was hardly desirable for him to share his life with a woman:

'A certain soldier had thrown off his sword-belt in church and taken his vows as a monk; he had made himself a cell in an isolated place, where he might live as a hermit. Meanwhile the adversary cunningly troubled his untaught mind with various thoughts, so that he wanted his wife,

93. Cover decorated with pigs, rabbits, roast fowls and bunches of grapes.

whom Martin had directed to enter a nunnery, to change her mind and live with him.'

So the honest hermit went to St Martin, who expostulated that a wife could not come back to live with her husband once he was a monk. But the hermit was unconvinced, and pleaded that now he was a soldier of Christ he would be able to keep his vow of chastity loyally:

'Then Martin said (and I will give you his exact words): "Tell me, when an army is preparing to give battle, or with bare steel fighting hand to hand with the enemy, have you ever seen a woman take her place in the ranks, or fight?" Then the soldier blushed in confusion, thanking Martin that he had not left him in his error, and had corrected him not by harsh rebukes but by a true and reasonable comparison such as suited a soldier.' (70: pp. 80–1.)

From anecdotes such as these we can understand the enormous success of St Martin's preaching. What he said was direct and easily understandable. But there was in him too a deep humanity and charity. There is a moving example of this in a story told by Gallus, and reported by Sulpicius Severus in his *Dialogues*, of how the saint had accepted communion with heretic bishops because it was the only way of saving the Priscillianists of Africa from being condemned to death:

'On the way back he was sad and lamented that he had even for an hour shared in a culpable communion. . . . His companions being a little way ahead, he sat down, turning over in his mind the cause of his grief, and by turns accusing and defending himself. Suddenly an angel stood before him and said: "It is right, Martin, that you should feel compunction; but you could have taken no other way out. Take courage again, possess your soul in constancy, or you will endanger not only your reputation but your salvation.' (70: p. 107.)

Anyone capable of such delicacy of feeling must have been a man of rare quality, and, as Camille Jullian says, it is one of St Martin's chief claims to glory that he did everything possible, even something which caused him great pain, to turn the Church aside from the paths of persecution.

94. Capital letter from illuminated missal, Tours, late 12th century.

## Squabbling over Relics

St Martin died on 8th November 397 at Candes, a parish of his diocese where he had gone on a visit. His holiness was already universally recognized; and Gregory of Tours tells us that no sooner was he dead than a hot dispute over the possession of his precious body broke out between the churches of Poitiers and Tours, in each of which in turn he had exercised his ministry:

'In the second year of the emperors Arcadius and Honorius the holy Martin, bishop of Tours, full of virtues and holiness, and doer of many good deeds to the sick, left this world at Candes, a village of his diocese, and passed to Christ in the eighty-first year of his life and the twenty-sixth of his bishopric. He passed at midnight, on a Sunday, in the consulship of Atticus and Caesarius. And many at his passing heard a chanting in the sky. . . .

'As soon as the holy man of God fell ill, as I have said, at Candes, the people of Poitiers and Tours came together to be present at his death. After his passing there arose great altercation between the two peoples.

95, 96. Details of Brescia casket. Ivory, 4th century.

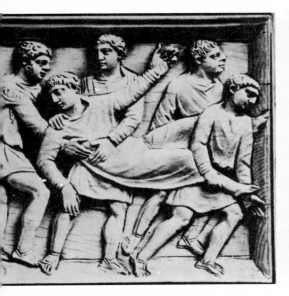

For the men of Poitiers said: "As monk, he was ours; he became abbot among us; we demand back him whom we entrusted to you. For you let it suffice that while he was a bishop in this world ye enjoyed his converse, sat at his table, were strengthened by his blessings, and above all made glad by his miracles. Let therefore all these things suffice for you; but be it permitted to us to bear away at least his lifeless body." To this the men of Tours made answer: "Ye declare that we should be content with the miracles done among us; but know that while his place was among you, he wrought more than he did here. For, to say nothing of the greater number, he raised two persons from the dead for you, and for us but one; and as he himself would often say, the power was greater in him before he was made bishop than after. Therefore it needs must be that what he left unfulfilled during his life among us he should complete now in his death." '

The men of Tours, who were by no means at a loss for arguments, then asserted that a bishop should be buried in the city where he had been ordained:

'The sun went down on their dispute, and it was full night. The doors were locked, and both parties kept watch over the body which lay between them. The men of Poitiers meant to carry it off by force upon the morrow, but Almighty God would not have the city of Tours deprived of its own patron. So in the dead of night the whole troop from Poitiers was overcome with sleep; of all the multitude there remained not one who kept vigil. Now when the men of Tours saw them fallen asleep they took up the mortal clay of that most holy body, and while some passed it out through a window, others received it outside; then they placed it in a boat, and the whole people went with it down the stream of the Vienne. And as soon as they entered the stream of the Loire, they steered for the city of Tours, with loud songs of praise and abundant chanting. Their voices roused the men of Poitiers, who, robbed of the treasure which they wished to guard, returned home sore confounded.' (*28*: vol. ii, pp. 29–30.)

Gregory of Tours inserted this picturesque story into his *History of the Franks* two hundred years after the saint's death. But we have a contemporary account of his death and burial in a letter from Sulpicius Severus to his mother-in-law Bassula. (*53*: p. 135.) Its tone, as befits its subject-matter, is grave and sorrowful. The writer tells how the whole city of Tours hastened out to meet the funeral procession, how more than two thousand weeping monks were there, how the choir of maidens followed, exhorting one another not to vent their grief in tears. But indeed it is not impossible to reconcile the two accounts. There may well have been a clash between the citizens of Poitiers and Tours, as Gregory of Tours relates, without Sulpicius Severus' having felt it necessary, or even fitting, to refer to it in his letter to his mother-in-law. Gregory of Tours, on the other hand, would have made the most of the incident; it was a victory for his diocesans, and the possession of the precious relics had decisively shaped the future of his town of Tours, making it a place of pilgrimage for the whole Catholic world. But true or false, the story of the incident is valuable in that it shows how rapidly in Gaul the religious spirit had degenerated into materialism. By Merovingian times, as we shall see, the miraculous powers attributed to the bodies of saints had become the essential part of religion.

*Part V*

# THE GERMANIC INVASIONS

# 14

# THE DAWN OF THE FIFTH CENTURY: THE GERMAN MENACE

## *The Hordes of Legend*

THERE is a myth of the great invasions which owes its wide currency to the old history books, and which fanciful pictures have imprinted on the minds of generations of children: the myth that hordes of Germanic and Tartar tribes were unleashed on the Roman Empire in the fifth century and toppled it to its ruin. Amid the flood of invaders one or two legendary figures stand out: Alaric, the leader of the Visigoths who forced the gates of Rome, and of course Attila the Hun, the 'scourge of God'.

The truth is more complex and less romantic. The peoples of the lands to the east of Europe did not wait for the decline of the Roman Empire before they flung themselves against the West. As early as the end of the second century B.C. a wave of Germanic invaders had broken upon Gaul—the Cimbri, from north Jutland, and the Teutones, who came originally from what is now Schleswig; and only the energy of the consul Marius prevailed against them, first at Aix-en-Provence in 103, and then, as the wave ebbed, at Verceil (Piedmont) in 101 B.C. This first Germanic invasion, which was indeed a migration of peoples, has been long and vividly remembered; even today the name of one of the tribes, the Teutones, is still applied to the German people.

This first fierce assault revealed the existence of an ever-present danger, and was perhaps one of the reasons behind the Roman conquest of Gaul; certainly the Romans saw the defence of the Rhine frontier against the tribes beyond as one of the essential duties laid on them.

The formidable Germanic tribes aroused a great deal of uneasy curiosity under the Early Roman Empire. But the mystery which surrounded them did not last long, for trading contacts were many. The historian Tacitus, whose father seems to have been procurator of Belgica and who was himself well informed by travellers and merchants, has painted a picture of them in his *Germania* which may not be strictly accurate, but is at least an attempt at a faithful portrait of their country as it was towards the end of the first century A.D.

'Germany [he writes at the beginning of his book] is separated from Gaul, from Rhaetia, and Pannonia, by the Rhine and the Danube; from Dacia and Sarmatia, by a chain of mountains, and, where the mountains subside, mutual dread forms a sufficient barrier. The rest is bounded by the ocean, embracing in its depth of water several spacious bays, and islands of prodigious extent, whose kings and peoples are now, in some measure, known to us, the progress of our arms having made recent discoveries.'

The impression made on the Roman visitor by this country 'covered with the gloom of forests, or deformed with wide-extended marshes', was anything but happy; it was the last place he would choose to settle, and Tacitus adduces the repellent aspect of the land as a conclusive argument in support of his contention that the Germans were indigenous to it.

97. Roman cavalryman at the gallop. Bronze from Tigring (Austria).

98. Troops on the march. Detail of marble sarcophagus, Arles.

'Putting the dangers of a turbulent and unknown sea out of the case, who would leave the softer climes of Asia, Africa or Italy, to fix his abode in Germany?—where nature offers nothing but scenes of deformity; where the inclemency of the seasons never relents; where the land presents a dreary region, without form or culture, and, if we except the affection of a native for his mother country, without an allurement to make life supportable.'

## Tacitus on the Germans

To Roman eyes, though, the inhabitants were more attractive than their country. Tacitus describes their physique as follows:

'[There is] a family likeness throughout the nation; the same form and features, stern blue eyes, ruddy hair, their bodies large and robust, but powerful only in sudden efforts. They are impatient of toil and labour; thirst and heat overcome them; but, from the nature of their soil and climate, they are proof against cold and hunger.'

Tacitus dwells on the very rudimentary economy of the Germans;

153

it must have made an impression on the Romans who traded with them. Barter was still customary, and in the time of Tacitus specie was familiar only to the tribes on the frontier where hucksters and wine-sellers had penetrated. Marc Bloch has ingeniously pointed out that the German word *Kaufmann* comes from the Latin *caupo*, a tavern-keeper. The wine trade was the first form of commercial business the Germans knew.

Tacitus notes that they did not hoard gold and silver:

'There are indeed silver vessels to be seen amongst them, but they were presents to their chiefs or ambassadors; the Germans regard them in no better light than common earthenware. It is, however, observable that, near the borders of the empire, the inhabitants set a value upon gold and silver, finding them subservient to the purposes of commerce. The Roman coin is known in these parts, and some of our specie is not only current, but in request. In places more remote, the simplicity of the ancient manners still prevails: commutation of property is their only traffic. Where money passes in the way of barter, our old coin is the most acceptable, particularly that which is indented at the edge, or stamped with the impression of a chariot and two horses. Silver is preferred to gold, not for caprice or fancy, but because the inferior metal is of more expeditious use in the purchase of low-priced commodities.' (*71*: vol. ii, pp. 311–15.)

Tacitus dwells on the moral virtues of the Germans, and it will be easy to see why. He paints an idyllic picture of their family life:

'The virtue of the woman is guarded from seduction; no public spectacles to seduce her; no banquets to inflame her passions. . . . Populous as the country is, adultery is rarely heard of: when detected, the punishment is instant, and inflicted by the husband. He cuts off the hair of his guilty wife and, having assembled her relations, expels her naked from his house, pursuing her with stripes through the village. To public loss of honour no favour is shown. She may possess beauty, youth and riches; but a husband she can never obtain. Vice is not treated by the Germans as a subject of raillery, nor is the profligacy of corrupting and being corrupted called the fashion of the age. . . . To set limits to population, by rearing up only a certain number of children and destroying the rest, is accounted a flagitious crime. Among the savages of Germany, virtuous manners operate more than good laws in other countries.' (*71*: vol. ii, p. 324.)

This is clearly an allusion to the licentiousness prevailing in the

Roman Empire and the impossibility of suppressing it by legislation. But has Tacitus achieved a good likeness in his portrait of German society? We may doubt it; as we shall see, the Franks who settled in Gaul later on could not be held up to the native Gallo-Roman population as models of the domestic virtues.

## People who Hate Peace

If we are to arrive at a fair assessment of Tacitus' work, we must find out what was at the back of his mind—what decided him to write his book. This is not hard to discover. He felt he had a duty to warn his compatriots that the proximity of a warlike people, wresting their living from an unproductive land, was a constant threat to the Empire. That is why he particularly stressed their martial qualities:

'A German transacts no business, public or private, without being completely armed. The right of carrying arms is assumed by no person whatever, till the state has declared him duly qualified. The young candidate is introduced before the assembly, where one of the chiefs, or his father, or some near relation, provides him with a shield and javelin. This, with them, is the manly gown: the youth from that moment ranks as a citizen; till then he was considered as part of the household; he is now a member of the commonwealth.' (71: vol. ii, p. 320.)

Then Tacitus explains the German custom of companionship. The chieftains, whom he calls *principes*, are recruited from the aristocracy. Each chieftain gathers round him a band of companions in arms, who form his escort; these the historian calls *comites* (counts). The close bonds of comradeship between them are especially obvious in battle:

'In the field of action, it is disgraceful to the prince to be surpassed in valour by his COMPANIONS; and not to vie with him in martial deeds is equally a reproach to his followers. If he dies in the field, he who survives him survives to live in infamy. All are bound to defend their leader, to succour him in the heat of action, and to make even their own actions subservient to his renown. This is the bond of union, the most sacred obligation. The chief fights for victory; the followers fight for their chief. If, in the course of a long peace, the people relax into sloth and indolence, it often happens that the young nobles seek a more active life in the service of other states engaged in war. The German mind cannot brook repose.' (71: vol. ii, p. 321.)

## Barbarian Infiltration

The warning is clear. Soberly and objectively, Tacitus reminded his fellow countrymen that the forests and marshes beyond the Rhine harboured warlike, well-disciplined peoples who loved war above the occupations of peace. Until the end of the second century the Roman armies kept watch and ward. But in the dark days of the third century, and the first German invasions, we see cracks appearing in the defence. It was then too that the barbarian infiltration began, and by degrees the Empire itself became barbarian. The catastrophe was delayed by the great emperors of the late third and fourth centuries, who to some extent restored the Empire. The respite they won for Rome lasted some hundred years.

The barbarization of the Empire began afresh, and continued at an even greater pace, under the Emperor Theodosius, who bore the un-deserved title of 'the Great', and his two very ordinary sons, Arcadius and Honorius, who divided the Empire between them on the death of their father in 395. From the late fourth century onwards, the Roman armies were submerged by the tide of barbarian mercenaries. At its

99. Bust of a young German in the service of Rome, wearing a slave's collar. Found at Welschbillig.

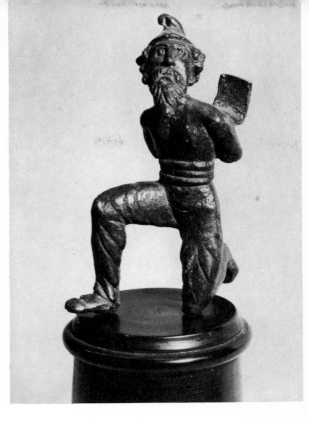

100. Barbarian in Phrygian cap, hands bound and kneeling on one knee.

wits' end, the government instituted the system of 'hospitality', which settled a multitude of German 'nations' on the soil of Gaul: Visigoths, Burgundians, Alans, Franks. To them was entrusted the duty of policing and defending their own districts.

So widely was the system adopted that the great invasions of the fifth century usually meant in fact that fresh barbarian invaders found themselves face to face with barbarians already settled on imperial territory.

This universal barbarization was symbolized by an event that shook the civilized world to its foundations—the 'fall of the Eternal City', the capture of Rome by the Visigoth Alaric on the night of 24th August 410. The threat which had hung over Italy for the last ten years had forced Stilicho, the barbarian *magister militiae* of the feeble Emperor Honorius, to recall troops from the Rhine frontier. This left the door open to the plundering hordes from beyond the Rhine, and the first years of the fifth century were darkened by a number of great raids into Gaul.

157

101. Head of barbarian
with half-closed eyes. Gilt
bronze. Found at
Avenches (Switzerland).

## The Terrible Invasion of 406

The most terrible of all these raids was launched on the last day of the
year 406. Our main source of information about it is a famous letter
written by St Jerome. Though he had retired to a monastery in Bethlehem in 386, the great doctor still followed with concern the tragedy
being played out in the West. He was a firm believer in the greatness of
Rome, and the penetration of the barbarians into the Western Empire
filled him with foreboding. In the preface to his history he openly
expresses his anxiety over the future of the world: 'But since the
barbarians still rage through the land, all things are uncertain.'

His distress found expression more than once in the voluminous
correspondence which he kept up to the end of his life. Writing to
the young widow Geruchia, who was thinking of marrying again, he
tries to dissuade her by depicting the world on the verge of catastrophe.

True, he begins with more personal arguments:

'You set before me the joys of marriage. . . . The good that we hope
for in marriage is not so great as the evil which may befall us, and which
is much to be feared. Passion satisfied always leaves remorse behind it; it
is never sated, and dies only to be rekindled. It waxes and wanes with
intercourse, and obeys no reason, being directed by impulses. But, you
will say, my great fortune, and the administration of my property, need
a man's authority. . . . Do not your grandmother, your mother and aunt,

enjoy the authority they formerly had, and high regard, since they are received by the whole province and the princes of the Church? . . . As if you could not have servants of suitable age, whether slaves or freedmen, at whose hands you were reared in childhood, to direct your household, answer for you in all public matters, pay your taxes; to revere you as their protectress, cherish you as their nurseling, venerate you as their saint! Seek ye first the kingdom of God, and all these things shall be added unto you.'

Then, perhaps suspecting that these arguments may not carry much weight, St Jerome ends his exhortation with a dark picture of the times, in the hope that this will turn the young woman's thoughts from marriage. The day of Antichrist is at hand: 'Woe unto them that are with child, and to them that give suck in those days!' And he completes the text with the very pertinent observation: 'Both these things are the fruit of marriage.'

102. Barbarians. Detail from tomb of Jovinus at Rheims.

'If up to now we few still enjoy peace, it is not by our merits, but by the mercy of the Lord. Countless and savage tribes have seized the whole of Gaul. All that lies between Alps and Pyrenees, all that is enclosed between the ocean and the Rhine, is laid waste by the Quadi, the Vandals, Sarmatians, Alans, Gepids, Herulians, Saxons, Burgundians, the Alemans, and—alas for the state—the Pannonians now our enemies: "for Assur is come with them." Mainz, once an illustrious city, has been taken and overthrown; several thousands have been massacred in the church there. The people of Worms have been destroyed after a long siege; the mighty city of Reims, Amiens and Arras, the Morini, the most remote of all peoples, the citizens of Tournai, of Spires and Strasburg, have fallen to Germany. Aquitania, Novempopulana, the provinces of Lugdunensis and Narbonensis have all been pillaged, except for a few towns. And those which escape the sword from without are laid low by famine from within. I cannot without tears speak of Toulouse, which owes its survival up to the present to the merits of her holy bishop Exuperius. All Spain, even now on the verge of destruction, daily trembles to remember the invasion of the Cimbri, and in her fear suffers continually what others have suffered once and for all.

'I will say no more [St Jerome goes on], lest I should seem to despair of God's mercy.'

But he does not fail to point the moral:

'Tell me, dearest daughter in Christ, are you going to marry in the midst of all these disasters? Whom will you take as husband, then—a man who will flee battle, or one who will seek it? You know the result in either case. Instead of the nuptial song, the harsh note of the terrible trumpet will assail your ears: and for your bridal attendants you may well have mourners.' (*33*: col. 1055.)

St Jerome's well-known description of the invasion of 406 must be studied in its context, however; its author's enthusiasm for the cause, whether good or bad, which he was pleading to the young widow may well have encouraged him to exaggerate the darkness of the picture.

# 15

# VISIGOTHS AND BURGUNDIANS

THE Antichrist whose coming St Jerome anticipated with such real or simulated apprehension did not in fact make his appearance on earth; a new world was slowly built up on the ruins of the Western Empire, whose death throes lasted until 476. From this slow incubation emerged medieval Europe, and in Gaul the Frankish kingdom.

Modern historians have studied with intense care and interest the process of decomposition and the task of rebuilding which characterized what was both the twilight of the ancient world and the dawn of the Middle Ages. Just as our present-day journalists feverishly pursue the interviews that may lay bare the secrets of current events, our historians have subjected all the various contemporary witnesses, letter-writers, poets, apologists and chroniclers, to close interrogation, and their intricate inquiries have thrown at least some light on a period which, despite their efforts, remains very obscure.

For our part we shall not attempt to do more than set down here a few pictures of the period. Their very diversity indicates the complexity of the problem, a complexity which seems to grow ever greater, the more impartial is our study of all its aspects.

## The New Masters

The Visigoths played a leading part in the history of fifth-century Gaul. They came in the great raid described by St Jerome, surging into

103. Princess Placidia, with her children Valentinian III and Honoria. Painted glass disc from Byzantine cross (before 425).

southern Gaul under their king Athaulf. After a defeat at Marseilles they seized Bordeaux and Toulouse, whose fall was one of the disasters the great doctor feared at the time of his letter to the young widow Geruchia. But Athaulf's greatest success was winning the hand of Princess Placidia, sister of the Emperor Honorius.

The marriage seems to have changed his whole outlook. If we are to believe the historian Paulus Orosius, the barbarian became a Roman:

'The Gothic peoples at that time were under the rule of King Athaulf who, after the capture of Rome and the death of Alaric, had succeeded him on the throne and taken to wife, as I said, Placidia, the captive sister of the emperor. This ruler, an earnest seeker after peace, preferred to fight loyally for the Emperor Honorius and to employ the forces of the Goths for the defence of the Roman state. For I have myself, while at the town of Bethlehem in Palestine, heard a certain man of Narbo, who had served with distinction under Theodosius and who also was a pious, sensible and serious person, tell the most blessed priest Jerome that he himself had been a very intimate friend of Athaulf at Narbo, and that he had often heard what the latter, when in good spirits, health and temper, was accustomed to answer in reply to questions. It seems that at first he ardently desired to blot out the Roman name and to make all the Roman territory a Gothic empire in fact as well as in name, so that, to use the popular expressions, *Gothia* should take the place of *Romania*, and he, Athaulf, should become all that Caesar Augustus once had

162

been. Having discovered from long experience that the Goths, because of their unbridled barbarism, were utterly incapable of obeying laws, and yet believing that the state ought not to be deprived of laws without which a state is not a state, he chose to seek for himself at least the glory of restoring and increasing the renown of the Roman name by the power of the Goths, wishing to be looked upon by posterity as the restorer of the Roman Empire, since he could not be its transformer.' (57: p. 395.)

A good deal has been written on this sudden change of attitude. It shows that the far-sighted among the barbarians would rather settle in the Roman Empire than destroy it, for they knew uneasily that they had nothing to set in its place.

Athaulf's diplomacy was well rewarded, though not until after his death. In 418 Honorius, the emperor of the West, settled the Visigoths in Aquitania as federates (*foederati*). Gradually nibbling away the neighbouring provinces, their kings succeeded in the course of the fifth century in making themselves masters of central Gaul; and by skilful political manoeuvring they insinuated themselves into the good graces of the Gallo-Roman aristocracy. Our evidence for this comes from a great lord who was also a scholar, Sidonius Apollinaris; we shall meet him later in our story.

He has left us a flattering portrait of Theodoric II, king of the Visigoths, who succeeded to the throne when his father was killed at the Battle of the Catalaunian Fields in 451:

'He is a man worth knowing [writes Sidonius to his brother-in-law Agricola], even by those who cannot enjoy his close acquaintance, so happily have providence and nature joined to endow him with the perfect gifts of fortune.

'And first as to his person. He is well set up, in height above the average man, but below the giant.'

Sidonius notes the slightest details of his person with the most minute care, and not without some affectation of style; here are a few typical examples, which may well strike the reader as a little odd:

'The upper ears are buried under overlying locks, after the fashion of his race. The nose is finely aquiline; his barber is assiduous in eradicating the rich growth on the lower part of the face.'

The rest of the description is in keeping with this sample; more interesting is the picture Sidonius gives us of the king's daily routine:

## Twenty-four Hours in the Life of a King

'Now for the routine of his public life. Before daybreak he goes with a very small suite to attend the service of his priests. He prays with assiduity, but, if I may speak in confidence, one may suspect more of habit than conviction in this piety. Administrative duties of the kingdom take up the rest of the morning. Armed nobles stand about the royal seat; the mass of guards in their garb of skins are admitted that they may be within call, but kept at the threshold for quiet's sake; only a murmur of them comes in from their post at the doors, between the curtain and the outer barrier. And now the foreign envoys are introduced. The king hears them out, but says little; if a thing needs more discussion he puts it off, but accelerates matters ripe for dispatch. The second hour [7 a.m.] arrives; he rises from the throne to inspect his treasure chamber or stable.

'On ordinary days his table resembles that of a private person. The board does not groan beneath a mass of dull and unpolished silver set on by panting servitors; the weight lies rather in the conversation than in the plate; there is either sensible talk or none. The hangings and draperies used on these occasions are sometimes of purple silk, sometimes only of linen; art, not costliness, commands the fare, as spotless-

104. 'And now the foreign envoys are introduced. The king hears them out.'
Tours Pentateuch, 7th century.

105. 'The siesta is always slight.'
Tours Pentateuch, 7th century.

ness rather than bulk the silver. Toasts are few, and you will oftener see a thirsty guest impatient, than a full one refusing cup or bowl.

'The siesta after dinner is always slight, and sometimes intermitted. When inclined for the board-game, he is quick to gather up the dice, examines them with care, shakes the box with expert hand, throws rapidly, humorously apostrophizes them and patiently awaits the issue. Silent at a good throw, he makes merry over a bad, annoyed by neither fortune, and always the philosopher.

'About the ninth hour [3 p.m.], the burden of government begins again. Back come the importunates, back the ushers to remove them; on all sides buzz the voices of petitioners, a sound which lasts till evening, and does not diminish till interrupted by the royal repast; even then they only disperse to attend their various patrons among the courtiers, and are astir till bedtime.

'When he rises to withdraw, the treasury watch begins its vigil; and sentries stand on guard during the first hours of slumber.' (66: vol. i, pp. 2–5.)

From this description of a day in the life of King Theodoric II, the reader might well think that the Visigoths were going to settle in Gaul for the express purpose of taking over from the dying Western Empire. Things turned out very differently; the successors of Theodoric II alienated the Gallo-Roman population by their violence and their malignant Arianism. Clovis, king of the Salian Franks, was quick to see how he could supplant the Goths.

## The Romance of a Nation

The Burgundians played a less spectacular part than the Visigoths at the time of the great invasions; but they have given their name to one of France's fairest provinces, Burgundy, and the misfortunes that befell

106. 'He is quick to gather up the dice.' Twelve-lined gaming-board in white marble; found at Autun.

them in the first half of the fifth century have been immortalized in the German epic of the Nibelungs.

The Burgundians are first mentioned by Pliny the Elder (59: vol. i, p. 345.)

They came from the island of Bornholm, and seem to have taken advantage of the breach made by the 406 invasions to occupy Worms and establish themselves on the banks of the Rhine in 413. Apparently they then tried to extend their territories. They paid dearly for their ambition; the patrician Aëtius came out against them, and in 436 a great part of their nation was massacred by his Hunnish mercenaries.

Our only records of this disaster are one or two notes in the annals, as dry as they are brief. The most informative is in the chronicle of Prosper of Aquitaine:

'At this same time [435] Aëtius crushed in battle Gunther, the king of the Burgundians, who lived in the interior of the Gauls, and granted him peace at his prayer; but he did not enjoy it for long, for the Huns utterly destroyed him, with all his people.' (62: p. 475.)

This information is confirmed by an even briefer mention in the anonymous chronicle known as the *Chronica Gallica*, under the year 436:

'A memorable war broke out against the nation of the Burgundians, in which almost all the nation, with its king, was wiped out by Aëtius.' (39: p. 18.)

## The Song of the Nibelungs: Saga of a Burgundian Royal House

But imagination has embroidered the theme magnificently. The extermination of the Burgundians so briefly noted by the annalists must have created a sensation, to judge by the adjective 'memorable' used by one of them; and it became the historical foundation of the Nibelungenlied composed by an anonymous German poet early in the thirteenth century. Scholars, both German and French, have tried to trace the slow development of the legend, and to show by what devious and distant ways a short news item factually reported by sober chroniclers must have travelled before, eight centuries later, it became the theme of a heroic poem in thirty-nine 'adventures'.

Scandinavia and Iceland, where the poems of the *Edda* were composed, were the most important stages in this roundabout journey, and everyone knows that the thirteenth-century poem was not the last metamorphosis that the legend underwent. In the nineteenth century Richard Wagner took it, transformed it by his magic art, and made it the theme of his tetralogy.

In the strange grandiose drama of the *Nibelungenlied* the Burgundians hold the centre of the stage, with their king Gunther (the Gontier of history) and his sister Kriemhild, the heroine of the drama. She marries Siegfried, the son of the king of the Netherlands, who is assassinated by a traitor; she then marries Etzel, king of the Huns, who is none other than Attila, and to avenge Siegfried contrives the massacre of the Burgundian warriors, her fellow countrymen, who had come to the court of king Etzel at her invitation.

Here are the opening lines of the poem:

'In old tales they tell us many wonders of heroes and of high courage, of glad feasting, of wine and mourning; and herein ye shall read of the marvellous deeds and of the strife of brave men.

'There grew up in Burgundy a noble maiden, in no land was a fairer. Kriemhild was her name. Well favoured was the damsel, and by reason of her died many warriors. Doughty knights in plenty wooed her, as was meet, for of her body she was exceeding comely, and her virtues were an adornment to all women.

'Three kings noble and rich guarded her, Gunther and Gernot, warriors of fame, and Giselher the youth, a chosen knight. The damsel was their sister, and the care of her fell on them. These lords were courteous and of high lineage, bold and very strong, each of them the pick of knights. The name of their country was Burgundy, and they did great deeds, after, in Etzel's land. At Worms, by the Rhine, they dwelled in might with many a proud lord for their vassal.' (56: p. 1.)

The last lines of the poem have a sombre, tragic grandeur. Kriemhild, now the wife of Attila, in her implacable desire to avenge Siegfried's death, not only kills Hagen, his murderer; she sacrifices her own kin, in particular her brother Gunther, king of the Burgundians. But she in turn perishes, at the hand of old Hildebrand who is revolted by her cruelty:

' "I will end the matter," said the queen. Then she bade them slay her brother, and they smote off his head. She carried it by the hair to the knight of Trony [Hagen, the king's vassal, who had murdered Siegfried]. He was grieved enow.

'When the sorrowful man saw his master's head, he cried to Kriemhild: "Thou hast wrought all thy will. It hath fallen out as I deemed it must. The noble king of Burgundy is dead, and Giselher the youth, and eke Gernot. None knoweth of the treasure now save God and me. Thou shalt never see it, devil that thou art."

'She said: "I come off ill in the reckoning. I will keep Siegfried's sword at the last. My true love wore it when I saw him last. My bitterest heart's dole was for him."

'She drew it from the sheath. He could not hinder it. She purposed to slay the knight. She lifted it high with both hands, and smote off his head.

'King Etzel saw it, and sorrowed. "Alack!" cried the king; "the best warrior that ever rode to battle, or bore a shield, hath fallen by the hand of a woman! Albeit I was his foeman, I must grieve."

'Then said Master Hildebrand: "His death shall not profit her. I care not what come of it. Though I came in scathe by him myself, I will avenge the death of the bold knight of Trony."

'Hildebrand sprang fiercely at Kriemhild, and slew her with his sword. She suffered sore by his anger. Her loud cry helped her not.

'Dead bodies lay stretched over all. The queen was hewn in pieces. Etzel and Dietrich began to weep. They wailed piteously for kinsmen and vassals. Mickle valour lay there slain. The folk were doleful and dreary.

'The end of the king's high tide was woe, even as, at the last, all joy turneth to sorrow.

'I know not what fell after. Christian and heathen, wife, man and maid, were seen weeping and mourning for their friends.

'I will tell you no more. Let the dead lie. However it fared after with the Huns, my tale is ended. This is the fall of the Nibelungs.' (56: pp. 234–5.)

107. Merovingian belt-plate in cloisonné work.

On this poignant note of pessimism the *Nibelungenlied* ends. In fact a less pitiful fate awaited the Burgundians than the poet would have us believe. The author of the *Chronica Gallica*, who records their memorable defeat in the year 436, is careful to reassure us on the fate of the many survivors, and when he comes to the year 443 he tells us in seven words what happened to them: *Sapaudia Burgundionum reliquis datur cum indigenis dividenda*—'Savoy was given to those who were left of the Burgundians to be shared with the natives.' (*39*: p. 19.)

So the Burgundians were settled in Sapaudia as federates of the Empire, and from this modest beginning grew the Burgundian kingdom, which lasted until 535.

How far did Sapaudia extend? A good many historians have set themselves the task of tracing its boundaries. Here we need do no more than note that this is the first appearance of Savoy in the pages of history.

*a*

108. Burgundian belt-plates:
*a*. gold.
*b*. iron inlaid with silver.

*b*

# 16

# IN THE WAKE OF ATTILA

To TRY to reduce the great invasions to a gradual infiltration of barbarian elements into a diseased and dying Empire is to over-simplify history. But that is how the great French historian, Fustel de Coulanges, saw them; his great mistake was not making enough allowance for the complexity of human phenomena.

As the tragic fifth century wore on, the monotonous process of decomposition was broken by shattering blows of which the most terrible was the invasion of Gaul by Attila's Huns. The Huns were barbarians of Turco-Mongol stock, whose savage hordes appeared in Europe in the second half of the fourth century, on the shores of the Caspian. By the end of that century they had established themselves as masters of a vast area corresponding to modern Hungary, Moldavia and southern Russia.

The historian Ammianus Marcellinus has painted an unlovely portrait of them:

## *The Huns—'Wild Beasts Walking Upright'*

'The people called Huns, slightly mentioned in the ancient records, are a race savage beyond all parallel. At the moment of their birth the cheeks of their infant children are deeply marked by an iron, in order that the usual vigour of their hair, instead of growing at the proper season, may be withered by the wrinkled scars; and accordingly they grow up without any beards, and consequently without any beauty, like eunuchs.'

The author adds that you might fancy them two-legged beasts. Their way of life is uncouth:

'They are so hardy that they require neither fire nor well-flavoured food, but live on the roots of such herbs as they get in the fields, or on the half-raw flesh of any animal, which they merely warm rapidly by placing it between their own thighs and the backs of their horses. They never enter a house unless under the compulsion of some extreme necessity; nor indeed do they think people under roofs as safe as others.'

They are entirely nomadic:

'None of them plough, or even touch a plough-handle: for they have no settled abode, but are homeless and lawless, perpetually wandering with their waggons, which they make their homes; in fact they seem to be people always in flight. Their wives live in these waggons, and there weave their miserable garments; and here too they sleep with their husbands, and bring up their children till they reach the age of puberty; nor, if asked, can any one of them tell you where he was born, as he was conceived in one place, born in another at a great distance and brought up in another still more remote.' (3: pp. 577–9.)

Their way of life was somewhat modified in the course of the fifth century. We know from the Greek Priscos, who accompanied the ambassador of the emperor of the East on a mission to Attila, that the king of the Huns had his palace somewhere in Pannonia, and the chronicler describes the sumptuous feast to which he was bidden. Like many Orientals, Attila was not only a warrior; he was just as much— perhaps even more—a very cunning diplomatist. Dissembling with the emperor of the West, coquetting with him even while in a flagrant piece of double-dealing he was offering the king of the Vandals an alliance against Rome, early in the year 451 he unleashed his forces without warning in a savage attack on the West.

His onslaught came like a thunderbolt; but it had one fortunate result—it banded together against the invader all the forces of Gaul, 'Romans' and barbarians alike, whether federate or independent, under a general who knew his own mind, the *magister militiae* Aëtius.

109. 'They gave the city to the flames . . . No spot in the town remained unburned.'
Tours Pentateuch, 7th century.

173

## The Sack of Metz

Hagiography, impartially mingling legend and history, soon took a hand in the tragic story of the campaign which ended in the death of Attila. The first act in the drama was the sack of Metz. The town was burned down on 7th April (Easter Eve):

'The Huns, therefore, issuing from Pannonia, reached the town of Metz [says Gregory of Tours] on the vigil of the feast of Easter, devastating all the country. They gave the city to the flames, and slew the people with the edge of the sword, and did to death the priests of the Lord before the holy altars; no spot in the town remained unburned save the oratory of the blessed Stephen, protomartyr and deacon. The story of this oratory, as I heard it from certain persons, I will now relate. They say that before the coming of the enemy, one of the faithful in a vision saw the blessed deacon Stephen conferring with the holy apostles Peter and Paul about this destruction, and heard him say: "I beseech you, O my lords, that by your intercession ye suffer not the city of Metz to be burned to the ground by the enemy, for there is in it a place in which relics of this your humble petitioner are preserved; but rather let the people perceive that my power somewhat availeth with the Lord. But if the evil doing of the people is waxed so great that the city needs must be given to the flames, at least suffer not this oratory to be burned." They answered: "Go in peace, most beloved brother, this oratory of thine shall alone be spared in the fire. For the city we shall not obtain this grace, seeing that the sentence of divine judgment is already gone forth upon it. For the sin of the people is grown great, and the sound of their wickedness is gone up before the Lord. For this cause shall this city be burned with fire." '

And Gregory adds:

'It is therefore beyond doubt that by their intercession the oratory remained unburned.' (28: vol. ii, pp. 45–6.)

## Paris Saved by a Virgin

Marcel Poëte in *Une Vie de Cité* has called Paris 'the town on the road'. Her inhabitants had good reason to fear that the road would be Attila's route, when he invaded Gaul and set his face towards the valley of the Loire. Panic was averted by a woman, originally from Nanterre, whom the townspeople already revered for her piety, her ecstasies and her gifts of prophecy. The biographer of St Geneviève, writing shortly after her death, records her successful efforts with a simplicity that carries conviction:

'Rumour, which is said to give true tidings as well as false, spread it abroad that Attila, king of the Huns, surpassing himself in savagery, had decreed that all Gaul should be laid waste and brought under his dominion. The citizens of Paris, terror-stricken, began to labour to transfer their possessions and resources to other and safer towns. But Geneviève called the married women together, and urged them to apply themselves to fasting and prayer and vigils, so that like Judith and Esther they might escape the enemy attack that hung over them. They were of one mind with Geneviève, and for several days, keeping vigil in the baptistery, they devoted themselves to God in fasting and prayer. In like manner she urged their husbands too not to take their possessions out of Paris, for the raging hordes would lay waste the cities they believed to be safer, while Paris would not be defiled by the enemy but saved through Christ's protection.

'But some of the citizens of Paris rose up against her at this, saying she was a false prophetess who had appeared in their times, because she forbade them to move their goods to safer towns from the city of Paris, which she claimed was not going to be destroyed. These citizens were already discussing whether they would punish her by stoning her, or by throwing her into a deep abyss, when, with God's approval, an archdeacon arrived from the town of Auxerre, who, though St Germanus was now dead, had formerly heard him bear witness to Geneviève. [St Germanus, bishop of Auxerre, had foretold that Geneviève would be great before the Lord.]

'The archdeacon came upon those who were holding meetings in different places to discuss how to put her to death, and when he knew their purpose he said to them: "O citizens, do not commit this execrable crime; for our bishop St Germanus has told us that this woman whose death you would compass was chosen by God in her mother's womb, and here I show you the eulogies he has bequeathed to her." And so, when the citizens discovered from the testimony of St Germanus that Geneviève was a most faithful servant of God, and saw the eulogies which had been sent to her and which the archdeacon had brought, they were filled with the fear of God, and wondered at the archdeacon's words; and abandoning their wicked plan, they put an end to their plotting.' (39: pp. 27f.)

This anecdote is entirely credible. Men who face the threat of invasion have two alternatives: to stand their ground or to take to flight.

The first course needs the more courage. The patron saint of Paris had the good sense to counsel it, and the strength of mind to impose her will on the townspeople, terrified as they were at the approach of Attila; their descendants have not forgotten her courageous stand.

## Defeat at Orleans

Attila swept through Reims and Troyes, leaving Paris on his flank, and came to Orleans, the gateway to Aquitania. If we can believe a story told to Gregory of Tours a hundred years later, this was the turning-point in the campaign of the Hun king, who had so far met no obstacle in his path:

'But Attila, king of the Huns, going forth from Metz, subdued many cities of Gaul; and he came to Orleans, and battered it with rams, striving so to take the city. At that time the most blessed Anianus was bishop in this city, a man eminent in wisdom and renowned for holiness, the records of whose virtuous deeds are faithfully preserved among us. When the beleaguered people cried out to their bishop to know what they should do, he, trusting in God, enjoined them all to prostrate themselves in prayer, and with tears to implore the help of God, ever present in time of need. And while they prayed according to his bidding, the bishop cried: "Look forth from the city wall, if haply the pity of God succour us." For he deemed that by the mercy of the Lord Aëtius should come, whom he had visited in Arles, foreseeing that which might come to pass. So they looked out from the wall, but saw no man. Then he said: "Pray in faith; for this day shall the Lord deliver you." And while they continued praying he said: "Look once more." And when they looked they saw none that might succour them. He said to them a third time: "If ye seek Him in faith, the Lord cometh among us right soon." Again with many tears and lamentations they besought the compassion of the Lord. But when their prayer was done, they looked forth from the wall a third time as the old man bade them, and behold they saw afar off as it might be a cloud rising from the earth. And they brought the bishop the news, and he said: "It is the succour of the Lord." And now the walls were already shaking under the shock of the rams, and on the point of falling, when behold Aëtius came; and Theodoric, king of the Goths, and Thorismond, his son, with their armies swiftly advanced upon the town and cast forth and flung back the enemy. The city thus freed by the intercession of the blessed bishop, they put Attila to flight.' (*28*: vol. ii, p. 46.)

110. Valentinian III trampling underfoot Attila in the shape of a man-headed snake. He holds a cross on a long shaft in his right hand, and in his left a globe surmounted by a figure of Victory presenting a crown to him. The legend reads: VICTORIA AUGUSTORUM, RM (Rome). Reverse of gold solidus of Valentinian III.

'It ends as dramatically as the story of Bluebeard,' says Ferdinand Lot. (*48*: p. 106.) It is indeed very possible that the denouement of the Bluebeard story was inspired by the account in Gregory of Tours' *History*, and this seems all the more likely as the Bluebeard legend must have originated on the banks of the Loire.

Whatever the truth of the matter, what is noteworthy in the story of the siege of Orleans is the leading part played by Anianus—or St Aignan, to give his name its French form. In the mid fifth century, the provincial governors were as powerless as the imperial government, and almost without authority; while municipal government had crumbled into decay. In most cases it was the bishops who shouldered the task of civic administration. The reverence which the people accorded them as their religious leaders gave them the prestige that was needed.

## The Battle of the Catalaunian Fields

The combined forces led by Aëtius did not suffer Attila's hordes to retreat unmolested. The armies met at the place called *Campus Mauriacus*, which has been identified as Moirey, on the road from Sens to Troyes. The historian Jordanes, in his *History of the Goths*, reports that the battle 'of the Catalaunian Fields' was 'fierce, fluctuating, violent and stubbornly contested, such that in all antiquity there is no record of the like'. (*39*: p. 33.) His account was unfortunately written a hundred years after the event. If we are to believe the ancients, he adds:

'. . . the stream of this memorable battlefield, flowing between low banks, was increased by the blood from the wounds of the slain, and swollen not with rains, as was its wont, but with this unaccustomed flow, it became a torrent by the addition of so much blood. And those who were driven to the stream by the burning thirst that resulted from their wounds drew up from it liquid polluted by the slaughter; and so, constrained by their miserable fate, they were fouled as they drank the blood which they had shed when wounded.'

Our only reason for quoting this excursion into melodrama is to show how far an historian of some repute can go in bad taste. Preferable to his turgid account of the battle is the short notice given under the year 451 by Prosper of Aquitaine in his *Chronica*. He was born about 390, and so was an oldish man at the time of the Hun invasion. Without striving for effect, he emphasizes the grave risk Aëtius took in joining a battle whose outcome was doubtful to the very end of the engagement; legend had not yet embroidered the theme when he wrote:

'After the assassination of his brother, Attila, enriched by the possessions of the murdered man, led many thousands of men from the neighbouring tribes to a war which he declared he was waging against the Goths alone, since he was anxious to preserve Roman friendship. But when, after he had crossed the Rhine, many Gallic towns had experienced his savage assaults, both the Gallo-Romans and the Goths quickly agreed to join their armies together to withstand the fury of these arrogant foes. Such was the foresight of the patrician Aëtius, that with the warriors he hastily gathered from all quarters he was able to meet the opposing host with an equal force. Although in this conflict, since neither side gave way, the numbers of the slaughtered cannot be reckoned, yet it is evident that the Huns were the vanquished, because the survivors lost confidence in the outcome of the fighting and returned to their own country.' (62: pp. 481–2.)

# 17

# COUNTRY HOUSE LIFE IN THE FIFTH CENTURY

## *Contemporary Evidence*

THOSE who write about the history of the distant past are often tempted, if their period is marked by great wars or revolutions, to remember only the outstanding events, and to forget that everyday existence persued its humdrum way through all the upheavals of public life. A frightening number of periodicals and documents will call our descendants to order if they show signs of forgetting this when they come to write the history of the twentieth century. But the case is different for the fifth century; very few eye-witnesses of the age of the 'great invasions' took the trouble to describe how life was lived in the Gaul of their day by lord and peasant. Nevertheless two very different writers, Sidonius Apollinaris and Salvian, have left us their impressions. Let us turn to them now for our information, as we turned to Ausonius in the century before.

## *Sidonius Apollinaris*

Sidonius Apollinaris, the son and grandson of praetorian prefects, belonged to the Gallo-Roman aristocracy. He was an important figure; born at Lyons, he became bishop of Auvergne late in life after holding high civil office and moving in society. He was a prolific writer. His extensive correspondence, which he carefully collected himself into nine books, and his numerous occasional poems, tell us a good deal about the life of the aristocracy of Gaul in the fifth century. Their evidence is extremely valuable, even though the author's affectations of style make them at times tedious reading.

Sidonius married well while still a young man; his wife Papianilla was the daughter of an Arvernian noble called Eparchius Avitus, who in 455 became a Roman emperor, though only briefly. Papianilla brought Sidonius as dowry a magnificent estate called *Avitacum* after her father. Nothing remains of the estate but the name Aydat, now that of a commune in pleasant country some fourteen miles from Clermont-Ferrand; but we still have the detailed description of his luxurious home which Sidonius wrote for one of his friends:

## An Aristocrat's Home

'We are at the estate known as Avitacum, a name of sweeter sound in my ears than my own patrimony because it came to me with my wife. Infer the harmony which it established between me and mine; it is God's ordinance; but you might be pardoned for fearing it the work of some enchantment.'

After a somwhat laboured description of the country round, Sidonius comes to the baths:

111. Marble bath, 3rd century.

112. Terra cotta perfume-jar.

'On the south-west are the baths, which so closely adjoin a wooded eminence that if timber is cut on the hill above, the piles of logs slide down almost by their own weight, and are brought up against the very mouth of the furnace. At this point is the hot bath, which corresponds in size with the adjoining *unguentarium*. The chamber itself is well heated from beneath; it is full of day, and so overflowing with light that very modest bathers seem to themselves something more than naked. Next come the spacious *frigidarium*, which may fairly challenge comparison with those in public baths. The architect has inserted two opposite windows about the junction of walls and dome, so that if you look up you see the fine coffering displayed to the best advantage. The interior walls are unpretentiously covered with plain white stucco. No frescoed scene obtrudes its comely nudities, gracing the art to the disgrace of the artist.'

Leaving the baths—and we have cut short his description of them— Sidonius takes us to the women's withdrawing-room:

'On leaving this chamber you see in front of you the withdrawing-room; adjoining it is the store room, separated only by a movable

113. Narcissus admiring his reflection. Mosaic from Vaison-la-Romaine.

114. 'From here one enters a smaller chamber or dining-room ... furnished with a dining-couch'. Tombstone from Arles.

partition from the place where the maids do our weaving. On the east side a portico commands the lake, supported by simple wooden pillars instead of pretentious monumental columns. On the side of the front entrance is a long covered space unbroken by interior divisions; at the end it is curtailed by a section cut off to form a delightfully cool bay, and here, when we keep open festival, the whole chattering chorus of nurses and dependants sounds a halt when the family retires for the siesta.

'The winter dining-room is entered from this crypto-porticus; a roaring fire on an arched hearth often fills this apartment with smoke and smuts. But that detail I may spare you; a glowing hearth is the last thing I am inviting you to enjoy just now. I pass instead to things which suit the season and your present need. From here one enters a smaller chamber or dining-room, all open to the lake and with almost the whole expanse of lake in its view. This chamber is furnished with a dining-couch and a gleaming sideboard.'

This is where Sidonius receives his friends:

183

115. Roman oil-lamps, terra cotta.

'The meal over, we pass into a withdrawing-room, which its coolness makes a perfect place in summer. Facing north, it receives all the day-light but no direct sun.'

After describing all the buildings, Sidonius suggests a stroll outside:

'If you leave the colonnade and go down to the little lakeside harbour, you come to a greensward, and, hard by, to a grove of trees where everyone is allowed to go. There stand two great limes, with roots and trunks apart, but all boughs interwoven in one continuous canopy. In their dense shade we play at ball when my Ecdicius honours me with his company.' (66: vol. i, pp. 36–41.)

Country-house life, in fact—the kind of life that the Gallo-Roman aristocracy of the fifth century found most to their taste, now that the towns had been turned into fortresses and could offer few of the amenities of life to their inhabitants.

## 'Youth's a stuff will not endure'

It is easy to find parallels between the way of life of these fifth-century aristocrats and that of the wealthy French of the nineteenth century. Read, for instance, the letter which expresses Sidonius' concern over a

116. Silver funnel with strainer, from Chaourse (Aisne).

117. Silver pan, with handle decorated with a bust of Tutelis, from Reignier (Haute-Savoie).

118. Dancing girl. Ivory plaque, 4th century.

119. Marine animal and shells. Amber amulet, Roman.

young friend who had squandered part of his inheritance on an extravagant mistress, but had finally left her and put his affairs in order by marrying a rich heiress, to the great satisfaction of his friends and relations:

'Your holiness [he wrote to Bishop Ambrose] has interceded before Christ with effect on behalf of our well-beloved friend (I will not mention his name—you will know whom I mean), the laxity of whose youth you used sometimes to lament before a few chosen witnesses of your sorrow, sometimes to bemoan in silence and alone. For he has suddenly broken off his relations with the shameless slave-girl to whose low fascination he had utterly abandoned his life; by this prompt reformation he has taken a great step in the interests of his estate, of his descendants, and of himself. He dispelled his inheritance until his coffers were empty; but when he once began to consider his position, and understood how much of his patrimony the extravagance of his domestic Charybdis had swallowed up, not a moment too soon he took the bit in his teeth, shook his head, and stopping his ears, as one might say, with

120. Boys extracting thorns. Bas relief, Gallo-Roman.

Ulysses' wax, he was deaf to the voice of evil, and escaped the shipwreck that follows meretricious lives. He has led to the altar a maid of high birth and ample fortune, and for that we must give him credit. It would of course have been a greater glory to have abandoned the voluptuous life without taking to himself a wife; but few of those who forsake error at the call of virtue can begin upon the highest level, and after indulging themselves in everything, cut off all indulgence at one stroke.

'It is now your part by assiduous prayer to obtain for the newly married couple good hope of issue; and then, when they have one or two children (perhaps even in that we concede too much), to see to it that this stealer of unlawful joys shall abstain thereafter even from lawful pleasures.' (*66*: vol. ii, pp. 184–5.)

It would seem from this letter that Sidonius looked on marriage as a *pis aller;* but he had had experience of married life himself before he was ordained. It is obvious too—and this is a more significant point— that long families were not greatly esteemed in fifth-century Gaul.

187

## *Pleas for a Crook*

Sidonius' besetting sin was inquisitiveness about the private lives of his contemporaries. But when he passed on to a confidant the details he had collected, he did it good-humouredly, without malice, and often with the intention of putting things right, for he was by nature a peace-maker. A good example is his appeal to the bishop of Marseilles, Graecus, on behalf of a young protégé of his from Auvergne, Amantius, who had got himself married under false pretences. The story, which Sidonius tells at some length, is an interesting one.

He begins by enlisting the bishop's sympathies for Amantius. He tells of his humble beginnings, his impecunious but free-born family, his father who was an honest man but so close-fisted where his children were concerned that Amantius was compelled to leave home. The young man went to Marseilles, where Eustachius, who had been bishop before Graecus, found him lodgings and the office of reader. The young man made many friends by his exemplary conduct, and even won the good graces of the count of the city:

'It chanced [Sidonius explains] that near the house where he lodged there resided a lady whose disposition and income were all that he could have desired; she had a daughter, not quite marriageable, but no longer a child. He began to attract the girl by pleasant greetings, and by giving her (as, at her age, he quite properly could) the various trifles and trinkets which delight a maid's fancy; by such light links he succeeded in closely attaching her heart to his own. Time passed; she reached the age of marriage. You already guess what happened. This young man, without visible relations or substance, a foreigner, a minor who had left home without his father's leave or knowledge, demands the hand of a girl equal to himself in birth, and superior in fortune. He demands and, what is more, he obtains; he is recognized as suitor. For the bishop actively supported his reader, and the count encouraged his client; the future mother-in-law did not trouble to investigate his means; the bride approved his person. The marriage contract was executed, and some little suburban plot or other at Clermont was put into settlement and read out with much theatrical parade. This legal trick and solemn swindle over, the pauper lover carried off the wealthy bride. He promptly went into all his wife's father's affairs, and got together some nice little pickings for himself, aided all through the imposture by the credulity of his easy-going and free-handed mother-in-law; then, and not till then, this incomparable charlatan sounds the retreat and vanishes

121. 'This young man demands the hand of a girl equal to himself in birth.' Christ crowning a bridal couple; gold-painted glass cup, 3rd–4th century.

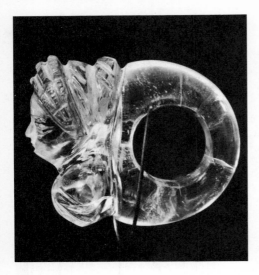

122. Crystal ring from Glanum.

into Auvergne. After he had gone, the mother thought of bringing an action against him for the absurd exaggerations in the contract. But it was rather late for her to begin lamenting the exiguity of his settlement, when she was already rejoicing at the prospect of a wealth of little grandchildren.

'"That is the story of this accomplished young man," Sidonius ends: "as good in its way as any out of Attic comedy or Milesian fable".' (66: vol. ii, pp. 100–1.)

All the same, he has no hesitation in recommending his protégé to the bishop, turning a blind eye on his ungentlemanly behaviour and admitting with disarming frankness that he still has a kindly feeling for the young reprobate.

## The Seamy Side of an Election

Sidonius was no doubt blasé about the morals of his contemporaries, and that explains why he was so tolerant. Intrigue in particular, as we saw in his portrait of the Goth king Theodoric, he felt to be entirely natural, and certainly it did not shock him even when it came near to vitiating the election of a bishop. In this letter to his friend Domnulus, an honorary quaestor and poet, he gives the inside story of the election of a bishop at Chalons-sur-Saône:

'When the episcopal council met, it found that the opinion of the citizens was not unanimous, and that there existed private factions of the kind so ruinous to the public welfare. The presence of three candidates aggravated these evils. The first had no moral qualification whatever, but only the privilege of ancient lineage, of which he made the most. The second was brought in on the applause of parasites, bribed to support him by the free run of a gourmand's table. The third had a tacit understanding with his supporters, that if he attained the object of his ambition, the plundering of the Church estates should be theirs.' (*66*: vol. ii, p. 46.)

## King Euric and the Bishops

But now we turn to more serious matters. Towards the end of Sidonius' life, when he was bishop of Auvergne, the king of the Visigoths, the Arian Euric, launched a violent persecution of the Catholics. Sidonius defended his co-religionists valiantly; he realized that the cause of the Empire was lost, and bowed to the inevitable; but he did everything in his power to prevent the Empire dragging the Catholic faith down with it in its fall. He says as much in a letter to his colleague Basilius, bishop of Aix, perhaps the most moving he ever wrote. Faced with this threat to the faith, all his decadent affectations of style vanish:

'Neither a saint like you can fitly here discuss, nor a sinner like myself indict, the action of Euric the Gothic king in breaking and bearing

123. Dancing cupids; small ivory plaque, 2nd century.

down an ancient treaty to defend, or rather extend by armed force the frontiers of his kingdom. . . . I must confess that, formidable as the mighty Goth may be, I dread him less as the assailant of our walls than as the subverter of our Christian laws. They say that the mere mention of the name of Catholic so embitters his countenance and heart that one might take him for the chief priest of his Arian sect rather than for the monarch of his nation. . . .'

Then comes a dark picture of the devastated churches of the Visigothic kingdom. No candidates for the episcopacy come forward. In the parishes everything is going to rack and ruin; the churches are shut and falling into decay.

Sidonius ends with a vehement warning, an adjuration to the few bishops who still occupy their sees:

'Do your best, as far as the royal condescension suffers you, to obtain for our bishops the right of ordination in those parts of Gaul now included within the Goth boundaries, that if we cannot keep them by treaty for the Roman State, we may at least hold them by religion for the Roman Church.' (*66*: vol. ii, pp. 107–9.)

# THE LAWLESS MISERY OF THE FIFTH CENTURY

As a distinguished French Latinist, A. Loyen, once pointed out, the lower classes hardly ever come into the letters or poems of Sidonius Apollinaris. It goes against the grain to write about them, or to come into any sort of contact with them. He is forced to find room on his estates for a number of Burgundian federates, but the proximity of the barbarian 'who spreads rancid butter on his hair' is repugnant to him, and he congratulates his old friend Catullinus on having no such disagreeable neighbours: 'I am fain to call your eyes and ears happy, happy too your nose, for you don't have a reek of garlic and foul onions discharged upon you at early morn from ten breakfasts.' (67: vol. i, p. 213.)

## Social Injustice

So his writings give us an incomplete picture of contemporary Gaul. One panel of the diptych is missing; the people are not represented. Very seldom does Sidonius allude to the social movement of the Bagaudae which shook Gaul in his day, and he certainly does not understand it; he sees the victims of the economic crisis as no better than brigands. But another fifth-century author, Salvian, has written with outspoken bluntness of the popular revolts of his time, inveighing passionately against the officials of the dying Western Empire and the great Gallo-Roman landowners, exalting the virtues of the barbarians to show up the vices of the wealthy Gallo-Roman aristocrats.

Salvian was a priest, settled in Marseilles, who may have been born at Trèves and was at one time a hermit at Lérins; he wrote his *Treatise of God's Government* between 439 and 451; in it he tries to justify the ways of Providence by showing that the misfortunes which befell the Romans of his time were the retribution their crimes so well deserved.

## Salvian's Indictment

Salvian was a man of the people and something of an anarchist, and his diatribe was aimed chiefly at the wealthy and at government officials:

'Some may think that all this Wickedness, this whole Catalogue of base enormous Crimes I have mention'd, are only deeds of Slaves and Men of desperate Fortunes, but nothing that bears the Face of a Gentleman can ever be so wicked. Pray what is the Merchant's Life but Perjury and Cheat? The Courtier's but Iniquity? The Lawyer's Calumny, and the Soldier's Plunder?' (65: pp. 75–6.)

The 'courtiers' of this translation are the curials, officials who were responsible for the allocation of taxes, and were particularly unpopular. Salvian continues his denunciation of them:

'For what either City, Town, or Village is there, where there are not as many Tyrants as there are Magistrates? Altho' it may be, they please themselves with the Name, because it makes them look Big and Stately:

124. Youth carrying a faggot. Engraved crystal vase.

125. A man of the fifth century. Sarcophagus from Charenton-sur-Cher.

For so 'tis with all Thieves, who pride and glory when they are reported to be much more daring than they really are. What place is there then, as I said, where the very Bowels of Widdows and Orphans are not devour'd by the Governours of Cities, and with them those of almost all holy men?'

And Salvian notes bitterly that no one protests or dares to interfere:

'For who can assist the Distressed and Afflicted, when even the Christian Priests do not withstand the oppression of wicked Men?

'And thus it comes that the Poor are Oppress'd, Widdows mourn, Orphans are trod underfoot, insomuch, that many of them, well born and genteely bred, fly over to the Enemy, for Fear of Dying here under the publick Persecution, going to seek the *Roman* Humanity among the *Barbarians*, because they cannot undergo barbarous Inhumanity among the *Romans*. And altho' they differ from those they fly to, both in their Rites, and Language; and, as I may so say, in the ungrateful Scent of their Bodies and awkward Cloathing, yet they had rather bear with a different Habit among the *Barbarians*, than with raging Injustice among the *Romans*. And therefore from all Parts they straggle either to the *Goths*, or the *Bacaudae*, or to some other of the Conquering Barbarians, and they do not repent their Journey. For they had rather live

8

126. Bulla of a doctor's
slave, no doubt Roman.

free under a seeming Captivity, than be real Captives under a seeming
Liberty. So that the name of *Roman* Citizens, formerly esteem'd not
only very high, but purchas'd at a great Price, is now voluntarily
rejected and fled from, and is reckoned not only cheap and contemptible,
but abominable and a burden.' (*65*: pp. 136–8.)

## The Ruin of the Countryside

After exposing the iniquities of the Roman fiscal system, which lays the
whole burden of taxation on the poor without allowing them any benefit
from the reliefs recently introduced, Salvian wonders why all the
peasants have not yet gone over to the barbarians:

'And really, it seems a little strange to me, that all the Poor and
meaner Sort, who are assess'd to the Taxes, do not all go over, and there
seems to be only one Reason why they have not done it; Because they
cannot carry over with them the diminutive Remnants of their Fortunes,
their poor lots and Families. . . . Since they cannot accomplish this,
which, it may be, they had rather, they strike up with the only Method
that is left them. They throw themselves into the Guardianship and
Protection of the Great ones. They surrender themselves to rich Men's
hands, and entirely put themselves under their Power and Jurisdiction. I
should not take this to be any great Burden or Misfortune, but should
rather commend this Power of the Great ones, to whom these poor
People surrender themselves, if they did not sell their Protections, and
when they gave them such Shelter, they did it out of Charity or good

196

Nature, and not for sordid Lucre. But 'tis very hard and cruel, that they only seem to Protect them, that they may Plunder them; they defend them only on Condition, that they may make those who are miserable already, to be much more so. For all who are under this seeming Protection, make over almost All their whole Estates to their Guardians, before they can procure the Favour; and so the Children lose their Inheritance, that Fathers may gain a Protection. The defence of the Parents is procur'd with the Beggary of the whole Family. And these are the Grand Helps and Protections of the Great ones. They give not a Cross to those who are under their Patronage, but keep all to themselves. And thus the Parents for some small while, have a little Advantage, that afterward the Whole may be taken from their Children. So that the Great ones sell, and sell at the highest Rate they can, every Favour that they do. And what I call selling, I wish they would sell after the usual Method; for then, it may be, the Buyer might reserve somewhat for himself. But this is a new and unheard of Way of Buying and Selling. The Seller delivers nothing, and yet receives all. The Buyer receives nothing, and yet utterly loses all.'

And Salvian has not finished yet.

'How intolerable and monstrous [he goes on], and so far from being endur'd by Mankind that 'tis not to be heard by them, is this, that many of these pitifully Poor, miserable Wretches, who are robb'd of all that little they had, and driven from their little Lands, even when they have thus lost their Estate, yet still pay the Tax for the Estate thus taken from them; and tho' they have lost the Possession of that, their Capitation does not leave them. They have not one jot of Property, and yet they are over-borne with Taxes!'

The practice which so rouses Salvian's indignation is well known: it is the *precarium*. A small farmer at his wits' end would put himself under the protection of a rich man, ceding the ownership of his little property in return for the privilege of continuing to farm it at a rent, without any guarantee of occupation.

Salvian then goes on, in one of those *crescendos* he used so effectively, to censure no less severely another practice of the rich:

'When they have either lost their Houses and Lands by Oppression, or have been driven from them by the Tax-gatherers, and find they cannot hold them, they seek out for the Lands of some Great Man, and so become Farmers to the Rich.'

Then indeed their condition is pitiable, and Salvian maintains that they have become no better than slaves:

'After the pattern of *Circe*, that most powerful Enchantress, who was said to change Men into Beasts, all of these who are admitted within the Lands of Great Men, are perfectly Metamorphos'd, as by a Draught of *Circe*'s Bowl. For those whom they receive as Foreigners and Aliens, they presently seize as their proper Goods; and those who are well known to be Gentlemen, are converted into Slaves.' (*65*: pp. 145–8.)

Salvian's description of this misery and his picture of the pitiable condition of the peasantry in his time explain the state of anarchy and

127. 'Those who are well known to be Gentlemen, are converted into Slaves. . . . The Seller delivers nothing, and yet receives all. The Buyer receives nothing, and yet utterly loses all.'
Paying the rent; scene from a Gallo-Roman tombstone.

endemic revolt which prevailed in different parts of Gaul in the fifth century, and which has been given the name, perhaps originally Celtic, of the *Bagaudae*. A few contemporary annalists refer to the Bagaudae, but unfortunately not in very explicit terms. The most detailed references are those in the *Chronica Gallica* for the years 435 and 437, i.e., about the time Salvian was writing his treatise:

'435. Further Gaul, following Tribatton, the leader of the rebellion, forsook the Roman alliance; and this was the beginning of the conspiracy which involved almost all the slave population of Gaul in the Bagaudae.
'437. When Tribatton had been captured and the other ringleaders either taken prisoner or killed, the rising of the Bagaudae died down.'
(*39*: pp. 18–20.)

## The Bagaudae

We must look to Salvian again for details, unfortunately somewhat marred by rhetorical effects, about the revolutionary movement of the Bagaudae, which seems to have originated in north-west Gaul:

'I shall now speak of the *Bacaudae* [says Salvian] who being pillag'd, distress'd, and murder'd by cruel and unjust Judges, after they had lost the Privilege of the Roman Liberty, have now also lost the Honour of the Name. What is only their Misfortune is thrown upon them as a Crime, and we impute a Name on their Calamity, which we our selves have been the Occasion of: We call them Rebels, and lost Wretches, when we our selves compell'd them to the Crime. For how came the *Bacaudae* to be such, but by our Injustice, and the Wickedness of their Judges, but by the Proscription and Rapine of those who converted the publick Tribute to their own private Gains, and have made the Peoples Taxes only a Prey for themselves? Who like the most Savage Beasts, have not so much governed those put under their Care, as they have devour'd them, not being satisfied with the Spoils of the Men, as most Thieves are used to be, but have torn them piecemeal; and, as I may say, have gorg'd themselves with their very Blood. And thus it came that the Men being suffocated and murder'd by the notorious open Robberies of their Governours, began to be in a manner *Barbarians*, because they were not permitted to be Romans. They were satisfied to be what they were not, because they were not suffer'd to be what they had been; and were forc'd at least to defend their Lives, because they saw plainly they had utterly lost their Liberty already.

199

'And what are we doing now [asks Salvian] but the very same thing that was done before, that is that they who already are not *Bacaudae*, shall be forc'd to be such.' (*65*: pp. 139–40.)

It is a dark picture of anarchy and revolt gaining foothold in Gaul and flourishing unchecked because the dying Empire is powerless against them.

## The Britons Emigrate : St Guénolé

One of the consequences of the Bagaudae troubles was the arrival of British settlers in Armorica. Early in the fifth century the Roman emperors had ceased to exercise any effective power in the north-west of Gaul, and the Britons took advantage of the anarchy reigning in Armorica to infiltrate and settle there. They came from Cornwall and Wales, fleeing before the Scots and even more the Anglo-Saxon invaders of Britain, and landed on the Atlantic and Channel coasts of Brittany. Gradually they took possession of the countryside, which must by then have been much depopulated. They brought with them their Celtic tongue, their religion and their customs, and so Armorica became Brittany.

It would be interesting to know how this colonization was effected; unfortunately contemporary records are silent on the subject. It was not until the ninth century, when a knowledge of Latin had penetrated into the ecclesiastical circles of this Celtic population, and more especially when the religious orders established in Brittany had abandoned the Irish rule for the Benedictine, that historical texts, written in Latin, begin to make their appearance there. It was piety that inspired their authors, and they tell the story of half-historical, half-legendary saints who were—and still are—the objects of touching popular devotion.

One of the most interesting of these works is the *Life of St Guénolé*, who founded the abbey of Landévennec. It was written by an anonymous monk and reworked by one of the abbots of Landévennec called Gourdisten. The two pious authors recount naïvely, but not without a good deal of fanciful embellishment, how the saint's parents landed on the Channel coast.

They were, we are told, among the few Britons who succeeded in leaving their native shores at the time when the brutal race of Saxons was invading their homeland:

'Among them was an illustrious man, by name Fracanus, in whom was the hope of a blessed progeny. He was a cousin of Catovius, a British king who was much renowned among his contemporaries; and the holy seed lay hid in his loins. This Fracanus had twin sons, called Guenoc and Jacut. Their mother Alba was surnamed "the three-breasted", because she had three breasts, equal to the number of her sons; their sister was not counted in reckoning the number of breasts, for it is not customary for writings to include the genealogy of women. Fracanus, then, embarking in a ship, set sail for Armorica, where at that time there was reported to be a shady and quiet territory free from natural disasters. With a few companions he crossed the British sea, and a light breeze brought him to shore at a harbour which is called Bréhec. He at once explored the surrounding countryside, and finding a reasonably large territory surrounded on all sides by woods and thickets, and fertile by reason of the river (called the River of Blood) which watered it, he settled there prosperously with his family.

'At that time, when the number of his companions was gradually increasing, and in the midst of a flood of prosperity, a third son, to typify the Holy Trinity, was eagerly desired, as if it were altogether too little to have only two. The happy wife divined that she had conceived in her womb the child they longed for. The husband was glad at his wife's pregnancy and moved by great joyfulness of heart, hoping that this child would be his heir after him. So the long awaited day came, when the true light so long looked for was manifested in our land—the day which shone more brightly than any other for the western Armoricans. They called the new-born child by the pure name of Guénolé.' (*39*: p. 83.)

Obviously the story is nothing but legend. But it has a naïve charm, and shows us how monks of imagination, writing some four hundred years after the event, pictured the arrival of their predecessors on the shores of France.

# SECOND INTERLUDE IN BRITAIN

## The Romans Withdraw Through Gaul

Britain was more vulnerable than Gaul, being an island (no longer provided with an efficient navy) and now poorly defended by land also; for since the end of the third century the Roman generals in command of the British garrison had formed the habit of playing politics and declaring themselves emperor. The bad example was first set by Marcus Aurelius Carausius (a naval officer of Gaulish extraction in command of the fleet based on Boulogne) who set himself up in Britain and so violently resisted the central authority that Maximilian (co-emperor with Diocletion in charge of the northern provinces) was forced to recognize his sovereignty of Britain in 287. Without attempting to chronicle the series of revolts and mutinies which broke out in the course of the fourth century, we may draw attention to the rebellion of Constantine III, who, aiming at the imperial throne, led what remained of the Roman regular garrison out of Britain into Gaul and deliberately left the British civilians to their fate (407).

Now the situation was indeed critical, for the Britonś had to face enemies on three fronts at once, and all equally formidable. To the north the Caledonians, now known as Picts, remained unconquerable and less than ever restrained by the fortified zone which the Romans had built but no longer manned. To the west were the Scots from Ireland, who had taken to piracy on the high seas and to raiding up and down the west coast of Britain.

But above all, to the east and the south there were the Anglo-Saxons. This composite name (first used by Bede) embraces chiefly three groups of coastal Germanic tribes who, after a struggle lasting many generations, were to make themselves masters of Britain: the Saxons, the Angles and the Jutes. From the time of Carausius onwards the name of Saxons ('men of the *seax*', a type of short sword) had been borne by the tribes of Holstein and Lower Saxony. Bold and restless mariners, they had 'felt their way along the coast as far as the mouth of the Gironde' according to a recent historian of the Dark Ages. Place-names in the countryside around Bayeux attest the density of their occupation, temporary though it may have been, of the department of Manche; but Britain was to be their chosen settlement. The original home of the Angles marched with that of the Saxons: it was called Angel and situated on the east coast of Sleswig. North of them, in the Jutland peninsula, dwelt the Jutes; though the learned still dispute among themselves whether the province is called after the tribe, or *vice versa*.

The transformation of the land of Britain by the Anglo-Saxon settlement may be considered as the first page in the history of England. It is perhaps unnecessary to add that it is still a blank despite numerous chroniclers and annalists who have had the temerity to make their mark on it; some were English by birth, such as the compilers of the *Anglo-Saxon Chronicles* and the ecclesiastical historian, Bede; others were British, like the monk Gildas, or like Nennius and other compilers of the *History of the Britons*, whoever they were; but for the most part they wrote long after the events described and many had a great weakness for the marvellous.

Britain was attacked by the Saxons from the very year following the withdrawal of the Roman garrison; but the British themselves fought back spiritedly, and when Germanus, bishop of Auxerre, came to the island on a mission to refute the heresy of Pelagius, he witnessed and took part in a victory over a combined force of Picts and Saxons which the native British won near the still inhabited Roman town of Verulam, whose ruins now lie under the turf outside St Albans in Hertfordshire.

The success was short-lived, for a laconic note contained in a brief annal which is priceless because of its authenticity mentions under the year 442 that 'Britain which up to that time had suffered all sorts of disasters and setbacks, now fell under the dominion of the Saxons'. There is here no question of the conquest of the whole island; indeed more than two centuries will be necessary for the English to gain mastery within what had been roughly the frontiers of the Roman province. What this passage means is that the English had gained a firm foothold in Britain which they were never to yield.

The exact history of this beginning is hardly known, but legend has seized on it to stiffen and consolidate a very sparse documentation, and interwoven with the thread of events are a tale of treason and a drama of love. To one of the authors of the *History of the Britons* we owe the tale which has the air of legend, though certain present-day scholars are more tolerant than their predecessors and now attempt to see in it some moiety of historical fact. On this account alone it is worth our while to reproduce it here, but more so because the principal characters involved have been adopted by all the older histories of England and thereby gained an enormous notoriety:

'When the rule of the Romans came to an end in Britain, the British people themselves were in terror for forty years. Vortigern reigned in Britain, and as long as he reigned he was haunted by fear of the Picts and the Scots as well as of a Roman re-conquest and the hostility of Ambrosius [the last of the Romans]. At this time there came three ships out of Germany, bearing two brothers, Hengist and Horsa by name, who were exiles fleeing from that country.'

The chronicler then traces their genealogy, which we will not reproduce here, but which goes back to an ancestor called Geta, of whom it says:

'He was a son of God. But by this is not meant the Lord God of Hosts, but one of their idols whom they worshipped.

'Vortigern welcomed these men heartily and gave them for their dwelling-place that island which is called in their language Thanet, and in Welsh Rhuoim.

'It happened so, that when the Saxons had settled in the said isle of Thanet the king before-mentioned promised to give them provisions and garments regularly. This pleased them and they on their part promised to attack his enemies vigorously. But as the number of these barbarians increased, the British people were unable to provide enough food. When the foreigners demanded food and clothing according to the agreement, the Britons declared: "We cannot give you food and raiment because your numbers are increased, therefore leave us, for we have no need of you." Then the latter took counsel among their elders to denounce the treaty of peace.

'Now Hengist, who was educated, cunning and crafty, had observed the impotence of the king and the unarmed state of his people, and he undertook to negotiate with the British king, saying: "We are few in numbers, but if you wish we will send a message to our home inviting soldiers from there to come over and increase the number able to fight for you and your people." Now the said king ordered that this should be done and they sent messengers home. These messengers returned again across the valley of Thetis [the sea] with sixteen ships carrying picked warriors and also a young maiden, very fair of countenance and comely of form who was the daughter of Hengist.

'After the landing of the ships, Hengist made ready a feast for Vortigern at which his interpreter, by name Ceretic, was also present, and he ordered his daughter to pour them out all the wine and ale so that they drank and were drunken. Now while they drank, the devil entered into the heart of Vortigern so that he fell in love with the young girl and asked, through the interpreter, for her hand in marriage, saying: "Ask what you will for her even to the half of my kingdom." And Hengist, having taken counsel with his companions who had come with him from the isle of Oghgul[1] arguing how much they should ask as a bride price for the young girl, finally were all agreed to demand that province which is called in their language Canturguaralen and in our language Kent. He gave it to them while Guoyrangon was yet reigning in Kent and unaware that his kingdom had been given away to the heathens and he himself with it. It was not done, therefore, with his knowledge or consent. So the young girl was given over to Vortigern in marriage and he took her to his bed and loved her passionately.'

We shall not follow this chronicler further through the maze of legendary rather than historical happenings with which he fills the two-score years after the evacuation of Britain by the Roman army, that is up to the middle of the fifth century; the story in which we see Saxons actually taking possession of Britain. The sequel to the above story shows us Hengist, having completely beguiled Vortigern, bringing over yet another forty shiploads of soldiers who made themselves masters of Bernicia, a northern province beyond the Humber, while yet others occupied the city of Canterbury in the south.

The Anglo-Saxon advance seems to have called a halt at the end of the fifth century and during the first quarter of the sixth. If we are to give credence to the *History of the Britons*, it is during this period and after the death of Hengist that there took place in real life the exploits

---

[1] Presumably the province of Angel mentioned above.

of a legendary personage who was to be called to play a part of the very first importance in medieval literature. Arthur of Britain appears for the first time in the *History of the Britons*, having been previously quite unknown. Nevertheless, we should salute him in passing by reproducing this passage about him from the *History of the Britons*:

'At this time the Saxons were moving forward and increasing in numbers throughout Britain. After the death of Hengist, his son Octha left the northern parts of Britain and came to settle in Kent, and it is from him that the kings of that part are descended. Now in those days Arthur and the kings of Britain fought against the Saxons, but he was the leader in war. The first battle was fought at the mouth of a river called Glein. The second and the third and the fourth and the fifth on a river called Douglas, which is in Linnuis (Lennox). The sixth battle was at a river called Bassas, the seventh battle in the Forest of Caledonia. The eighth was at the fortress of Guinnion, where Arthur carried the image of St Mary, ever Virgin, on his shoulders and the heathen were put to flight the same day. There was great slaughter done by virtue of the Lord Jesus Christ and the Virgin Mary, His Mother. The ninth battle was fought in the City of the Legion [Chester—Deva in Latin— or Caerleon-on-Usk] the proper Latin name of which was Isca Silurum but which the Welsh in their language call "the Camp of the Legions". A tenth battle was fought on the banks of the river called Tribruit. The eleventh took place on the Hill of Agned. And the twelfth was the fight at Mt Badon where, in one day, 960 warriors perished in a single attack delivered by Arthur, and no other but he vanquished them. And he came off victorious from all these battles.'

Although this list has a legendary air, it is nevertheless not out of order to conclude that the British made worthy efforts to try to stem the progress of the invaders; but little by little they were overrun and the authors of the *History of the Britons* themselves recognized the fact for, after declaring that their hero Arthur came off victorious in all these campaigns, they add:

'The foe, who had been beaten in all these battles, sought reinforcements from Germany; and these continually increased in number as kings came over from Germany to reign over the Saxons who were in Britain, and this went on down to the time of King Ida, the son of Eobba who was the first king of Bernicia.'

This king is considered as having reigned in the middle of the sixth century. Now, what was the position at that time as between the native

British and the invaders from Lower Germany? It is worth while asking this question because, after an apparent pause, the advance of the latter continued in the second half of this century.

The British were still holding their own in the south-west, south of the Bristol Channel in a region then called Dumnonia; in what is now Wales; further north in Lancashire and the Lake District (where their territory extended up to the region of the Clyde; also in some parts of the West Riding of Yorkshire, where modern Leeds marks the centre of the British petty kingdom of Loidis). Thus, though repulsed in the west, the Anglo-Saxons strove to consolidate their position on the frontier, and those who had landed on the east coast founded different kingdoms up and down the island. Of these, tradition has recorded the names of seven and given rise to the nineteenth-century phrase 'Anglo-Saxon heptarchy' (though the period during which all seven flourished independently was short if it existed at all). These kingdoms were in fact territories settled by tribes whose chiefs, all belonging to families of divine origin, bore the name of king. They ate each other up until finally the three strongest emerged as survivors. In the south, Wessex has been proved by a recent historian to have had its beginnings in the merging of two converging westward drives, one taking off from the Saxon settlements of the upper Thames, and the other from a bridge-head on the coast of Hampshire. North of that came Mercia, the kingdom of the midlands, which absorbed East Anglia. Beyond the Humber, the two kingdoms of Deira and Bernicia merged to form Northumbria.

Precious as the data may be in regard to chronology and geography that we can extract by painful conjecture from chronicles in which history is lavishly watered with legend, the study of the psychology and social life of the invaders presents more and more interest as the progress of archaeology and linguistics brings us more material to supplement the deficiencies of documentary sources. Thus, a French historian of England, the late André Maurois, set himself the task of drawing a portrait of the Anglo-Saxons during a period of settlement which seems too striking not to be quoted here, at least in part:

'These Angles and Saxons are men of violent habit. . . . During the migration period they attached little importance to human life. Their favourite pleasure is war and their history is a history of hawks and crows. But underneath their native barbarism they have noble aspirations and there is a certain fundamental seriousness about them which banishes frivolous motives. Women in this society are chaste and marriage is pure. Once a free man has chosen the lord whom he will serve, he remains faithful to him. . . . Men of this breed are able to accept the discipline of a superior to whom they will pay devotion and respect. They are, moreover, religious because, far more than the inhabitants of milder climates, they have felt the terrible power of nature.'

Then he goes on to describe the landing of a Saxon war band and the installation, according to tribal custom, in villages comprising ten to thirty families. These villages are the cells of the Anglo-Saxon body politic, and the land surrounding them will be subjected to intensive cultivation, contrasted with the territory of the previous Celtic occupants, for the Saxons had a much more efficient agricultural technique than the former.

What must be stressed here is that in contrast to the Gallo-Romans the Britons, in what was to become England, seem to have exercised no permanent influence on the invaders. The Franks abandoned their Germanic language in favour of that spoken in Gaul, they adapted themselves to the civilization of the country and were rapidly converted to the Catholic religon as there practised. On the contrary, the Britons, who had forgotten the Latin language and were almost cut off from Roman civilization, never succeeded in imposing—and perhaps did not even try to impose—on the invaders a culture which was not superior to their own. And thus the Anglo-Saxons remained Germanic.

# Part VI

# GAUL UNDER THE FRANKS AND THE ROYAL HOUSE OF THE MERWINGS

# 19

# THE SALIC FRANKS

BISHOP SIDONIUS APOLLINARIS would have been much surprised if some prophet had told him that a few years after his death a chieftain of the Salian Frankish people would occupy almost the whole of Gaul and establish a great and lasting state: the Frankish kingdom. 'Without Clovis', says Ferdinand Lot, 'Gaul would not have become France, or else would have been an entirely different France, a little France, a dismembered Gaul.' (50: p. 44.) This may be going too far, for it is always difficult to determine how far any individual is responsible for the fate of a nation. But it would be difficult to overestimate the importance of his reign. We must now turn our attention to these Franks, who, as we saw in Chapter 9, made their first appearance in the third century.

The early history of this Germanic people lies hid in a mist so thick as to be almost impenetrable. Fortunately the great historian of the fourth century, Ammianus Marcellinus, has thrown a little light on the settlement of the Franks in what is now Belgium, which took place in 358, with the tacit consent of the Emperor Julian. Ammianus Marcellinus is the first historian to mention the people which gave its name to modern France.

'Caesar [he writes], passing his winter among the Parisii, was eagerly preparing to anticipate the Allemanni. . . . When all his preparations were made, he first marched against the Franks, that is against that tribe of them usually called Salii, who some time before had ventured with great boldness to fix their habitations on the Roman soil near Toxandria. But when he had reached Tongres, he was met by an embassy from this tribe, who expected still to find him in his winter quarters, offering him peace on condition of his leaving them unattacked and unmolested, as if the ground they had seized were rightfully their own.'

Ammianus Marcellinus reports that the emperor gave them an ambiguous reply, and sent them away with gifts:

'But the moment they had departed he followed them, sending Severus along the bank of the river, and suddenly came upon the whole settlement like a thunderbolt; and availing himself of his victory to make a reasonable exhibition of clemency, as indeed they met him with entreaties rather than with resistance, he received the submission of them and their children.' (*3*: pp. 140–1.)

The Belgian historian Godefroid Kurth has pointed out, however, that if Julian left the Salian Franks in occupation of their lands south of the Meuse, it was because they had already held them on sufferance for two generations (*38*: p. 112.)

It would be interesting to know what happened to the Salians in the next half century. Darkness falls once more, and we lose sight of them until the beginning of the fifth century; it is bishop Gregory of Tours who puts us on the scent again. An Arvernian of old Gallo-Roman stock, who had considerable influence with the Merovingian kings, he carefully reported in his *History of the Franks* all the meagre details he could collect about their origins, and more especially about their first kings:

## *Their Struggle to get a Footing—the Romance of Chlodion*

'Such are the accounts which the remaining chroniclers have left us of the Franks, but without recording any names of kings. It is a common tradition that this people issued from Pannonia and first colonized the banks of the Rhine; that then they passed the river and traversed Thuringia, setting over them, according to their country districts and cities, long-haired kings belonging to the first and, so to speak, the most noble family of their race. This is proved later by the victories of Clovis, as I shall subsequently narrate. Moreover, we read in the consular *Fasti*,[1] that Theudemer, king of the Franks, son of Richemer, and Ascyla

[1] A collection of annals, in which events were dated by the consulate in which they occurred.

his mother, were slain by the sword. Tradition has it that Chlogio, distinguished among his people for his capacity and most noble birth, was king of the Franks; he had his home at Dispargum,[1] in the land of the Thuringians. On this side, that is, towards the south, Romans were dwelling as far as the river Loire, beyond which lay the dominions of the Goths. The Burgundians, who belonged to the Arian sect, lived across the Rhone, on which is the city of Lyons. Chlogio sent scouts to the city of Cambrai, who first explored everything. Thereupon he followed in person, crushed the Romans, and took possession of the city. He remained there only a short time before he occupied the whole country. Some assert that Merovech, father of Chilperic, was of his family.' (*28*: vol. ii, pp. 53–4.)

Gregory adds sadly that the Franks were idolaters, and remained so up to the time of the memorable conversion of Clovis:

'But this people seems always to have followed idolatrous practices, nor had they any knowledge of the true God. They made them images of woods and waters, birds and beasts, and other elements, and were wont to worship them as God, and to offer them sacrifices. Oh, if that awful voice had but touched the fibres of their hearts, which spake through Moses to the people, saying: "Let there be no other gods but Me. Thou shalt not make to thyself any graven image nor adore any likeness which is in heaven, or in the earth, or in the waters.' (*28*: vol. ii, p. 54.).

Chlodion, or Chlogio, who lived in the first half of the fifth century, was the first historical sovereign of the Merovingian house. His existence is confirmed by his contemporary Sidonius Apollinaris, who in his panegyric on the Emperor Majorian refers to the progress of the Frank 'Clodio' in Artois. Here in the north-east corner of the country Chlodion began the Frankish conquest of Gaul.

## Childeric and Basina

Childeric I, possibly Chlodion's grandson, who was the father of Clovis, brings us to the mid fifth century. We know Childeric chiefly through Gregory of Tours, in whose pages he appears as a man of dissolute life:

'But Childeric, who reigned over the Franks, was sunk in debauchery, and began to dishonour their daughters. For which cause they were wroth, and expelled him from the kingdom. And when he learned that

[1] This place has not been identified.

128. Portrait of Childeric I on his signet ring.

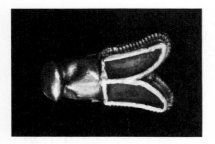

129. Cicada in gold and garnet cloisonné work from the tomb of Childeric I, adorning his royal mantle.

130. Merovingian spear-head.

214

they were minded to slay him, he fled into Thuringia, leaving behind a friend who should essay to soothe their fury by smooth words, and send him a token when he might return to his country. For this purpose they divided a gold coin. Childeric took one half with him, and his friend kept the other, saying: "Whenever I send thee this part, and by joining the two halves thou make a single *solidus*, then with a mind free from anxiety thou mayest return to thine own land." Childeric therefore departed into Thuringia and took refuge with King Bisinus and Basina his queen. And after his expulsion, the Franks unanimously chose for their king Aegidius, who, as I stated above, had been sent from Rome as master of the soldiery. But in the eighth year of his reign over them the faithful friend, who had succeeded in secretly pacifying the Franks, sent a messenger to Childeric bearing the half of the divided *solidus* which he had kept. Then Childeric, receiving it as a sure sign that the Franks wished him back, returned from Thuringia at their invitation and was restored to his kingdom. The two being now joint kings, the above-mentioned Basina left her lord and came to Childeric. To his anxious question why she had come to him from so great a distance, she is said to have replied: "I know thee capable and strenuous in action, therefore am I come to dwell with thee. For be sure that if in the parts beyond the sea I were acquainted with one more capable than thou, I should in like manner have sought him for my husband." At which answer he rejoiced, and was united with her in wedlock. And she conceived and bore a son, and called him Clovis. And he was a great man and a famous warrior.' (*28*: vol. ii, p. 56.)

Childeric died at Tournai, and his tomb was discovered by chance nearly twelve centuries later. On 27th March 1653, workmen digging near the church of St Brice at Tournai found a burial, identified as that of King Childeric by the inscription on his signet ring. He had been buried in ceremonial dress. The magnificent grave goods were deposited in the Cabinet des Médailles at the Bibliothèque Nationale, but only a part is still there, the rest having been stolen in 1831.

## *The Legend of Trojan Origin . . .*

No doubt Gregory of Tours was over-credulous; but he was a conscientious historian too, not without common sense, and prepared if need be, as we have seen, to admit his ignorance. Those who came after him had fewer scruples, and with their assistance some very odd legends were built up round the origin of the Franks.

## . . . *according to Fredegar and . . .*

The chronicle of Gregory of Tours was continued by a writer errone-
ously named Fredegar in the sixteenth century; he is the first author to
refer to the Trojan origins of the Franks. Was this seventh-century
historian, then, the inventor of the legend? Probably not, for he was too
stupid to do more than echo what he heard from others. The reader may
judge from this typical extract from his *Chronicle*:

'The Franks had Priam as their first king; when Troy was taken by
the guile of Ulysses they went out from there; afterwards they had a
king, Frigas; they had divided into two groups, and one went to
Macedonia; the others, who were with Frigas and so were called
Phrygians, ranged across Asia and settled on the banks of the River
Danube and on the shores of the sea. They divided into two parts again,
and one part went into Europe with their king Francio. And wandering
through Europe, they occupied the banks of the Rhine with their wives
and children, and tried to build a city not far from the Rhine named
after the fashion of Troy. A beginning was made, but the work was
never finished. The other part, which had remained on the banks of
the Danube, elected a king by name Turcoth, from whom they took the
name of Turks; and the others were called Franks from Francio. For
a long time, with their dukes, they refused to accept foreign domination.'
(26: vol. ii, p. 93.)

After repeating some ill-digested facts from Gregory of Tours'
*History of the Franks*, Pseudo-Fredegar instructs his readers on the
origins of the Merovingian house:

'Then, the dukes having died out, kings were created in France from
among the descendants of the former kings. . . .
'The Franks, who diligently sought to choose a long-haired king such
as had reigned before, elected one taken from the race of Priam, Frigas
and Francio, by name Theudemer, son of Richmer, who had been
killed by the Romans in the battle recorded earlier. He was succeeded on
the throne by his son Chlodion, a man who was of great service to the
nation.'

It would be an idle and thankless task to pick out all the errors and
absurdities in this odd document. But it is worth noting the various false
and nonsensical etymologies it contains, because they show a strangely
childish process of reasoning. The kings Frigas and Francio were thought
up to explain the words 'Phrygian' and 'Franks'. 'Turcoth' is there for

the same reason; the Turks are indeed in strange company here. Finally we may add that the city which the Franks are said to have partially built and then abandoned is perhaps none other than Thuringia (*Thoringia*), whose name in Latin is not unlike Troy (*Troia*); in his ignorance our author may have taken Thuringia to be the name of a city, as others have thought the Piraeus to be a man.

131. Merovingian hoard from Pouan (Aube): Collar, bracelet, signet ring, in solid gold.

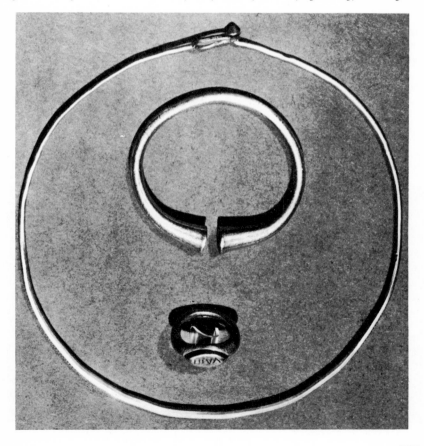

## . . . *the Monk of St Denis*

A later writer, the author of a chronicle called the *Liber historiae Francorum*, who was perhaps a monk at St Denis and wrote shortly before 736, gives an account of the origins of the Franks which is less hesitant and incoherent, but quite as fanciful. It is worth quoting, for it represents an important stage in the development of the Trojan legend:

'Let us set forth the beginnings of the kings of the Franks, their origin and that of their nation, and their deeds [he begins his book]. There is in Asia a stronghold of the Trojans where is the city called Ilium, where Aeneas reigned. The people were strong and valiant, and their men warlike and exceedingly impatient of control. . . .

'But the kings of the Greeks rose up against Aeneas with a great army, and made war on him with great slaughter, and many of the Trojans fell there. So Aeneas fled and shut himself into the city of Ilium, and they besieged the city for ten years. And when it was subjugated, the tyrant Aeneas fled to Italy to recruit men for the war. And other princes, Priam and Antenor, with the rest of the Trojan army, to the number of twelve thousand, took ship and sailed to the banks of the river Tanais

132. Great square-headed brooch found at Pompey (Meurthe-et-Moselle), 6th century.

[Don]. They sailed to the swamps of Maeotis [Sea of Azov], and made their way within the frontiers of the Pannonias, along the swamps of Maeotis, and began to build a city which as a memorial of their race they called Sicambria. They lived there many years and grew to be a great nation.' (*44*: p. 241.)

The author goes on to say that at that same time they responded to an appeal from the Emperor Valentinian, who was anxious to rid himself of the savage Alani and promised a ten-year remission of tribute to anyone who could drive them out. This the Trojans successfully did.

'Then it was [notes the chronicler] that the emperor Valentinian called them Franks, that is, in the Attic tongue, fierce, because of the hardiness and boldness of their character.'

We may note in passing that this explanation is entirely groundless, and proves nothing but the author's ignorance. He adds that after ten years Valentinian sent his officers to the Franks to collect the taxes due from tributary peoples, since the period of exemption had come to an end. But the Franks refused, and massacred the tax-collectors.

'When the emperor heard this, he was inflamed with great rage and anger, and mobilized an army of Romans and other peoples with Aristarcus as *magister militiae*, and sent it against the Franks. There was great slaughter of both peoples. The Franks, seeing that they could not withstand so great an army, fled after their army had been cut to pieces; and there Priam fell, the bravest of them all. So leaving Sicambria, they came to the farthest parts of the Rhine, to the strongholds of Germany, and lived there with their prince Marcomir, son of Priam, and Sunno, son of Antenor, and lived there many years. After the death of Sunno, they determined to have one king over them, as other peoples did. Marcomir counselled them thus, and they chose his son Faramond, and made him their ruler as a long-haired king. Then they began to have laws, which the chief men of the nation drew up. . . .

'When king Faramond died, they raised Chlodion, his long-haired son, to the throne of his father.'

The account of the monk of St Denis is as entirely legendary as that of Pseudo-Fredegar. The route which he claims was followed by the Trojans, who in the course of their wanderings became the Franks, is completely fanciful, and the city of Sicambria will not be found on any map.

But with the monk of St Denis, who had rather more education than his predecessor, the legend of the Franks' Trojan origins takes a new turn; King Faramond, for so long enthroned in the school history books as the first of the kings of France, makes his tardy entrance on the stage of history. Later he was relegated to the realm of legend, and school-children have long since forgotten good King Faramond, who not so long ago headed the glorious list of the sovereigns of France.

# 20

# CLOVIS: THE FOUNDER OF THE FRANKISH KINGDOM

THE digressions of the Merovingian chroniclers on the origins of the Frankish monarchy have a literary interest in that they show us the birth of a legend which was widely used by medieval romance writers, and even more extensively by some of the great sixteenth-century poets, headed by Ronsard with his *Franciade*. But extravagant as they are, the historian too can learn from them, for they prove that the Salian Franks were upstarts who, in the way of upstarts, very early set about finding, or manufacturing, ancestors for themselves, by the strangest means, in the attempt to improve their standing with the indigenous Gallo-Romans.

## *A Royal Opportunist*

Undoubtedly they owed their success to the foresight and boldness of Clovis, who seized his opportunity in the confusion that followed the gradual decline of the Western Empire and its unexpected fall in 476; he became a convert to Catholicism at the psychological moment, and being wiser in his generation than the kings of the Visigoths and Burgundians who remained Arians, he thus won the favour of the only moral power still surviving, the episcopacy. He was then able to conquer the whole of Gaul and build up his authority on firm foundations.

MAP 4  GAUL ON THE ACCESSION OF CLOVIS

Three-quarters of a century after his death in 511, his conversion could still rouse the pious Gregory of Tours to enthusiasm, unedifying as the king's life had been. Indeed, the pages Gregory devoted to Clovis in his *History of the Franks* have even been dismissed as simply an improving tale, a collection of pious legends. (*29*: p. 240.) But this judgment seems unduly severe when we remember that Clovis' widow, Queen Clothild, lived in retirement at Tours after her husband's death, until an advanced age. Many of the anecdotes Gregory relates probably go back to the old queen, turning over her memories in her declining years at Tours.

## The Soissons Ewer

Several of these stories are so well known that there would be no point in repeating them were they of less historical importance. One of the most familiar is the story of the Soissons ewer, the first of the anecdotes which Gregory tells about Clovis:

'At this time [about 486] many churches were plundered by the troops of Clovis, because he was yet fast held in pagan errors. Thus it happened that a ewer of great size and beauty had been taken, with other ornaments used in the service of the church. But the bishop of that church sent messengers to the king, asking that if no other of the sacred vessels might be restored, his church might at least receive back this ewer. When the king heard this he said to the envoy: "Follow us to Soissons, for there all the booty is to be divided and if the lot gives me the vessel, I will fulfil the desire of the bishop." When they were at Soissons, and all the spoil was laid out in open view, the king said: "I ask you, most valiant warriors, not to refuse to cede me that vessel" (he meant the ewer of which I have spoken) "over and above my share." After this speech all the men of sense replied: "All that is before our eyes, most glorious king, is thine; we ourselves are submitted to thy power. Do now that which seemeth good to thee, for none is so strong as to say thee nay." At these words a soldier of a vain, jealous, and unstable temper raised his axe and smote the ewer, crying with a loud voice: "Naught shalt thou receive of this but that which thine own lot giveth thee." While all stood astounded at this act, the king suppressed his resentment at the wrong under a show of patient mildness; he then took the ewer and restored it to the bishop's envoy. But the wound remained hidden in his heart. After the lapse of a year, he commanded the whole army to assemble with full equipment, and to exhibit their arms in their

223

'Thus it happened that a ewer of great size and beauty had been taken.'

133. Silver flagon, 4th century Christian art.

134. Helmeted soldier carrying pitcher. Small bronze from Mâcon.

brightness on the field of March. The king went round inspecting them all; but when he came to the man who struck the ewer he said: "None hath appeared with his arms so ill-kept as thou; neither thy lance, nor thy sword, nor thy axe is fit for use." He then seized the axe, and threw it on the ground. As the man bent down a little to take it up, the king swung his own axe high and cleft his skull, saying as he did it: "Thus didst thou treat the ewer at Soissons.' (28: vol. ii, pp. 65–6.)

Louis Halphen has noted in this story several of the devices used by the authors of lives of saints, in particular the theme of the soldier who flouts God's representative and is punished for his sacrilege exactly a year later. But though the basis of the anecdote may be legend, the picture as a whole is painted from life. The armies commanded by the Frankish kings were small forces of free men. Their leader was in constant and direct touch with his soldiers; they had elected him and felt they had a right of interpellation; every now and then he reviewed them, just as a captain in our modern armies inspects his company.

## A Momentous Conversion

Gregory's account of the conversion of Clovis is still more widely known. It may be a little romanticized, but, on the whole, as we shall see, it carries conviction.

The starting-point of this memorable conversion was the king's marriage to a Burgundian princess, Clothild, a pious Catholic who missed no opportunity of urging her husband to adopt her religion.

Gregory of Tours tells of the king's marriage, and goes on:

'Of Queen Clothild the king had a first-born son whom the mother wished to be baptized; she therefore persistently urged Clovis to permit it, saying: "The gods whom ye worship are naught; they cannot aid either themselves or others, seeing that they are images carved of wood or stone, or metal. Moreover the names which ye have given them are the names of men and not of gods. Saturn was a man, fabled to have escaped by flight from his son to avoid being thrust from his kingdom; Jupiter also, the lewdest practiser of all debaucheries and of unnatural vice, the abuser of the women of his own family, who could not even abstain from intercourse with his own sister, as she herself admitted in the words "sister and spouse of Jove". What power had Mars and Mercury? They may have been endowed with magical arts; they never had the power of the divine name. But ye should rather serve Him, who at His word

225

135. 'She ordered the church to be adorned with hangings and curtains.' Interior of a church with rich hangings, and a votive crown above the altar. Tours Pentateuch, 7th century.

created out of nothing and adorned the heaven with stars; who filled the waters with fish, the earth with animals, the air with birds; at whose word the lands are made fair with fruits, the trees with apples, the vines with grapes; by whose hand the race of man was created; by whose largess every creature was made to render homage and service to the man whom He created." Though the queen ever argued thus, the king's mind was nowise moved towards belief, but he replied: "It is by command of our gods that all things are created and come forth; it is manifest that thy god availeth in nothing; nay more, he is not even proven to belong to the race of gods." But the queen, true to her faith, presented her son for baptism; she ordered the church to be adorned with hangings and curtains, that the king, whom no preaching could influence, might by this ceremony be persuaded to belief. The boy was baptized and named Ingomer, but died while yet clothed in the white garment of his regeneration.' (*28*: vol. ii, pp. 67–8.)

This tragedy strengthened the king in his unbelief, and Gregory tells how he repeatedly reproached the queen:

' "If the child had been dedicated in the name of my gods, surely he would have survived, but now, baptized in the name of thy God, he could not live a day." The queen replied: "I render thanks to Almighty God, Creator of all things, who hath not judged me all unworthy, and deigneth to take into His kingdom this child born of my womb." '

The chronicler adds that afterwards she bore another son who was baptized and received the name of Chlodomir:

'When he too began to ail, the king said: "It cannot but befall that this infant like his brother shall straightway die, being baptized in the name of thy Christ." But the mother prayed, and God ordained that the child should recover.'

These touching and accurate details may well be taken as proof of the authenticity of the story. If the baby had not in fact died after being baptized, what motive could Gregory have had for inventing the untoward incident?

Meanwhile the queen's ceaseless exhortations had failed to convert the king. His convictions were shaken only after the vow he made at Tolbiac, in the course of a battle against the Alemanni which seemed on the point of turning into a defeat.

'It befell that when the two hosts joined battle [says Gregory] there was grievous slaughter, and the army of Clovis was being swept to utter ruin. When the king saw this he lifted up his eyes to heaven, and knew compunction in his heart, and, moved to tears, cried aloud: "Jesus Christ, Thou that art proclaimed by Clothild Son of the living God, Thou that art said to give aid to those in stress, and to grant victory to those that hope in Thee, I entreat from a devout heart the glory of Thy succour. If Thou grant me victory over these enemies, and experience confirm that power which the people dedicated to Thy Name claimeth to have proved, then will I also believe on Thee and be baptized in Thy Name. I have called upon mine own gods, but here is proof that they have withdrawn themselves from helping me; wherefore I believe that they have no power, since they come not to the succour of their servants. Thee do I now invoke, on Thee am I fain to believe, if but I may be plucked out of the hands of mine adversaries." And as he said this, lo, the Alemanni turned their backs, and began to flee.'

Clovis had won a complete victory. The account of the battle ends: 'This happened in the fifteenth year of his reign.' This corresponds to the year 496, and the traditional date, after much controversy, is now accepted by most scholars.

On his return Clovis told the queen how he had won his victory. The opportunity was too good to be missed:

'The queen commanded the holy Remigius, bishop of Reims, to be summoned secretly, entreating him to impart the word of salvation to the king. The bishop, calling the king to him in privity, began to instil into him faith in the true God, Maker of heaven and earth, and urged him to forsake his idols, which were unable to help either him or others. But Clovis replied: "I myself, most holy father, will gladly hearken to thee; but one thing yet remaineth. The people that follow me will not suffer it that I forsake their gods; yet will I go, and reason with them according to thy word." But when he came before the assembled people, or ever he opened his mouth, the divine power had gone forth before him, and all the people cried with one voice: "O gracious king, we drive forth our gods that perish, and are ready to follow that immortal God whom Remigius preacheth." News of this was brought to the bishop, who was filled with great joy, and commanded the font to be prepared. The streets were overshadowed with coloured hangings, the churches adorned with white hangings, the baptistery was set in order, the smoke of incense spread in clouds, perfumed tapers gleamed, the whole church about the place of baptism was filled with the divine fragrance. And now

136. St Remigius baptizing Clovis in the presence of Queen Clothild. Detail from diptych of the life of St Remigius, 9th century.

the king first demanded to be baptized by the bishop. Like a new Constantine, he moved forward to the water, to blot out the former leprosy, to wash away in this new stream the foul stains borne from old days. As he entered to be baptized the saint of God spoke these words with eloquent lips: "Meekly bow thy proud head, Sicamber; adore that which thou hast burned, burn that which thou hast adored." ' (*28*: vol. ii, pp. 68–70.)

Gregory of Tours then records that 'the king, confessing Almighty God, three in one, was baptized in the name of the Father, the Son, and the Holy Ghost, and anointed with holy chrism, with the sign of the Cross of Christ;' and that more than three thousand of his warriors were likewise baptized.

Students of archaeology and the liturgy alike will find much of interest in this description. In the sixth century there were still very few parishes in each diocese, and the great religious ceremonies were staged in the mother church of the city, later known as the cathedral. The most important of these ceremonies, at this period of mass conversions, was baptism, which was administered by total immersion in the font. A special place was set apart for the purpose, the baptistery, which was often a separate building adjoining the church. Another example has come to light during recent excavations on the hill at Cimiez (Nice), which have uncovered a fifth-century cathedral with a baptistery beside it.

## The Crusade Against Alaric II

Clovis won his first victory at Soissons in 486, over the son of the patrician Aegidius, Syagrius by name, who even though the Western Empire had fallen was fighting to save the last shreds of Roman dominion in northern Gaul.

When the power of Rome disappeared for good, two aspirants to the mastery of Gaul were left confronting each other: Alaric II, king of the Visigoths, and Clovis, king of the Franks. A clash was inevitable. But as Clovis had been converted to Catholicism, his war against the Arian Alaric II became a crusade with the backing of the Gaulish episcopate, and God Himself, if we are to believe the author of the *History of the Franks*, looked with favour on Clovis' cause.

As Clovis was marching through Touraine to attack the Visigoths encamped near Poitiers, he thought to obtain the protection of St Martin, whose body lay at Tours:

'The king sent messengers to the church of the saint, with these words: "Go now, and haply ye shall bring some good auspice of victory from that sacred house." He entrusted them with offerings to be set in the holy place, saying: "If Thou, O Lord, art my helper, and if Thou hast determined to deliver into my hands this unbelieving people, ever set against Thee, deign of Thy favour to give me a sign at the going into the basilica of the blessed Martin, that I may know that Thou wilt deign to show Thy servant Thy favour." '

137. 'The king sent messengers to the church of the saint . . .' Tours Pentateuch, 7th century.

The king's envoys hastened to the shrine of the saint as they had been ordered, and as they entered the basilica the precentor broke into the antiphon:

' "Thou has girded me, O Lord, with strength unto the battle; Thou hast subdued under me those that rose up against me. Thou hast also made mine enemies turn their backs upon me, and Thou hast destroyed them that hate me." The messengers, hearing these words chanted, gave thanks to God, and vowing gifts to the blessed confessor, joyfully returned with their news to the king.'

After giving this sign of his willingness to extend his protection to Clovis, St Martin lost no time in keeping his promise. Here again is the pious bishop of Tours:

'When Clovis had reached the Vienne with his army he was wholly at a loss where to cross the stream, for it was swollen with heavy rains. That night he besought the Lord that He would show him where he might pass, and lo! at dawn a hind of wondrous size entered the river at God's bidding, and where she forded the host saw that it could cross.'

The other great saint of Gaul as well, Hilary, bishop of Poitiers, guided Clovis on his road to victory:

'When the king came to the neighbourhood of Poitiers, but was abiding at some distance in his tents, he saw a fiery beacon issue from the church of the holy Hilary and come over above his head; it signified that aided by the light of the blessed confessor Hilary he might more surely overcome the host of those heretics against whom the saint himself had so often done battle for the faith.' (*28*: vol. ii, p. 76.)

The two armies met at Vouillé, some twelve miles south of Poitiers (507); the army of the Visigoths was routed, and King Alaric perished in the *mêlée* by the hand of Clovis himself. A thanksgiving pilgrimage to St Martin of Tours crowned the triumphant campaign; the Frankish king had won the whole of the kingdom of the Visigoths, together with the treasure Alaric had kept at his capital, Toulouse.

## Clovis as Consul

'His victory being complete [says Gregory of Tours], he returned to Tours and made many offerings to the holy shrine of the holy Martin.

138. 'From that day he was hailed as Augustus'. A fifth century consul.
Felix diptych (428).

'Clovis received letters from the Emperor Anastasius conferring the consulate, and in the church of the blessed Martin he was vested in the purple tunic and in a mantle, and set the diadem upon his head. Then, mounting his horse, he showered with his own hand in the generosity of his heart pieces of gold and silver among the people all along the road between the gate of the atrium of the holy Martin's church, and the church of the city. From that day he was hailed as Augustus. He left Tours and came to Paris.' (*28*: vol. ii, p. 78.)

Much has been written about this ceremony and the nature of the consulate which the Emperor Anastasius conferred on Clovis; Ferdinand Lot thinks it was nothing more than 'one of the decorations so eagerly sought by barbarian princes.' (*50*: p. 36.) But perhaps this minimizes the importance of the emperor's action. To understand it we must try to put ourselves back in the sixth century, at a time when the Roman Empire, which preserved and monopolized the traditional title of *respublica*, still enjoyed universal prestige even though Rome was no longer the seat of an emperor. Rome was still the indivisible and sovereign state; the barbarian kingdoms were as yet only *regna*, ephemeral creations which had to wait for the institution of the coronation ceremony before they could assume a spiritual and religious character.

Leaving Tours, Clovis went on to Paris. That is an important point. For the first time Paris is a real capital, the seat of a king. Clovis died there in 511 at the age of forty-five, after reigning for fifteen years, and the *History of the Franks* tells us that he was buried in the church which he and Queen Clothild had built, the basilica of the Holy Apostles Peter and Paul. (Afterwards, when the relics of St Geneviève were laid there, it was renamed after the patron saint of Paris; it stood on what is now the site of the Panthéon and the rue Clovis.)

The name by which Clovis is known in French history has its origin in a misunderstanding. The manuscripts of Gregory of Tours give him the Latin name Chlodovechus, of which the French form is Louis. Clovis, the founder of the Frankish kingdom, was in fact the first of the long line of kings of France who bore the name Louis. But it is too late now to correct the mistake; it has been hallowed by long use.

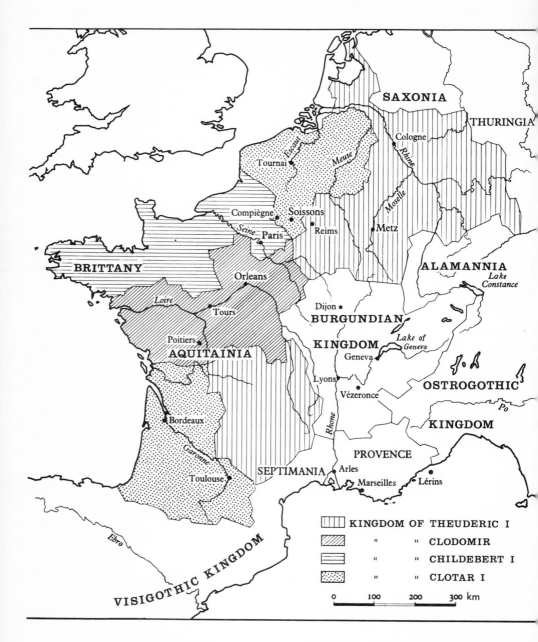

SAXONIA

THURINGIA

Cologne

Tournai

*Escaut*

*Meuse*

*Rhine*

*Moselle*

Compiègne    Soissons

*Seine*    Paris

Reims

Metz

BRITTANY

ALAMANNIA
*Lake Constance*

Orleans

*Loire*

Tours

Dijon

BURGUNDIAN

*Lake of Geneva*

Poitiers

AQUITAINIA

KINGDOM

Geneva

Lyons

OSTROGOTHIC

Vézeronce

Bordeaux

*Garonne*

*Po*

KINGDOM

Toulouse

SEPTIMANIA

PROVENCE

Arles

Marseilles    Lérins

*Ebro*

KINGDOM OF THEUDERIC I

"          "    CLODOMIR

"          "    CHILDEBERT I

"          "    CLOTAR I

VISIGOTHIC KINGDOM

0    100    200    300 km

MAP 5    PARTITION OF GAUL AMONG THE SONS OF CLOVIS

# SONS AND GRANDSONS OF CLOVIS

CLOVIS created the Frankish kingdom. He also founded a royal house, the Merovingian (the latinised form of the patronymic Merwing) dynasty. But this was small credit to him. 'Treachery, cruelty and lust' were the vices which characterized it. (*47*: p. 279.)

Clovis left four sons at his death. The eldest, Theuderic, was the son of a concubine; the other three, Chlodomir, Childebert and Lothar, were the fruit of his marriage to Clothild. The four sons divided the kingdom between them on their father's death (*see* Map 5, p. 234). They detested one another.

## *Enmity Between Brothers*

Gregory of Tours gives many instances of their mutual detestation. The story that follows shows that they were on occasion as stupid and capricious as they were wicked. The scene is laid in Thuringia, in the course of an expedition against King Hermenfred on which Theuderic had embarked with the help of his youngest brother Lothar:

'While the above-mentioned kings were in Thuringia, Theuderic sought to slay his brother Lothar. Having first set armed men in ambush, he invited him to his presence, as if he would discuss with him some privy matter. He had stretched tent-canvas from one wall to the other in a part of the house, and stationed the armed men behind it. But the hanging was too short, and the feet of the men showed below it. Lothar, warned already of the trap, entered the house accompanied by his men-at-arms. As soon as Theuderic saw that he knew all, he made up some story, and talked at random of one thing after another; at last, seeing no way of glozing over his treachery, he made him a present of a great silver salver. Lothar thanked him for the gift, bade him farewell, and returned to his lodging. Then Theuderic complained to his people that he had lost his silver dish without sufficient cause, and said to his son Theudebert: "Go to thy uncle, and ask him to give up to thee the present which I made to him." The boy went, and obtained his request.'

As Gregory says: 'Theuderic was very artful in this kind of trickery.' (*28*: vol. ii, p. 91.)

## Death of Chlodomir

Chlodomir was the first of the sons of Clovis to disappear from the scene. He was killed in 524, at Vézeronce (Isère), in the course of a war against the Burgundians. A Merovingian helmet, discovered in the locality and now in Grenoble Museum, is a vivid reminder of the battle:

'They joined forces at a place named Vézeronce in the territory of Vienne, and there gave battle to Godomer. But Godomer retreated with his army, pursued by Chlodomir, who was soon seperated by some distance from his own men. Thereupon the Burgundians imitated his battle-cry, shouting to him: "This way, this way! We are thy own men!" He was tricked and went, falling thus into the midst of his enemies, who cut off his head, fixed it on a pole, and raised it aloft.' (*28*: vol. ii, p. 89.)

## Undesirable Heirs

Chlodomir's three sons were given shelter by their grandmother Clothild, and her affection for them roused the jealousy of the Frankish kings, Childebert and Lothar in particular:

'During the sojourn of Queen Clothild at Paris, Childebert observed that his mother lavished all her affection on the sons of Chlodomir, whom I have above mentioned. This filled him with jealousy, for he feared that by her favour they might be admitted to a share in the kingdom. He therefore sent a secret message to his brother, King Lothar, to this effect: "Our mother keepeth our brother's sons ever at her side, and is fain to give them their father's kingdom; it were well,

139. Frankish helmet found at Vézeronce.

therefore, if thou camest with all speed to Paris, that we may take counsel together and consider what we should do in the matter; whether we should cut their long locks so that they may be held as the common sort, or whether we should put them to death and equally divide our brother's kingdom between us." Lothar was rejoiced at the message and came to Paris. Childebert spread the rumour among the people that this meeting of two kings had for its object the raising to the throne of the young boys. When they met, they sent to the queen, who was residing at the time in Paris, a request that she should let the boys come to them, as they wished to exalt them in the kingdom. Thereupon she rejoiced, perceiving nothing of their guile, and after giving the boys to eat and drink, sent them forth with these words: "I shall not feel that I have lost my son, if I see you raised to his place in the kingdom." So the children went, but were straightway seized and kept in custody, apart from their attendants and governors; they were in one place, their attendants in another. Then Childebert and Lothar sent to the queen that Arcadius, of whom I have spoken above, with a pair of scissors and a naked sword. Admitted to the queen's presence, he showed her both, and said: "Most glorious queen, our lords thy sons seek to know thy desire with regard to the boys; is it thy will that they live with shorn locks, or that they both be slain?" But she, terrified at these words and moved to violent

237

140. 'Lothar seized the elder boy by the arm, dashed him to the ground, and did him cruelly to death'. Carolingian ivory, late 9th century.

wrath, especially when she looked upon the drawn sword and the scissors, distraught by bitterness of grief, and not knowing in her trouble what words came to her lips, said simply: "If they are not to be raised to the throne, I had liever see them dead than shorn." But Arcadius took small account of her grief, nor cared to see what she might afterwards resolve after fuller reflection, but hurried back with his tale and said: "The queen approveth; finish the task which ye have begun; she herself desireth the completion of your design." They did not wait for more, but Lothar seized the elder boy by the arm, dashed him to the ground, and driving his dagger deep under his armpit, did him cruelly to death. At the sound of his cries his brother flung himself at Childebert's feet, clasped his knees, and cried amid his tears: "Help, dearest uncle, lest I too perish like my brother." Then Childebert, his face wet with

238

tears, cried: "I entreat thee, beloved brother, of thy pity grant me his life; only let him be spared, and I will pay whatsoever thou mayst ask in return." But the other, giving way to violent abuse, cried to him: "Cast him from thee, or thyself shalt surely die in his place. It was thou didst prompt to this business, and art thou now so swift to recoil from thy pledge?" At this rebuke Childebert pushed the boy from him and drove him to Lothar, who received him with a dagger-thrust in the side and slew him as he had done his brother. The attendants and governors of the young princes were then slain. After all were killed, Lothar took horse and rode away recking little of the murder of his nephews; Childebert withdrew to a suburb of the town. But the queen had the bodies of the two boys laid upon a bier, and to the sound of chanted psalms followed them in her measureless grief to the church of St Peter, where they were both interred, one having lived ten years, the other seven.' (*28*: vol. ii, pp. 101–2.)

The historian adds that the third boy, who was called Chlodovald, 'was saved with the help of brave defenders' from the murderous fury of his uncles. Disgusted with life in the world, he took the habit of a monk and in a place called Nogent, near Paris, founded a monastery to which he gave his name, St Cloud; this is preserved today in the name of the town which grew up under the walls of the abbey he founded.

A ninth-century hagiographer, in a *Life* of the saint so fortunately

141. Lothar I; Merovingian gold solidus.

delivered from his uncles, tells a curious story of a miracle said to have taken place when Chlodovald, fleeing from his native land, came to Provence, possibly to Lérins, to become a hermit:

'While he was building an oratory in the aforesaid district [says the biographer], a poor man came and asked alms of him. But the man of God, having nothing at hand to give the beggar, gave him the cowl he was wearing. The poor man took it and went away, and found lodging in the house of a pious man. After he had eaten and drunk and fallen asleep, and saw his house shining with a bright light; and he at once told his wife and when much of the night was passed, the goodman got up in the night, who had woken up. Realizing that this was no ordinary occurrence she said: "The pilgrim we took in has brought some divine gift with him." When they questioned the pilgrim in the morning, he told how he had received the cowl from the holy man as a present.' (*15*: p. 356.)

The pious author adds that the miracle was soon noised abroad throughout the countryside.

## *Lothar, the Polygamist*

Lothar I, the fourth and last of the sons of Clovis, was also the last survivor. The story of the murder of his nephews is all the proof that is needed of his inhuman cruelty. But that he had a cynical sense of humour too is shown by this anecdote from Gregory of Tours:

'I will now tell how it was that King Lothar married his wife's sister [Aregund]. When he was already wedded to Ingund, and loved her with his whole heart, she made him the following suggestion: "My lord hath done with his handmaid according to his pleasure, and taken her to his bed; now to make my reward complete, let my lord hear the proposal of his servant. I entreat him graciously to choose for his servant my sister an able and rich husband, that I be not humbled but exalted by her, and thus may give thee yet more faithful service." On hearing this, the king, who was most amorous by temperament, began to desire Aregund, and betaking himself to the domain where she lived, he married her. When she was his, he returned to Ingund and spoke as follows: "I have done my best to procure for thee the reward which thy sweetness asked of me. I sought a man wealthy and of good wit, whom I might give in marriage to thy sister, but I found none better than myself. Know therefore that I have taken her to wife, which I believe will not displease thee." '

With a man like Lothar protest was useless, if not positively dangerous, and his wife finding herself thus supplanted dared say no more than: 'Let my lord do that which seemeth good in his sight; only let his hand-maid live in the enjoyment of his favour.' (*28*: vol. ii, p. 117.)

Only when, at the end of the most un-Christian of lives, they lay at the point of death did most of the Merovingians collapse like pricked balloons. Panic-stricken at the prospect of everlasting punishment, they strove to placate the King of Heaven by belated prayer and almsgiving. To turn aside his vengeful wrath they had recourse to the intercession of influential intermediaries such as St Martin, as did King Lothar when in 561 he felt his death near. Gregory of Tours, whose patron saint was the great prelate St Martin, makes a point of recording his last hours:

'In the fiftieth year of his reign, King Lothar sought the threshold of the blessed Martin, bringing many gifts. Arriving at Tours, he went to the tomb of the aforesaid bishop, where he recounted all the evil acts which by negligence he might have committed, and with many a groan, prayed the blessed confessor to implore the Lord's mercy on his offences, and by his intercession wash away the sins which he had thoughtlessly committed. Returning in the fifty-first year of his reign, he was seized with a fever while hunting in the forest of Cuise, and thence went back to his domain of Compiègne. There he was grievously vexed by the fever, and cried: "Welladay! what think ye? What manner of king is He above, who thus doeth to death such great kings?" In the midst of this weariness of spirit, he gave up the ghost.' (*28*: vol. ii, p. 133.)

## *Heirs to the Kingdom*

After Lothar's death, his four sons shared the kingdom of the Franks between them; since the death of Clovis it had been enlarged by the annexation of the kingdom of the Burgundians 534. (*See* Map 6, p. 246.) The heirs of Clovis' other sons were already dead, or else were swept aside; the kingdom was shared out as though it were a private patrimony, a family inheritance, regardless of the public interest, and with all the incidents that are apt to occur when the co-heir to an estate is avaricious and unscrupulous:

'Now Chilperic [says Gregory of Tours], after the funeral of his father, took possession of the treasures which were amassed in the

Treasure from the tomb of Aregunda, wife of Lothar I, in the Abbey of St Denis.

142. Belt-plate in silver-gilt filigree with stone and glass settings.

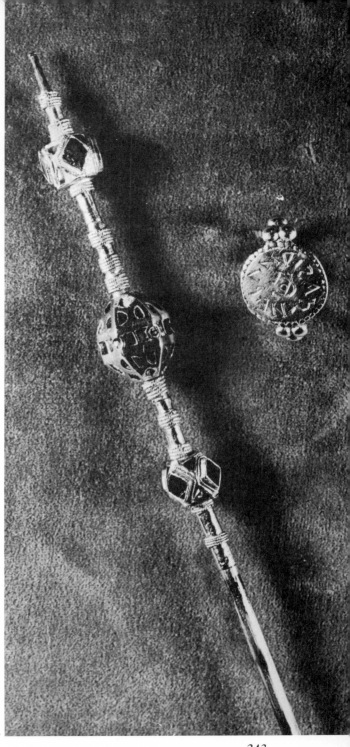

143. Great pin in gold, silver and garnets; Aregunda's signet ring, gold.

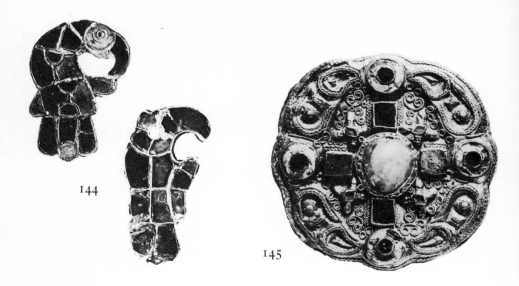

144

145

royal villa of Berny;[1] he then sought those Franks whom he deemed best able to serve him and won them by gifts to his allegiance. Soon after, he entered Paris, and seized the residence of King Childebert. But it was not given him to hold it long, for his brothers made common cause to drive him forth; and thus the four, Charibert, Guntram, Chilperic and Sigibert, made lawful division, and the kingdom of Childebert, with Paris for his capital, fell to Charibert; the kingdom of Chlodomir to Guntram, his capital Orleans; to Chilperic the kingdom of his father Lothar, with his royal seat at Soissons. Sigibert, for his part, received the kingdom of Theuderic, with his residence at Reims.' (28: vol. ii, pp. 133–4.)

Of all the line of Frankish kings in the sixth century, Sigibert was the only one whose private life will bear inspection. We have plenty of gossip from Gregory of Tours about the debauches of the others. Guntram, a foolish old man whom the chronicler, with an indulgence he had done nothing to deserve, calls 'Guntram the good', was hardly any better than his brothers; this anecdote shows how criminally weak he could be:

'Now the good king Guntram first took to his bed as concubine Veneranda, the handmaid of one of his subjects, by whom he had a son Gundobad. Afterwards he took to wife Marcatrude, daughter of

[1] Berny-Rivière, canton of Vic-sur-Aisne (Aisne), one of the chief domains of the Merovingian kings.

'He sent her with great treasures
to the king.'

144. Bird-head brooches incrusted with
garnets.

145. Composite disc-brooch in gold,
incrusted with glass, decorated with
stylized bird-heads.

146. Composite disc-brooch, in the form
of a four-leaved clover; gold, incrusted
with glass; in the centre a Roman gem
engraved with a figure of Mars.

146

Magnar, and sent his son Gundobad to Orleans. But when Marcatrude
had a son of her own, she was jealous of this boy, and went about to
compass his death; they say that she sent poison for him to drink, and
so destroyed him. After his death, she lost her own son by the judgment
of God, and incurred the hatred of the king, by whom she was put away,
dying not long afterwards. After her the king took to wife Austrechild,
also called Bobila.' (*28*: vol. ii, p. 135.)

## A Royal Marriage

The regrettable examples of his elder brothers determined Sigibert to
set his matrimonial sights higher:

'Now King Sigibert, seeing his brothers take to themselves unworthy
wives and even wed serving-maids, sent an embassy to Spain with many
gifts to demand in marriage Brunhild, daughter of King Athanagild.
For she was a girl of graceful form, fair to look upon; honourable and
comely, prudent in judgment, and amiable of address. Her father did
not refuse her, but sent her with great treasures to the king, who,
assembling the chief men of his kingdom, and making ready a feast,
received her as his wife with boundless delight. And because she was
subject to the Arian law, she was converted by the preaching of bishops
and the admonitions of the king himself, so that she confessed the
blessed Trinity in Unity, and received the holy chrism, remaining a
Catholic in the name of Christ until this day.' (*28*: vol. ii, p. 137.)

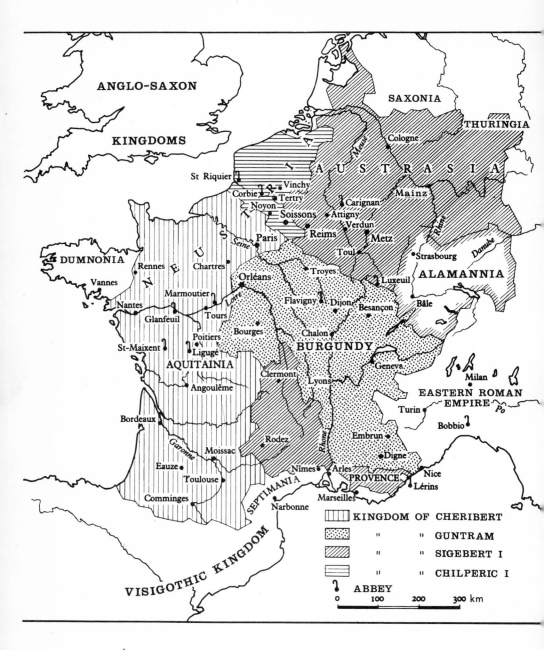

ANGLO-SAXON

KINGDOMS

SAXONIA

THURINGIA

Cologne

AUSTRASIA

St Riquier

Vinchy

Mainz

Corbie

Tertry

Carignan

Noyon

Attigny

Verdun

Soissons

Reims

Metz

DUMNONIA

Rennes

Chartres

Paris

Toul

Strasbourg

ALAMANNIA

Vannes

Orléans

Troyes

Luxeuil

Marmoutier

Flavigny

Dijon

Besançon

Bâle

Nantes

Tours

Glanfeuil

Bourges

Chalon

Poitiers

BURGUNDY

St-Maixent

Ligugé

Geneva

AQUITAINIA

Clermont

EASTERN ROMAN

Angoulême

Lyons

EMPIRE

Milan

Bordeaux

Turin

Bobbio

Moissac

Rodez

Embrun

Eauze

Digne

Toulouse

Nîmes

Arles

Nice

Comminges

Marseilles

PROVENCE

Lérins

Narbonne

SEPTIMANIA

KINGDOM OF CHERIBERT

"        "   GUNTRAM

"        "   SIGEBERT I

"        "   CHILPERIC I

ABBEY

0    100    200    300 km

VISIGOTHIC KINGDOM

MAP 6  PARTITION OF GAUL AT THE DEATH OF LOTHAR I

The poet Fortunatus, who was born in Italy in 530 and lived there until 565, wrote an epithalamium in honour of the bride and groom. As court poet he carried on the tradition of Sidonius Apollinaris into the sixth century. We need quote only a few lines of this poem, a mixture of affection and banality which has practically no interest for the historian. In this passage, where Venus hymns the charms of Brunhild, mythology seems to have gone to the poet's head:

'Then Venus began to sing the maiden's praises thus: "O virgin, who art my wonder and wilt be thy husband's delight, radiant Brunhild, brighter than the torch of heaven, whose glance outshines the rays of precious stones, another daughter of Venus, whose dowry is the kingdom of beauty, no Nereid from the deeps of the Iberian sea, swimming beneath the waters of Ocean, is like to thee; no Napaea [wood-nymph] is fairer than thou; the rivers themselves give thee place above their nymphs. Thy face of milky whiteness glows with a rosy flush. Lilies mingled with roses, where gold gleams amid purple, vie in vain with thy face and can never equal it. Sapphire, white diamond, crystal, emerald, jasper, all yield to thee. Spain has given birth to a new gem of flawless form, whose power has moved a king." '(25: vol. lxxxviii, col. 207.)

The poet adds that the gem has had to cross snow-covered mountains and venture among savage peoples to reach her betrothed, and he ends:

'Nothing can stand in the way of lovers whom it is the gods' wish to join together. Who would have believed, O Germany[1] that to thee would be given a Spanish queen, who would bring two precious kingdoms together under one yoke? No human effort could have compassed this wonder; for so difficult a matter the weapons of the gods are needed.'

We will quote no more. All that remains to be said is that Fortunatus had come straight from Ravenna, the seat of the representative of the Eastern Emperor, to the court of the king of Austrasia. In those barbarian circles the brilliant Italian culture Fortunatus brought with him made a great impression, and he was appointed official poet. But he was wise enough not to spend the rest of his life in the post. A few years later we find him at the court of St Radegund at Poitiers; the biography he wrote of her was to be his masterpiece.

---

[1] Sigibert was king of Austrasia, and his usual residence was Metz.

## Galswinth

By his marriage to Brunhild, King Sigibert brought into the royal house of the Merovingians a princess who had a decisive influence on the fortunes of the dynasty, and played a leading part in Frankish history. The wedding made a great impression at the time, as we know from Gregory of Tours and Fortunatus. So jealousy rather than concern for his own dignity was the motive which led Chilperic, Gregory of Tours' pet aversion, to follow his younger brother's example and seek the hand of Galswinth, Brunhild's sister:

'When King Chilperic saw this, although he already had several wives [says Gregory], he sent to demand her sister Galswinth, promising by the mouth of his envoys that he would forsake the others if only he were deemed worthy to receive a spouse befitting his rank and of blood royal. Her father believed his promises, and sent this daughter like the other with a rich dower to the king: Galswinth was the elder sister. When she was come to King Chilperic, he received her with great honour, and was joined to her in marriage, loving her dearly, for she had brought with her great treasures. But because of his passion for Fredegund, his former wife, a great quarrel arose between them. She so made constant complaint to the king of the wrongs which she had to endure, declaring that she had no part in his royalty; she craved his permission to return in freedom to her own country, leaving behind her the treasures she had brought with her. He cleverly dissembled, and appeased her with smooth words. At last he ordered her to be strangled by a slave, so that she was found dead in her bed. After her death, God showed forth a great miracle. A lamp was suspended by a cord above her tomb, and without being touched by any, this lamp fell to the paved floor. But the hardness departed from the pavement before it. It was as if the lamp sank into some soft substance; it was buried up to the middle without being broken at all. Which thing appeared a great miracle to all who saw it. The king made mourning for her death; but after a few days took Fredegund again to wife. Thereupon his brothers cast him out from the kingdom, deeming that the aforesaid queen was not slain without his prompting.' (28: vol. ii, pp. 137–8.)

Relentless civil war followed.

# 22

# GREGORY OF TOURS:
# BISHOP AND HISTORIAN

WE HAVE made considerable use of the works of Gregory of Tours in our preceding chapters; now we must introduce the author. He was by no means a vainglorious or egotistical writer; but though he never intentionally thrust himself forward, his historical works, the *History of the Franks* and his books of miracles, are apt to read like memoirs. One personal reminiscence follows another in his writings, so that, though we do not aspire to write his biography, we can with the help of his graphic anecdotes sketch in the portrait of one of the most attractive people who lived in the dark days he chronicled.

The reader will not hold it against him that he shares the excessive, almost childish, credulity of his contemporaries; and though some of the bishop's quirks may raise a smile, particularly his habit of retailing his ailments, yet the unassuming courage he more than once showed commands our respect.

## Memoirs of His Youth

Gregory's father, Florentius, was an Arvernian of senatorial family, with large estates in La Limagne, even in the sixth century a rich corn-growing district, which employed considerable labour at harvest time.

The future historian began to learn to read at the age of eight, in the household of his uncle St Nicetius, later bishop of Lyons, to whom his mother, being early widowed, had entrusted her son's education.

'I remember in my childhood [says Gregory of Tours, in the chapter in his *Lives of the Fathers* devoted to St Nicetius], when I was just beginning to know my letters and was about eight years old, he told me, unworthy as I was, to get into his bed, and he took me in his arms with the gentle affection of a father; but then, hastily taking the hem of his garment between his fingers, he wrapped himself in his tunic, so that I should not come in contact with his blessed limbs. See the precautions of the man of God, and take note of them, I beg of you! If he thus avoided contact with the limbs of a child, in whom there could be no incentive to concupiscence, no incitement to lust, how carefully he must have shunned anything which harboured a suspicion of lasciviousness!' (*27*: vol. i, p. 692.)

## Disarming Modesty

Gregory did not pursue his studies to a very advanced stage, either with St Nicetius or later with an uncle on his father's side, Gallus, bishop of Clermont, and he had no illusions about his knowledge of literature or even of grammar. In one of his prefaces he admits with charming modesty that his attainments leave much to be desired, excusing himself for aspiring to authorship and adding that he has done no more than collect the materials for others better equipped than he to put into shape. His modesty has had its reward, for the works of Gregory of Tours are still read in the twentieth century when most other products of early medieval hagiography are forgotten:

'One who is unlearned, condemned as clumsy and dull, is ashamed to enter upon something he cannot accomplish. But what can I do? I cannot refrain from bringing to the light of day the miraculous acts of holy men, which I have either observed myself or known through the reports of good and trustworthy men. But I fear, being without knowledge of rhetoric and the science of grammar, that when I begin to write the learned may say to me: "Witless clown, dost thou think to see thy name among those of writers? Or that experts will accept a work thus lacking in talent and grammatical knowledge; when thou hast no useful grounding in orthography, and canst not distinguish nouns, putting feminine for masculine, neuter for feminine, and masculine for neuter; not even giving their rightful place to prepositions whose use has been laid down by the authority of eminent teachers, but putting the accusative instead of the ablative, and the ablative instead of the accusative? Dost thou think not to appear as a lumbering ox joining in

147. Jar found at St Martin-de-Fraigneau (Vendée) bearing the inscription: 'Balm and oil of St Martin the bishop, for blessing'; 5th century.

the exercises of the wrestling-school, or a sluggish ass trying to run to and fro among tennis players?" '

The author continues his comparisons by likening himself to 'a crow who would cover his blackness with the feathers of white doves', or pitch that would change its dark hue to milky whiteness, and he ends:

'But I will answer them and say: "I do your work, and my uncouthness will exercise your skill; for if I am not mistaken, you may benefit from my writings, and what I describe in an unpolished and obscure style, you will be able to expand much more fully in clear and brilliant manner." ' (*27*: vol. i, pp. 747–8.)

## Miraculous Cures

It was the renown of St Martin and the miracles wrought on his tomb that one fine day brought the Arvernian Gregory, then a deacon, to Tours. Seriously ill, he came to pray the saint to heal him, and his prayer was answered. He gives a vivid, even a moving, account of his cure in the first book of the *Miracles of St Martin*:

'After all these things which were done for others, I shall now turn to what the miraculous virtue of the saint has performed for me, unworthy as I am. In the 163rd year after the blessed bishop Martin had been taken up into heaven, in the seventh year of St Eufronius' rule as bishop over the church of Tours, and in the second year of the reign of the most glorious King Sigibert [563], I suddenly fell ill with malignant pustules and fever, and being unable either to eat or drink I suffered so that I lost all hope of life on earth and thought only to prepare my burial. Death laid eager and unremitting siege to me, hoping to take my soul by storm from my body. Then, when I was already almost lifeless, I called on the name of the blessed bishop Martin, and recovered a little and began to prepare for my journey with effort that was still slow. For it was rooted in my mind that I ought to visit the place of his venerable tomb. I conceived so great a desire for this, that I thought it were better for me to die than to tarry longer. And so I, who was scarcely out of the fever of my illness, began to burn with the fever of desire. Without more delay, although I had hardly recovered strength, I hastily started on the journey with my company. After two or three stages, as I was going into a forest, I fell into a fever again and began to be so ill that everyone asserted that I was dying. My friends coming near and seeing me exhausted said: "Let us go back, and if it is God's will to call thee to himself, thou shalt die at home; but if thou escape death, thou shalt perform thy vow more easily. It is better to go home than to die in the wilderness." But when I heard this, weeping bitterly and bewailing my misfortune, I spoke to them, saying: "I adjure you by Almighty God and the day of judgment so greatly to be feared by all sinners, that you consent to what I ask. Do not abandon the journey we have begun. If I am worthy to see the basilica of St Martin, I thank my God; and if not, take my lifeless body and bury me there, for it is my determination not to turn back if I have not deserved to be presented at his tomb." Then all wept together, and we continued the journey we had begun. And the protection of the glorious Lord preventing us, we came to the basilica.' (*27*: vol. i, pp. 603–4.)

There the saint performed a twofold miracle. Among Gregory's fellow pilgrims was a clerk called Armentarius, very learned and with remarkable musical talent, who had lost his reason through 'a poison caused by malignant pustules'. He was taken to the basilica with Gregory, in the hope that he too might be healed.

'On the third night after our arrival in the holy basilica [Gregory goes on], we planned to keep vigil, and this we did. But when it was morning, after the bell had sounded for matins, we went back to our lodging, and resting on our beds, we slept until nearly the second hour [after sunrise]. When I awoke, all my weakness and bitterness of heart had disappeared, I felt that I had recovered all my former health, and joyfully I called my servant to attend on me. But Armentarius leapt up and stood before me, and said: "Master, I will do thy bidding." But I, thinking that he was still out of his senses, said: "If thou canst, call my servant." And he said: "I will do whatever thou commandest." Amazed, I asked him how this might be. He said: "I feel that I am completely sound in mind; but one doubt troubles me, that I know not how I am come hither." And he began to serve me, as he had been accustomed to do before his illness. Then rejoicing and weeping for joy, I offered thanks to Almighty God both for myself and for him, that by the intercession of our patron saint He had restored health of body to me, and health of mind to him, and that the faith of one had obtained healing for the other, who was mad and could not himself ask it. But I must not omit to say that on that day for the first time in forty days I took pleasure in drinking wine, when because of my illness I had till then detested it.'

After his miraculous cure, Gregory stayed at Tours and settled down there. In 573 he was made bishop, and continued in that office until his death, probably in 594. When he was raised to the throne of St Martin his gratitude to his famous predecessor knew no bounds, and he gave of his best in the service of the saint. Four of his books are devoted to accounts of miracles worked by St Martin. His chief concern, as we have seen, was to describe the miraculous cures which he had himself experienced. Here is a curious example, the passage where he tells how he was almost choked by a fish-bone but was saved by St Martin:

'I will begin this book with a miracle which I experienced not long since. While we were sitting at table together to break our fast, a fish was brought in on a dish. We made the sign of the cross over it and ate it, and one of the fish-bones stuck very painfully in my throat. It was so sharp that it pierced my throat, and so long that it stopped up my gullet, causing me violent pain; it hindered the sound of my voice, and prevented the passage of the saliva flowing from my palate. On the third day, when I could not cast it forth by coughing or spitting, I had recourse to the remedies I knew. I went to the tomb, prostrated myself on the pavement, and weeping and groaning I implored the confessor's

THE CHRONICLERS:
148. Fredegar holding his book.
Chronicle of Fredegar, *c.*715

149. Passage from the *Historia Francorum* of Gregory of Tours, dealing with the events after the death of Alaric. Manuscript written at the abbey of Luxeuil at the end of the 7th century.

help. Then getting up I touched my throat and gullet and the rest of my head with the veil which hung down. At once I was restored to health, and even before I had crossed the holy threshold I felt no exhaustion. What became of the injurious bone I know not.'

And he adds:

'One thing only I know, that I felt myself cured with such rapidity that it was as if someone had put in his hand and removed what had produced the injury to my throat.' (*27*: vol. i, p. 632.)

But it would be a grave injustice to dismiss Gregory of Tours as simply a collector of miraculous tales. His *History of the Franks* shows that he had the qualities that make a historian, and a rare gift of observation; and he was a courageous leader of the Church, with the strength of mind he needed to withstand so brutal a sovereign as Chilperic I.

254

## A Courageous Bishop

Opportunity to exercise it came with the trial of Praetextatus, bishop of Rouen, who was godfather to one of the king's sons, Merovech, and had blessed the marriage of the young prince with Queen Brunhild after the assassination of her husband Sigibert. Gregory came to the defence of his brother bishop, and opposed the wish of Chilperic and his wife Fredegund that Praetextatus should be publicly condemned by an assembly of the bishops of the kingdom summoned at Paris:

'The king [Chilperic] now withdrew to his lodging [writes Gregory of Tours], but we remained seated in the sacristy of the church of St Peter.[1] As we were taking counsel together, there suddenly arrived Aëtius, archdeacon of the church of Paris, who gave us greeting, and then said: "Give ear to me, O priests of the Lord here assembled; for

[1] See page 233.

either ye shall now exalt your name and shine with the grace of good renown or, lacking manhood to play the part that falleth to you, and suffering this your brother to perish, of a surety not a man of you shall henceforth be accounted the minister of God." Thus he spake, but not a bishop answered him a word, for they feared the king and his fury, by whose prompting these things were being done. As they remained absorbed in thought, with their fingers on their lips, I myself spoke as follows: "Hearken, I pray you, to my words, most holy priests of the Lord, ye before all who seem to have the confidence of the king. Give him now holy counsel and befitting bishops, lest in fury against a minister of God he perish by his wrath nor lose both kingdom and renown." When I had said this, all still held their peace.' (*28*: vol. ii, pp. 187–9.)

Gregory's efforts met with no success. The king learnt of his strenuous opposition from informers, and summoned him to his presence, determined to frighten him into conformity:

'Two sycophants among them [Gregory goes on], it is lamentable to say it of bishops, went to the king and told him that there was no greater enemy of his interests than myself. Forthwith one from the court was sent with all speed to command my presence. When I arrived, the king was standing in an arbour formed of branches, with Bishop Bertram [of Bordeaux] on his right and Ragnemond [of Poitiers] upon his left: before them was a bench covered with bread and various dishes. As soon as he saw me, the king said: "O bishop, it is thy part freely to deal justice to all, and lo! I receive not justice at thy hands; but I see thee consenting with iniquity, and in thee is fulfilled the proverb that crow picketh not out crow's eye." Whereto I answered: "If any among us, O king, would overstep the path of justice, it is in thy power to correct him; but if thou transgress, who may rebuke thee? For we may speak with thee indeed, and if thou wilt, thou hearest; but if thou wilt not, who shall condemn thee save He who hath proclaimed Himself to be very Justice?" He replied (for his flatterers had inflamed him against me): "All other men show me justice; with thee alone I find it not." '

The king's hypocrisy and his offer of succulent dishes left the bishop as unmoved as his anger:

'Then, as if to propitiate me, deeming that I did not see through his crafty dealing, he turned to a dish placed before him, and said: "These dishes I have had prepared for thee; there is nothing in this but fowl and a little pulse." But, knowing his insinuating arts, I said: "Our food should be to do the will of God, and not to take delight in these dainties, that in no case we transgress His commands. As for thee, who accusest others of injustice, promise first thyself to keep the law and the canons; then shall we believe that thou followest after justice." '

An attempt at bribery by Queen Fredegund, whose jealous hatred of Brunhild had made her the bitter enemy of Bishop Praetextatus, was met by Gregory with the same unflinching integrity:

'That night, when we had finished singing the nocturnal hyms, I heard a loud knocking on the door of my lodging, and learned from the servant whom I sent that messengers from Queen Fredegund stood without. They were introduced, and gave me greeting from the queen. These servants of hers then besought me not to oppose her interests; at the same time they promised me two hundred pounds of silver if, through my joining in the attack on him, Praetextatus were condemned. For they said: "We have now the promise of all the bishops; do not thou oppose alone." I made answer: "If ye gave me a thousand pounds of gold and silver, could I do aught but that which the Lord commandeth?" '

## Theology of a Frankish King

Gregory opposed King Chilperic with the same gentle obstinacy in other and very different circumstances. Chilperic fancied himself as a theologian, and conceived the odd ambition of forcing on the bishops of his kingdom his own idea of the Godhead, which was in fact the complete negation of the doctrine of the Trinity. In discussion with the king Gregory preserved his dignity and composure; he kept his temper, but in the end achieved his aim, and the king abandoned his absurd scheme:

'About the same time, King Chilperic wrote an ordinance enjoining that in the Holy Trinity we should make no distinction of Persons, but call it only God, declaring it unseemly that in the case of God we should speak of a Person, as if He were man in the flesh; moreover, he affirmed that the Father is the same as the Son, and the Holy Ghost is the same as the Father and the Son. "Even so," said he, "did He appear to the prophets and the patriarchs, so did the law itself proclaim Him." After he had ordered these arguments to be recited to me, he said: "This is my will, that such be thy faith, and that of the other doctors of the church." I made answer to him: "Most pious king, thou must abandon thy vain belief, and follow that which the Apostles, and after them the

257

Fathers of the Church, have handed down to us, that which Hilary and Eusebius taught, that which thou thyself didst confess in thy baptism." Then was the king wroth and said: "It is clear enough that in this matter I have strong enemies in Hilary and Eusebius." I replied: "Thou shouldest well perceive that neither God nor His saints be against thee. But know that in their Persons the Father is different from the Son, and the Son from the Holy Ghost. It was not the Father who was made man, nor the Holy Ghost, but the Son, that He who was the Son of God might for man's redemption be held the Son of man and of a virgin. It was not the Father who suffered, nor the Holy Spirit, but the Son, that He who was incarnate in the world might Himself be offered for the world. And that which thou sayest with regard to Persons is not to be understood corporeally, but spiritually. Therefore in these three Persons is one glory, one eternity, one power." Then he was angered, and said: "I will set forth these things to others wiser than thou, who will be of my mind." I retorted: "He who should be minded to follow that which thou dost propose will never be a wise man, but a fool." Thereat he gnashed his teeth, but held his peace. Not many days afterwards Salvius, bishop of Albi, arrived; and the king caused these opinions to be recited to him, begging him to express his agreement. But as soon as Salvius heard them, he rejected them with such abhorrence that if he could have reached the paper on which such things were written he would have torn it to pieces. So the king desisted from his purpose.' (*28*: vol. ii, pp. 217–18.)

That Chilperic thus relinquished his theological pretensions is a significant point, and evidence of the prestige the bishops commanded not only among the people as a whole, but among nobles and kings as well.

# 23

# ROYAL ADMINISTRATION UNDER THE MERWINGS

MODERN historians have strongly censured the government and administration of the Merovingians, and with good reason. For the Merovingian king the end and aim of government was the personal satisfaction of the monarch, and royal administration simply and solely the exploitation of the State by the king.

Decadence set in, swiftly and savagely, as soon as Clovis had conquered Gaul. Despotism would have triumphed completely but for the Church and her bishops, who kept alive some spark of the conception of the common weal. Not until the accession of the Carolingians and the reign of Pepin the Short was the situation righted.

One or two anecdotes from Gregory of Tours' inexhaustible supply will serve to illustrate and vindicate these assertions.

There were, strictly speaking, no functionaries, but the kings had servants who were charged with such domestic duties in their palaces as superintending the stables, and were also employed on military and diplomatic business. The king's creatures were installed in every town, holding all powers, living on the produce of the royal domains and on the various taxes they levied from the people. They were often robbers, and almost always totally uneducated.

## From Kitchen Boy to Count

There was for instance Leudast, the base-born count of the city of Tours, who treated Gregory abominably. Gregory describes his dealings with the count in detail in his *History*; here we shall quote no more than the historical sketch with which he prefaces his account:

'I am fain to tell somewhat of Leudast's career [says Gregory], beginning with his family, his native country and his character. There is an island off Poitou called Gracina, where Leudast was born to the serf of Leucadius, a vine-dresser of the domain. In due time summoned to service, he was assigned to the royal kitchens. But as in early life he had weak eyes ill fitted to endure the sharp smoke, he was transferred from the pestle to the baker's basket. He pretended to enjoy himself amid the fermenting dough, but escaped and forsook his service. Two or three times he was brought back after evasion; but as he could not be restrained, he was punished by the slitting of one ear. Then, as there was no possible means of concealing this branding mark, he took refuge with Queen Marcovefa, whom King Charibert loved exceedingly and had wedded in her sister's place. She received him kindly, promoted him in her service and assigned to him the care of her finest horses. As a result of this, his conceit and arrogance led him to solicit the office of count of the stables. No sooner was it his than he looked down on and slighted everyone; he was inflated with vain pride and gave way to lechery; he was inflamed with covetousness, and as the special favourite of his protectress was dispatched here, there and everywhere about her affairs. After her death, as his purse was well filled through his extortions, he offered presents to King Charibert and thus retained his old office. It was after this that he was nominated count of the city of Tours, for the sins of the people were now waxing gross.'

With this promotion, the one-time baker's boy grew more vain-glorious than ever:

'Such was his upstart arrogance [Gregory reports], that he came into the church house in his gorget and shirt of mail with his quiver hung about him, helmet on head and lance in hand; he could trust no man, being the enemy of all. When he sat in his court with the chief men of the country, lay or clerical, and marked any man pursuing justice, he straightway wrought himself into a fury and broke into abuse against the citizens. By his orders priests were dragged forth in manacles, and soldiers were beaten with clubs.' (*28*: vol. ii, p. 220.)

He had no greater respect for churches than for the clergy, and Gregory reports with righteous indignation that he was caught in the act of adultery in the very porch of the church.

## The Crimes of Duke Rauching

In the middle of the sixth century we find dukes being set above the counts; they were military commanders in charge of vast areas which included several counties. Their recruitment seems to have produced even worse results than that of the counts, and Ferdinand Lot describes the dukes who governed under Childebert II as ravening beasts. Rauching, to judge from Gregory of Tours' portrait of him, might have served as a model for them:

'Rauching, a man compact of all manner of vanities, puffed up with pride and insolent conceit, conducting himself towards those beneath him as one admitting no trace of humanity, raging against his people beyond all bounds of folly and malice, doing them unspeakable outrage. When a serf, according to usage, held a lighted candle before him as he sat at meat, he had his legs bared and fixed the candle light between his shins until it burned out; the same was done when a second taper was lit, until the shins of the serf were badly burned. If the man uttered a sound, or moved from his place, forthwith a naked sword threatened him; whereat Rauching exulted with great glee over the man's tears. There was one who had a story that at this time two of his serfs, a man and a girl, fell in love, as will often befall. After their affection had lasted for two years or more, they fled together and took refuge in the church. As soon as Rauching heard it, he went to the priest of the place and demanded the surrender of his two serfs, whom he professed to have forgiven. Thereupon the priest said to him: "Thou knowest what reverence is due to the house of God; it is not granted thee to take them back if thou promise not that they may remain in wedlock, and likewise that they be free from punishment." At this he stood silent a long while, pondering and doubtful what to do; but at length he turned to the priest and placing his hands upon the altar uttered this oath: "They shall never be put asunder by me; rather will I see that they remain united even as now. For though I was vexed that they acted without my consent, one thing I heartily approve, that the man doth not wed the maid of another lord, or the maid a man from another household." The priest in the simplicity of his heart believed the promise of that crafty man, and gave up the two serfs, as those whose pardon was assured. Rauching took charge of them, thanking the priest, and withdrew to his house. There he straightway bade fell a tree, and caused a section of the trunk to be split at the end with wedges and hollowed out; a pit was then dug in the earth to the depth of three or four feet, and this hollowed log placed in it by his orders. The girl was laid out in it as if she were a corpse, and the man cast in upon her; then the cover was put on and the earth filled in. So he buried them alive, uttering these words: "I have not gone counter to my oath that these two should never be put asunder." News whereof being brought to the priest, he ran thither with speed, and bitterly rebuking the man, hardly won from him leave to have the earth removed. The male serf was taken out alive, but the girl was found suffocated.' (*28*: vol. ii, pp. 170–1.)

The villainous duke met the fate he deserved. In 587 he fomented a plot against Childebert II, and King Guntram, who was the young prince's protector, seized the opportunity to have him assassinated. Gregory of Tours notes that much gold was found in his house.

## King Chilperic's Acts of Piety

A state so ill governed could hardly command the respect of its subjects, and the tax-collectors had great difficulty in keeping the royal coffers filled with contributions in money or in kind when everyone knew that they would be put to evil use. In the reign of Chilperic I there were even strikes against taxation, accompanied by riots. The worst disorders were in Limousin:

'Now King Chilperic ordered heavy new tax-assessment to be made in all his kingdom. For which cause many left their cities and their own possessions, and sought other kingdoms, deeming it better to migrate than to remain exposed to such risk of oppression. The people of Limoges, perceiving with what a burden they were to be laden, assembled on the first of March, and would have slain Mark the referendary, who had been ordered to carry out the plan; nor could they have been prevented, had not Bishop Ferreolus delivered him from his imminent peril. The mob seized the tax-collector's lists and burned them all to ashes.' (*28*: vol. ii, pp. 200–1.)

The taxes were so unpopular that when the agents of Childebert II arrived in Tours to levy fresh contributions, even so level-headed a man as Gregory of Tours flew to the rescue of his diocesans, and insisted that the collectors abate their demands out of respect for St Martin. To add to the confusion, the Merovingian kings, their personal treasury bulging with the proceeds of the taxes levied on their subjects, were sometimes overcome by remorse and thought to perform an act of piety by burning the rolls:

'In these days [says Gregory of Tours] Chilperic the king fell sick, and no sooner was he better, than his younger son, who was not yet reborn of water and the Holy Spirit, began to ail. Perceiving him near his end, they washed him in the water of baptism. He became a little better; but his elder brother Chlodobert was now attacked by the disease. When their mother Fredegund saw him also in peril of death, she repented all too late, and said to the king: "The divine mercy hath long borne with us in our misdeeds; often have we been seized with fevers and other ills, but there hath followed no amendment. And lo! now we lose our sons; lo! now they are slain by the tears of the poor, by the lamentations of widows, by the sighs of orphans, nor is there any object now left to us for which we may amass riches. We lay up treasures without knowing for whom we gather them together. Behold now our treasures are without an owner, having the taint of things plundered and accursed. Were not our store-chambers full of wine, our granaries of corn? Were not our treasuries filled with gold, with silver and precious stones, with necklaces and other royal ornaments? And lo! now we lose that which was loveliest of all that was ours. Come, therefore, if thou wilt, let us burn all the unjust tax-lists; let that be sufficient for our treasury which sufficed thy sire, King Lothar, before us." With these words the queen, smiting on her breast with her clenched hands, bade them bring her the books which had been brought from her own cities by Mark [the referendary], and cast them into the fire; then turning once more to the king, she cried: "Wherefore delayest thou? Do now as thou seest me do, that if we must needs lose our dear children, we may at least escape eternal punishment." Thereupon the king, smitten to the heart, cast all the tax-lists into the fire, and when they were consumed, sent messengers to forbid assessment in future.' (*28*: vol. ii, pp. 205–6.)

## 'Good King Dagobert'

Actions such as this are significant, because they are the negation of the State. The bloody fratricidal wars of the late sixth century, the incapacity and the wickedness of the great who governed the Frankish kingdom, had brought it to the brink of destruction.

There are a few slight signs of improvement at the beginning of the seventh century. The edict promulgated in Paris in 614 by king Lothar II, in a general assembly of nobles and bishops, shows an apparently sincere desire to reform the State.

The strong personality of Lothar's successor, Dagobert I (629–39) impressed itself on popular memory, and legend has seized upon him.

150. Dagobert I; gold solidus
struck at Limoges.

He began well enough. He dispensed justice energetically to his subjects.
On the death of his father he inherited the whole kingdom, and in-
augurated his reign in Burgundy and Neustria by a circuit thus described
by Pseudo-Fredegar, the insipid writer responsible for continuing the
work of Gregory of Tours:

'The arrival of Dagobert aroused such fear in the prelates and nobles
settled in the kingdom of Burgundy, and the other vassals, that all
men marvelled at it; it inspired great joy in the poor people who now
obtained justice. When he came to the city of Langres, he judged so
fairly between all his vassals, between rich and poor alike, that we may
believe it to have been altogether pleasing to God; no gift and no respect
for persons was allowed to intervene; justice alone prevailed, which was
acceptable to the Almighty. Then Dagobert went to Dijon, and staying
for some days in Losne he bent his whole mind to doing justice to all
the people of his kingdom; and being filled with the desire for good
works, he neither closed his eyes in sleep nor took food, having it ever in
the forefront of his mind that all men should return home from his
presence having obtained justice.' (*63*: pp. 149–50.)

An idyllic picture, but misleading. Our author, however, naïvely
unaware of what he is doing, soon brings us back to the realities of an
age still dominated by brute force:

'On the same day when Dagobert was preparing to leave Losne for
the council at Chalon [says Pseudo-Fredegar], before dawn, as he
entered the bath, he ordered the assassination of Brodulf, the uncle of
his brother Charibert.'

264

This murder does not seem to have weighed upon the king's conscience, for the chronicler adds:

'Then Dagobert went to Chalon, where he applied his mind, in his love of justice, to completing what he had begun.'

One of Dagobert's virtues was that he surrounded himself with honest and intelligent men. Most were clerics, like Eligius (St Eloi), a talented goldsmith, who became bishop of Noyon; the referendary Dado, better known under the name of Audoinus (St Ouen), to whom the see of Rouen was assigned; and Desiderius, whom Dagobert made his treasurer before nominating him to the bishopric of Cahors:

'Desiderius [says his anonymous biographer], devoting himself diligently to the service of God amid his very arduous duties in the palace, continued day and night in prayer. His friends were men of good faith, Paul [bishop of Verdun], Arnulf [bishop of Metz], Eligius and Audoinus, by whose example and encouragement he continually strove to amend his life and rise to better things. Meantime the mild and pious King Lothar paid his debt to nature and died peacefully, leaving his son Dagobert to rule the kingdom; Desiderius became so close a friend to Dagobert that he attained higher dignity than he had reached before.

'Indeed, King Dagobert entrusted to his discretion his richest treasures and all the furnishings of the palace; under the eye of Desiderius everything that had been given to the king was stored away; at his nod everything that was to be given by the king was brought out.' (*39*: p. 97.)

And other influences too were working on King Dagobert. While he was still a minor his father had sent him to be king of Austrasia, where he governed his kingdom under the tutelage of the mayor of the palace,

151. Signature of St Eligius on a charter of Clovis II for the abbey of St Denis, dated 22 June 654.

152. The cross of St Eligius in the abbey of St Denis; from an anonymous 16th century painting, the 'Mass of St Giles'.

153. Fragment of the cross of St Eligius in cloisonné work, which stood on the high altar in the abbey of St Denis.

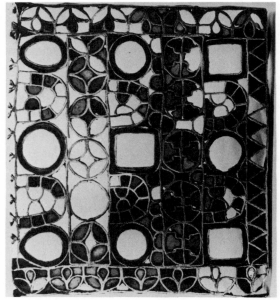

266

Pepin of Landen, and Arnulf, bishop of Metz. After the death of Lothar II these two continued his counsellors; they were the two grandfathers of Pepin of Herstal, the founder of the Carolingian house:

'From the time he began to reign up to then [i.e., till his father's death], he had availed himself chiefly of the counsels of the blessed Arnulf, bishop of the town of Metz, and Pepin, mayor of the palace, and he had exercised his kingly rule in Austrasia with such success that all men gave him the very highest praise. His power roused such fear that they were moved to surrender themselves to his sovereignty, and even the peoples settled on the borders of the Avars and Slavs besought him to attack those nations in the rear.'

The author adds that, after the blessed Arnulf's death, the king's counsellors were Pepin, mayor of the palace, and Cunibert, bishop of the town of Cologne.

But Dagobert's last years, after he had settled at Paris, belied the promise of his youth, and his biographer reluctantly admits as much:

'Returning to Neustria, Dagobert took a great liking to the residence of his father Lothar [probably Clichy], and was minded to live there permanently. And now he entirely forgot the justice he had once loved; his cupidity drove him to fall upon the possessions of the churches and his vassals, and all his cunning desire was to fill his treasuries afresh with spoils plundered from every quarter. He gave himself up to unrestrained sensuality, having three wives of the standing of queens, and many concubines. The queens were Nantechild, Vulfegund and Berchild. To include the names of the concubines would make this chronicle over-long, for they were very many. But though his heart was thus changed, as we have recalled, and his mind was withdrawn from God, yet afterwards—and please God he gained from it the true reward—he gave alms to the poor with unbounded liberality. If his greed had not stood in the way of his well-doing, it may well be thought that he would have deserved the everlasting kingdom.' (*39*: p. 89.)

Dagobert is often associated with the abbey of St Denis, though he did not found it, as is sometimes claimed; but he had a particular veneration for the famous house, which he proved by his many deeds of gift in its favour, and he was the first king of France to be buried there. With him begins the memorable history of St Denis as the burial ground of kings; and this too surely gives him a claim to the indulgence of heaven.

## The Donothing Kings

After Dagobert I the dynasty continued its progress downhill at an even faster rate. The last of the Merovingians mostly died young, and left few traces of their brief occupation of the throne. So posterity and the writers of text-books have left the specialists to unravel the tangled web of their genealogy and chronology, and without attempting to sort them out have lumped them all together under the contemptuous title of '*fainéant* kings'.

Usually these kings were under the thumb of their mayors of the palace, who combined the roles of steward of the royal household and prime minister; and the gradual rise to power of the Austrasian mayors of the palace, until with Pepin the Short they finally reached the throne, is the chief event of internal politics between 639 and 751.

Charlemagne's biographer, Einhard, has painted for all historians to come the collective portrait of the last Merovingians:

'The Franks in olden times [he tells us in the first chapter of his *Life*] used to choose their kings from the family of the Merwings, which royal line is considered to have come to an end in the person of Hilderic III, who was deposed from the throne by command of Stephen, the Roman pontiff, when his long hair was cut off and he was placed in a monastery. [It was in fact Pope Zacharias, not Stephen, who deposed Childeric III.]

'Although the line of the Merwings actually ended with Hilderic, it had nevertheless for some time previously been so utterly wanting in power that it had been able to show no mark of royalty except the empty kingly title. All the resources and power of the kingdom had passed into the hands of the prefects of the palace, who were called the "mayors of the palace", and by them the supreme government was administered. Nothing was left to the king. He had to content himself with his royal title, long hair and hanging beard. Seated in a chair of state, he used to display an appearance of power by receiving foreign ambassadors on their arrival, and by giving them on their departure, as if on his own authority, those answers which he had been taught or commanded to give.

'Thus, except his useless title, and an uncertain allowance for his subsistence, which the prefect of the palace used to furnish at his pleasure, there was nothing that the king could call his own, unless it were the profits of a single farm, and that a very small one, where was his home, and where he had such servants as were needful to wait on him, and who paid him the scanty deference of a most meagre court.

'Whenever he went anywhere he used to travel in a wagon drawn by a yoke of oxen, with a rustic oxherd for charioteer. In this manner he proceeded to the palace, and to the public assemblies of the people held every year for the dispatch of the business of the kingdom, and he returned home again in the same sort of state.' (*21*: pp. 26–8.)

It is a fanciful portrait, painted some eighty years after the last Merovingian had lost his throne, and it cannot be taken as an accurate picture of things as they were; for instance, Einhard has given long beards to the youths who succeeded one after the other to the throne. But his main object was to cast ridicule on the dynasty which the house of Pepin had supplanted.

*Part VII*

# CHRISTIAN LIFE UNDER THE MERWINGS

# 24

# RELIGIOUS FAITH AND PRACTICES

THE Merovingian period would indeed seem a melancholy age if we looked no further than the kings who held the stage and the men who ruled the Frankish kingdom in those three centuries. But there are other aspects of the time which are less misleading and more moving.

In particular, from the fourth century onwards Christianity in its Catholic form took root in Gaul and gradually won the dominating position in public and private life which it was to hold all through the Middle Ages. It is interesting to see how the new religion gradually came to permeate the whole heart and mind of the people.

We can trace its progress from the very beginning through material remains: baptisteries annexed to cathedral churches, where the bishop administered baptism with due ceremony, in early times by total immersion of the catechumens in the baptismal font; cemeteries with sarcophagi whose carvings make an interesting contrast with the decoration on the tombs of late pagan times; beautifully engraved reliquaries to house the precious relics of the saints.

## New Converts

But the psychology of the new converts makes no less absorbing a study. The people of Gaul, both the Gallo-Roman natives of the country who had begun to embrace Christianity at the end of the third century, and the barbarians, whether Frankish, Burgundian or Visigoth, who had come over to Catholicism in a body at the time of the baptism of Clovis, did not break completely with the religion of their fathers. By long habit they were still attached to pagan practices which the bishops regularly deplored when they met in synod:

'For we have learnt [said the Fathers assembled at a council at Tours in 567] that some are still to be found who cling to the ancient error and celebrate the kalends of January,[1] though Janus was a man of the heathen, perhaps a king, who could not be a god; and whoever believes in one God, the Father who reigns with the Son and the Holy Spirit, cannot be said to be wholly a Christian if over and above this belief he still keeps something of paganism. There are also those who on the feast day of St Peter's chair [22 February] offer masses for the dead and who, returning to their own homes after Mass, revert to the errors of the heathen and after receiving the body of the Lord partake of food consecrated to the devil. We call upon both pastors and priests to make it their constant care to cast out from the Church by their holy authority those whom they see persisting in this folly, or acting towards all kinds of stones or trees or springs or sacred places of the heathen in a way which does not accord with the doctrine of the Church; and not to allow any who still observe pagan customs to share in the service of the holy altar. For what is there in common between Christ and demons who do not make atonement for offences deserving judgment, but rather add to them?' (*16*: p. 133.)

In fact conversion to Catholicism did not mean that the mainly uneducated peoples of Gaul at once abandoned their accustomed habits of mind; and, even in the case of those who gave up their pagan superstitions, the most material practices of their new religion were those they adopted most readily.

## Relic-hunting

The most popular of all these practices was the pursuit of relics.

According to the hagiographers and chroniclers of Merovingian days, relics of the saints worked countless miracles; indeed the host of reliquaries which have survived from the early Middle Ages provides material evidence of the popularity of the cult.

So widespread was it that relic-hunting became a serious occupation.

---

[1] Solemn feasts of pagan Rome which celebrated the new year. Their memory persists in our New Year's Day, 1st January, which corresponds to the first day of the January kalends.

The most questionable methods were used to secure fragments of relics. The following anecdote about Gundovald, a pretender to the Frankish throne, illustrates this well. The story is particularly significant because it shows that two important figures in the second half of the sixth century, Duke Mummolus and the metropolitan bishop of Bordeaux, Bertram, were perfectly ready to compromise themselves in their efforts to secure a certain means of victory for the usurper they served:

'Seeking every means of helping forward his cause, [Gundovald] was told by some one that a certain king in the East had possessed himself of a thumb of the holy Sergius the martyr [a Syrian martyr of the third or fourth century], that he had inserted it in his right arm, and that whenever he was in straits how to drive back his enemies, putting his trust in this protection, he lifted up his right arm, and the multitude of his adversaries fled away, as though vanquished by the power of the martyr. Hearing this, Gundovald began diligently to inquire if there were anyone in that place who had succeeded in getting relics of Serbius the martyr. Thereupon Bishop Bertram told him of one Eufronius, a merchant, because he had a grudge against this man. He had once caused him to be tonsured against his will, because he coveted his possessions; but Eufronius, disdaining the act, migrated to another city, and when his hair had grown again he returned. The bishop therefore said: "There is here a Syrian, Eufronius by name, who hath made his house a church, and placed there relics of this saint, and by the saving virtue of the martyr he hath been witness of many miracles. Once the city of Bordeaux burned with a great fire, but his house, surrounded though it was by flames, was nowise touched of them." At these words Mummolus at once hurried to the Syrian's house, accompanied by Bishop Bertram; they pressed upon the man, and bade him show the sacred relics. He refused; but reflecting that a trap was perhaps being laid for him through some grudge, he added: "Trouble not an old man, nor do wrong to the saint, but take these hundred gold pieces to depart." When Mummolus still insisted on seeing the relics, he offered two hundred pieces; but even so he could not obtain his withdrawal unless the relics were displayed. Mummolus now ordered a ladder to be set against the wall (for they were hidden in a casket in the upper part of the wall over against the altar), and commanded his deacon to go up. He mounted the steps and grasped the casket, but was shaken with such trembling that none thought he would reach the ground again alive. But, as I have said, he laid hold of the casket, which was hanging from the wall, and took it down. Mummolus searched the contents, and found a bone from the saint's finger, which he did not

154

CHRISTIAN SARCOPHAGI:

154. Paris, cemetery of St Germain-des-Prés. Plaster coffin, 6th century.

155. Notre-Dame de Vie. Base of the tombstone of Bishop Boethius, who died in 604.

156. Arles. Marble. Jesus teaching the disciples.

157. Bordeaux, crypt of St Seurin. Marble, decorated with vine-branches and doves, 5th century.

158. Toulouse, St Sernin cemetery. White marble, 5th century, decorated with scenes from Meleager's hunt.

155

156

157

158

277

fear to strike with a knife; first he hacked it on the upper side, then on the lower. After many fruitless blows, the small bone remained unbroken; at length it split into three parts, which vanished in different directions; methinks it little pleased the martyr that such treatment befell it. Eufronius now wept bitterly, and all prostrated themselves in prayer, beseeching God and His grace to restore to them that which had been removed from their mortal sight. After the prayer, the fragments were found, and Mummolus, taking one of them, departed.' (*28*: vol. ii, pp. 308–9.)

The theft brought no good fortune to its perpetrators. Gundovald's campaign to secure the Frankish throne came to a tragic end at Comminges, where he sought refuge and was killed (585). As for the piratical Duke Mummolus, he was assassinated soon afterwards.

## Champions of the Ascetic Life

Still, in the number of the Merovingian Christians there were sincere neophytes too, eager to dedicate themselves body and soul to their new faith. Many, like the anchorites of the Thebaid, renounced the world and retreated to desert places to lead a life of asceticism.

They were most numerous in the sixth century, and throughout France we can still find traces of the pious recluses of Merovingian times. Round some a local cult grew up, and their memory lives on in place-names; so St Amador is commemorated in Rocamadour (Lot) St Ceneri at Saint-Céneri (Orne), St Eparchius in Saint-Cybard in Charente and Dordogne, the hermit Hospitius in the Cap de Saint-Hospice in the Cap Ferrat peninsula (Alpes-Maritimes).

Many of them have found a pious biographer. Most of these lives of the hermits are based on legend; but we have a few more reliable sources of information, in particular Gregory of Tours, and what he tells us is especially valuable because this form of asceticism gradually gave way to another kind of religious life, the life of the monastic community.

## The Hermit and his Wooden Saucepan

The life of these hermits was cruelly monotonous. Absorbed in their devotions, they lived in natural shelters or in huts built with their own hands. Wild herbs, or the vegetables they grew themselves, were all their

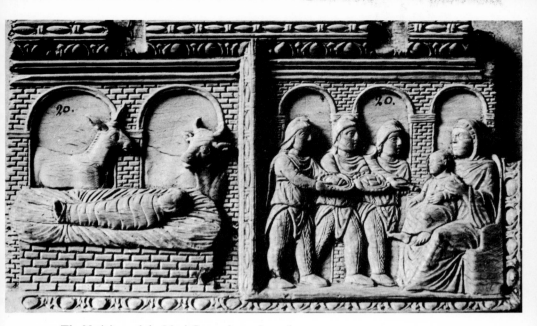

159. The Nativity and the Magi. Ivory plaque, late 5th century.

food. Such was the hermit with the wooden cauldron whom we find in the pages of Gregory of Tours:

'I remember I once heard of a man living in a deserted part of a certain region, whom his brother, living near by, came to visit with lively affection, and was received lovingly. They went into his little hut, and when they had prayed they sat down. As they talked at length about the Word of God, the old man got up from his stool and went into his little garden and gathered vegetables for their meal. Lighting a fire, he put over the flames a wooden cauldron, and filled it with water and the vegetables, and drew up the fire, making it burn so fiercely that it might have been thought the cauldron was made of bronze. When the visitor saw this, he was amazed, and asked how this was. The old man answered: "I have lived in this deserted place for many years, but at God's command I have always prepared in this cauldron the food for the refreshment of my frail body." '

As a conscientious chronicler, Gregory adds:

'This tale I once heard. And I have recently seen an abbot, who said that the man was nicknamed Ingenuus, or Artless; and he asserted that he had often eaten with him cabbage and cress cooked in that vessel. He

279

160. Reliquary from St Benoît-sur-
Loire. Gilt copper with repoussé
decoration, 7th century.

confirmed on oath that he had seen the cauldron standing over the fire
and boiling violently, and yet its base was always wet, so that it might be
thought that someone was constantly keeping it damp.' (27: p. 809.)

Gregory's scrupulous accuracy in this description has earned our
gratitude. No doubt his main purpose was to establish the authenticity
of the miracle of the wooden cauldron; but incidentally he has provided
us with some valuable details about the kind of life lived by a hermit of
his time, and this to us is the interest of his account.

## Recluses

Some hermits lived a life of even more rigorous discipline, confined in
their cells like the priest Gregory came across at Gourdon in Charolais,
who, he says, 'often put an end to fevers and toothaches by his prayers'.
(27: p. 802.) He emphasizes that the saint was a recluse, that is, he
never left his cell, and anyone who wanted him must seek him there.

So unnatural a way of life could have disastrous effects on those who
practised it, and the bishop of Tours had too much common sense and
honesty to blink the fact. He gives us an example in a chapter of his
*History* headed 'Of the anchorites who are tempted':

'Since the prince of darkness hath a thousand harmful arts, I will
relate what recently befell certain hermits and persons dedicated to God.
I have mentioned in an earlier book Winnoch the Breton, who, after he
was ordained priest, vowed himself to such abstinence that he used only

skins for clothing, and, for food, uncooked herbs of the field; while he would do no more than set the wine-cup to his mouth, seeming rather to touch it with his lip than to drink. But the pious were free-handed; he was too often given brimming cups of wine, and learned, alas! to drink beyond measure, being so overcome by his potations that he was often seen drunk.' (*28*: vol. ii, p. 358.)

## Vulfolaic, the Saint on the Pillar

Examples of this kind are rare, and in many cases a laudable spirit of emulation, a desire to equal the asceticism of the Eastern anchorites, spurred pious fanatics on to practices of excessive severity; so St Simeon Stylites, who died in 459 after spending twenty-six years of his life on top of a pillar at Antioch, found an imitator in the Ardennes at the close of the sixth century:

'Proceeding on my journey [says Gregory of Tours, who enjoyed travelling about Gaul], I reached the town of Yvois [now Carignan (Ardennes)], where I was kindly welcomed by the deacon Vulfolaic and conducted to his monastery.'

Gregory of Tours was inquisitive by nature; during his stay in the monastery it occurred to him to ask Vulfolaic, who was a Lombard by birth, how he had been converted and admitted to minor orders:

'At first he could not bring himself to tell the story, desiring with his whole heart to avoid all vainglory. But I adjured him with dread oaths, and enjoined him not to keep back any of these things that I asked, promising not to reveal to any man that which he should relate.'

161. Small reliquary in the shape of a purse. Copper with glass settings, 6th-7th century.

In the end the deacon yielded to the bishop's insistence, and Gregory of Tours proceeded to betray his confidence by repeating all his secrets in the *History*.

Was it so great a sin?

'I was still a little boy [said Vulfolaic] when I heard the name of the blessed Martin; although I knew no whit whether he was martyr or confessor, what good he had done in the world, or what region had the glory of receiving his blessed limbs in the tomb, I already used to keep vigils in his honour.'

After learning to read and write, Vulfolaic was taken on pilgrimage to St Martin at Tours by Aredius, the abbot of a monastery in Limousin. (This monastery was later called after the abbot, Yriez or Yrieix in the vernacular, and from it grew the town of Saint-Yrieix in Haute-Vienne.) The abbot collected some dust from the tomb of St Martin and put it into a small box; this box the deacon carried home, hung round his neck:

'On our arrival at his monastery in the territory of Limoges, he took the box to put it in his oratory; and the dust increased so much that it filled not only the whole box, but pressed through at any joint where it could find a way out. "From the light shed by this miracle, my heart more than ever burned to stay all its hope on the wonder-working power of the saint. I sought the territory of Trèves, and on this mountain where now thou standest I built by my own toil the dwelling which thou seest. I found here an image of Diana which the heathen people worshipped as a god. I also set up a column, on which I stood suffering great torture, with no covering for my feet. And so, when winter came, in its due course, I was in such wise pinched with the icy cold that often the severe frost made the nails drop from my toes, while frozen water hung from my beard like melted wax of candles. For this district had a name for its many hard winters." I then asked him, being very curious to know, what kind of food or drink he had and how he had cast down the idols of that mountain; and he continued thus: "My drink and my food consisted of a little bread and green vegetables, with a small measure of water. But when crowds began to flock to me from the neighbouring estates, I proclaimed without ceasing that Diana was naught, the images naught, and naught the rites which they practised; I said that the songs which they sang amidst their cups and their rank debauches were their shame. Rather let them pay worthy sacrifice of praise to Almighty God, who made heaven and earth. Moreover, I would often pray that the

162. Horn box for relics, 8th century.

Lord would vouchsafe to cast down the image and shake this people from their heathenry." '

Then the deacon told how his prayer had been granted, and the idol demolished in the teeth of opposition; his story is proof that even at the close of the sixth century paganism still had its followers.

But Vulfolaic was not yet out of his troubles:

' "But at the hour when I came home to eat [after the destruction of the idol], my whole body from my head to the soles of my feet was so covered with pustules, that there might not be found void of them even the space that a finger-tip would cover. Then I went into the church alone, and stripped myself before the holy altar. For I had there a flask of oil, which I had brought from the church of the holy Martin; and therefrom with my own hands I anointed well my every limb; and so I was laid in a deep sleep. But about midnight I awoke; and as I rose up to recite the appointed prayers I found all my body sound, as if never a sore had been seen upon me. I knew that those sores were not otherwise sent than by the malice of the Enemy." '

The end of Vulfolaic's story should be noted. Reading between the lines, we can see that even within the Catholic Church the moderates and the fanatics sometimes came into conflict:

' "And as ever in his spite he [the devil] striveth to harm those who seek God, there came now to me bishops whose duty it rather was to

283

exhort me wisely to complete the work that I had begun. But they said: 'The way which thou followest is not the right way; nor shalt thou, in thine obscurity, be compared to Simeon of Antioch, the Stylite. The situation of this place will not suffer thee to endure this torment. Come down rather, and dwell among the brethren whom thou hast gathered round thee.' At these words, because it is imputed as a sin not to render obedience to bishops, I of course came down, went with them, and likewise ate." '

But this act of submission cannot have convinced the bishop of the diocese that Vulfolaic would not go back to his pillar, and he thought it prudent to have it destroyed:

' "But on a certain day [the deacon goes on] a bishop induced me to go out to an estate at some distance; he then sent workmen with crowbars, hammers and axes, and they dashed to pieces the column on which I was wont to stand. On the next day I returned, and found all shattered, and wept sore. But I might not set up again that which they had destroyed, for fear that I might be called refractory to the orders of the bishops. Thereafter I have been content to dwell among the brethren, as now I do." ' (*28*: vol. ii, pp. 339–41.)

The decision which the deacon finally accepted, though unwillingly and only under pressure from the bishops, was certainly a wise one. His example is typical. It shows that the hermit's existence could never be anything but the exception, because it was antisocial, and even unnatural when carried to excess. It was the monastery, with its communal life, which became the usual refuge of the soul seeking holiness. From the sixth century onwards Gaul was full of religious communities, both of men and women. They became the cog-wheels not only of Christianity, but of social and economic life in the medieval world.

# 25

# THE BEGINNINGS OF MONASTIC LIFE

A SOLITARY life in the wilderness had its perils, and they were not overlooked by the more far-seeing of the Egyptian anchorites. That is why one of them, St Pachomius, judged it best to steer his companions into the coenobitical way of life, allowing his monks to live in separate cells, but requiring them to take their meals together and to pool the fruits of their labours.

This was the beginning of the monastic system, which took root in Gaul at the end of the fourth century. The first monasteries are attributed to St Martin: Ligugé near Poitiers where he settled after he was ordained priest, and then, after his elevation to the episcopate, Marmoutier where he lived with eighty disciples.

## The Abbey of Lérins

But the first monastery in Gaul to be founded on the exact lines of St Pachomius' reform was the abbey of Lérins. It was established during the first quarter of the fifth century on one of the two islands of the Lérins archipelago, two and a half miles off the coast of Cannes. Its founder, St Honoratus, who gave his name to the island, belonged to a wealthy family of northern Gaul. His life was written in the form of a sermon by his friend and compatriot St Hilary, whom Honoratus persuaded to come to Lérins, and who succeeded him as bishop of Arles.

Honoratus was converted to Christianity in the face of his parents' opposition; he was young when he left home, and with his brother Venantius and the old saint Caprasius made a long pilgrimage to the East which took them to the Peloponnese. As his biographer says, it was a stern test for the tender and delicate constitution of young men brought up in luxury. Venantius succumbed; Honoratus came back to the West in a state of exhaustion, and finally found himself on what is now the French Riviera:

'So he sought out a certain island which was uninhabited because it was so rugged, and unvisited for fear of its poisonous creatures, and which lay not far from the range of the Alps. Apart from the solitude it offered, he was attracted to the neighbourhood of Bishop Leontius, a holy man and most blessed in Christ, with whom he had ties of affection. But many tried to hold him back from this new venture; for the people round about said that it was a fearful wilderness, and did all they could, with an ambition inspired by faith, to keep him in their own country. But he found it difficult to suffer the society of other men, and longed to be cut off from the world by the straits that lay between. He had ever in his heart or on his lips . . . the promise Christ made to the disciples in the Gospels: "Behold, I have given you power to tread upon serpents and scorpions." '

He saw this saying as a prophecy, and it confirmed him in his decision:

'So he went on fearlessly, and dispelled his companions' fears by his own unconcern. The terrors of the wilderness fled; the host of serpents gave way before him.'

But there was more to do than rid the island of its dangerous denizens. He needed to make it habitable, to build dwelling-places, for though he intended to live far from the world he was eager to share his love of solitude and retirement with a few devout companions:

'By his diligence a temple for the Church's worship arose, sufficient for the needs of God's elect, and buildings suited to be the dwelling-places of monks. Water, which had been unknown there for many ages, flowed copiously, and as it welled forth it renewed two miracles of the Old Testament; for when it sprang from the rock it was sweet, amid the saltness of the sea.' (32: cols 1249–72.)

Lérins drew men from far and wide:

'All the countryside eagerly sent thither those who were seeking God.

Whosoever longed for Christ sought out Honoratus; and indeed whosoever sought out Honoratus found Christ.'

The success of his monastery was due in large measure to the saint's gift for handling men; he was an excellent psychologist:

'It is hardly to be believed with what care he saw to it that no one was afflicted by sorrow or tormented by thoughts of the world. He perceived what troubled anyone as easily as if he bore everyone's mind within his own. Moreover he ensured by kindly management that no one was weighed down by too much work, and no one grew slothful through too much inactivity. With tender care he measured out to each of the brethren their very sleep, if so it may be said.'

His solicitude was inspired and guided by a very human charity:

'Lest anything had been left undone for anyone, his mind was constantly returning to their needs: "This one feels cold; that one worries; the work is too hard for another, or the food is unsuitable; yet another has been hurt by someone else." ' (*32*: col. 1257.)

The monastery at Lérins very soon became not only the heart of the religious life of fifth-century Gaul, but the most active of its intellectual centres, a haven of learning amid the rising sea of barbarism. Men of great eminence found shelter there—St Hilary, St Valerianus, St

163. Buckle of St Caesarius' belt; ivory 6th century.

Vincent of Lérins, the polemist Salvian. St Eucherius, bishop of Lyons, always remembered with tender affection the years he had spent at Lérins with his wife and his two sons:

'Indeed I owe reverence to all those places which have been made illustrious by the holy men who have retired to them; but chiefly do I honour my beloved Lérins, which tenderly takes into her arms those who come to her as travellers shipwrecked in the storms of earthly life; and softly leads to her shady groves those who still burn from the heat of the world, that there they may recover and draw breath in the deep shadow of the Lord. Worthy indeed is she to nurture so many glorious hermits and priests who are the envy of the world!' (*22*: cols. 710–11.)

One of Lérins' most famous sons was St Caesarius, who followed St Honoratus and St Hilary as bishop of Arles in 502. He too had a deep attachment to the island where he had been grounded in the life of religion, and expressed it in a vivid metaphor in one of his sermons:

'Blessed and fortunate island of Lérins which, though small and low, has raised countless mountains to the skies.' (*14*: vol. i, p. 13.)

An outstanding theologian, he remained faithful to the ascetic ideals of his youth, and as bishop of Arles not only founded two religious communities, one for men and one for women, but was the first in Gaul to formulate rules of monastic life.

The rule for convents he drew up in 524 divided the nuns' time between the various processes of spinning and weaving, and the copying of manuscripts. It was extremely successful, and was adopted by Queen Radegund for the convent of the Holy Cross at Poitiers.

## Radegund, Queen and Nun

Radegund was a woman in love with an ideal, who saw charity as the foundation of Christian life and practised it unfalteringly; her story is profoundly moving. Thanks to the biography written by her contemporary Fortunatus, we know the saintly queen better than any other of the holy women of Merovingian times.

She was the daughter of Berthar, king of the Thuringians; she was taken prisoner when the Thuringians were overwhelmed by the Franks, and fell to the lot of King Lothar. But Fortunatus makes it clear that though she was married to a prince of this world she was not separated

164. Life of St Radegund, late 11th century manuscript. 'She was sent to the blessed Médard at Noyon' (above). 'He laid his hand on her and consecrated her deaconess'.

from the prince of heaven (25: col. 496.), and she continued to live a life of self-denial at the Frankish court. He notes that by the intervention of providence an evil chance may sometimes lead to salvation. The murder of her innocent brother was the opportunity for Radegund, as shocked by the crime as she well might be, to take the veil:

'She was sent by the king [says Fortunatus] to the blessed Medard at Noyon, and earnestly besought him to consecrate her to the Lord when she had changed her garments. But he, remembering what the apostle had said: "Art thou bound unto a wife? Seek not to be loosed," hesitated to let the queen put on the habit of a nun. Moreover nobles came and troubled the holy man, pulling him back roughly from the altar, even in the very church, to prevent his veiling the king's wife, saying that it was not meet that a priest should take away from a prince a woman who was not public property, but publicly married to him. When the holy woman knew of this, she went into the sanctuary and put on the garb of a nun and went up to the altar, addressing the blessed Medard in these words: "If thou delayest to consecrate me, and fearest man more than God, the soul of one of thy flock, O shepherd, will be required of thee." Shaken by the vehemence of her protestation, he laid his hand on her and consecrated her deaconess.' (25: col. 502.)

St Radegund retired to Poitiers, to a convent which took the name of Holy Cross from the precious relic from the East she procured for it; there she lived as the humblest of nuns, to the admiration of Fortunatus:

'While the nuns still slept she used to clean and polish their shoes, and took them back to each nun. During Lent she took a little rest only on Thursdays and Sundays. The rest of the time, except for Easter Day and the great festivals, she led always an austere life, as far as her health permitted, sleeping on ashes and wearing a hair-shirt, rising to chant hymns before the community was up. In the work of the monastery she was never content unless she was the first to give her service, and she punished herself if another was quicker than she to do some good work. When it was her turn she swept the floors and corners, cleaning whatever was dirty, first clearing away the filth, not shrinking from carrying away what others shuddered to see. . . . She brought wood in her arms, encouraging the flames by blowing on the fire and using tongs. If she fell, she never gave up even though she was hurt. She waited on the sick when it was not her week, cooking their food herself, washing the faces of those who were ill, bringing them hot water, visiting them with encouragement, and returning fasting to her cell.

165. Reliquary of the True Cross which once belonged to St Radegund. Cloisonné work, 6th century.

'Who shall tell the zeal with which she hastened to the kitchen when her week came round? When wood was needed, no nun was so willing to carry the load alone. She drew water from the well and poured it into the vessels. She cleaned cabbages, washed vegetables, and blew on the fire to revive it. She busied herself with cooking the food without fearing to scorch herself, then took the pans from the fire herself, washing the dishes and bringing them to table. When the meal was over she rinsed the plates, cleaned the kitchen and removed all the dirt, carrying all the refuse out to the appointed place.' (25: col. 507.)

## St Columbanus versus Brunhild

Gradually, but slowly, monastic life was organized. In Italy in the mid sixth century St Benedict of Nursia instituted a rule—the Benedictine rule—which towards the end of the following century outstripped all others in popularity; and in 590 an Irish monk, St Columbanus, landed on the Continent and founded many monasteries in Gaul. He laid upon them the stern rule of the monastery of Bangor in Ireland where he had

MEROVINGIAN MANUSCRIPTS:

166. The Virgin holding a cross and a censer. Gellone sacramentary, executed at Flavigny *c.* 780.

167. Zoomorphic capitals from a manuscript executed at the abbey of Corbie in the 8th century.

lived till then. The most famous of his foundations was the abbey of Luxeuil. His growing reputation brought him into collision with Queen Brunhild, the widow of Sigibert,[1] a despotic old woman who ruled her two grandsons Theudebert and Theuderic, the kings of Austrasia and Burgundy, with a rod of iron:

'By the fourteenth year of the reign of Theuderic [says the chronicler Pseudo-Fredegar] the fame of the blessed Columbanus was growing on all sides in the provinces of Gaul and Germany, and he was extolled and venerated by all; so much so that King Theuderic often came to him at Luxeuil and in all humility sought the intercession of his prayers. As he came very frequently, the man of God began to rebuke him, asking why he involved himself in adultery with concubines and did not rather enjoy the comforts of lawful wedlock; for the royal line should spring from an honourable queen, and not seem to issue from brothels. The king accepted all that the man of God said, and replied that he would abstain from all that was illicit; but then the old serpent entered into the mind of that second Jezebel, his grandmother Brunhild, and by the sting of pride roused her against the man of God. For she feared that the king would cast his concubines aside and set up a queen in his court, and so deprive her of part of her dignities and honour.' (63: p. 134.)

Brunhild's jealousy had been awakened, and St Columbanus had made himself an implacable enemy:

[1] See p. 245.

'When one day she saw him come into the courtyard, she brought to the man of God the sons who had been born to Theuderic in adultery. When he saw them, he asked what they wanted of him. Brunhild answered him: "They are the king's sons; strengthen them with thy blessing." But he replied: "Know that they will never bear the royal sceptre, for they have come forth from brothels." In fury she sent the children away. As the man of God left the king's court, just as he crossed the threshold, there was a great crash which spread terror everywhere but did not abate the wretched woman's fury.'

Brunhild's bitter enmity continued. She forced her grandson Theuderic, who was too timid not to carry out her orders, to exile St Columbanus to Besançon, and finally to expel him from the kingdom. Brunhild intended that he should return to Ireland. Abbot Jonas, who wrote a biography of the saint, gives us the details of his journey. From Nevers he was taken down the Loire, through Orleans where on the king's orders he was forbidden to visit the churches, then through Tours where his guards obligingly allowed him to turn aside to pray at the tomb of St Martin. Then he disembarked at Nantes, where, abbot Jonas tells us, he was welcomed by the highest authorities:

'Suffronius, bishop of the town of Nantes, with Count Teudoald, according to the king's command prepared to embark St Columbanus and send him to Ireland. But the man of God said: "If there is a ship returning to the territories of Ireland, let it take on board my baggage and my companions; meantime a skiff shall bear me down the Loire until I reach the open sea." So they found a ship which was loaded with Scottish merchandise, and put on board all his baggage and his companions. The ship, by the help of oars and favouring breezes, reached the high seas; but then great waves arose and forced the ship back to land, and grounded it on the beach so that it could not be moved. Then the waves ebbed and the sea was calm. The hull remained high and dry for three days. Then the captain understood that he was detained thus because of the baggage and the companions of the man of God. At length they decided to throw out of the ship all that belonged to the man of God. And immediately the great waves returned and carried the ship to the open sea. And all men marvelled, and recognized that it was not God's will that he should go back to Ireland again.' (*34*: col. 1037.)

St Columbanus was no slower than they to grasp the meaning of the miracle. We will not follow all the stages of his wanderings; but after visiting the king of Neustria, Lothar II, the sworn enemy of Brunhild, and receiving every encouragement from him, he finally arrived in Italy and founded an abbey at Bobbio, where he died.

## Tragic End of the Queen

As for Queen Brunhild, the Jezebel of Merovingian times, she met a tragic end. In 613, while she was still ruling Burgundy, after the death of her grandson Theuderic, in the name of her great-grandsons, she made a rash attack on her nephew Lothar II. This was lunacy, for her arrogance had ended by making her a host of enemies, even in her own household. Betrayed by the mayor of the palace and most of the nobility of Burgundy, she was handed over to her enemy:

'Brunhild was brought into the presence of Lothar [says the Pseudo-Fredegar], who held her in the greatest hatred. He accused her of having compassed the death of ten Frankish kings: Sigibert, and Merovech, his father Chilperic, Theudebert and his son Lothar, Lothar's son Merovech, Theuderic and the three sons of Theuderic who had just perished.[1] For the space of three days she underwent a variety of tortures. Then he ordered her to be mounted on a camel and led through the whole army. Finally she was bound by her hair, one foot and an arm to the tail of a wild horse, so that she was torn limb from limb by its hoofs in its swift career.' (*63*: p. 141.)

This forceful, headstrong queen, who so rashly measured swords with the powers of her day, has passed into legend. Her attack on the king of Neustria resulted in her death by tortures which are remembered even today; but her quarrel with St Columbanus brought a curse on her which has lasted more than ten centuries. Not until the nineteenth century were the accusations brought against her judged fairly in the light of historical criticism. Since then there has been a swing to the opposite extreme, and attempts have been made to turn her into one of the great figures of history. Where texts are few and ambiguous, it is easy enough to romanticize history.

[1] Of the ten kings Brunhild was accused of murdering, Sigibert was her husband; there is nothing to suggest that she contrived his death. Merovech, the son of Chilperic I, married her after Sigibert's death; his father Chilperic was assassinated in 584 during a hunting party. Theudebert was Brunhild's grandson, Lothar her great-grandson, and Merovech the infant son of Lothar II. Theuderic, another of her grandsons, died of dysentery, and his sons were killed on the order of Lothar II. The allegations prove nothing but Lothar's bad faith.

# THIRD INTERLUDE IN BRITAIN

## Christian Missions to Britain and Ireland

The conversion of Gaul to Christianity had been slow but steady and continuous, and the Franks, answering the call of the Gallo-Roman bishops, made no resistance to the adoption of the Catholic religion after the conquest of the country whose inhabitants to a man were Catholic. The conversion of the British Isles was a very different matter and forms a drama in several acts, many of which are intimately concerned with Gaul also.

The church had already been established in Britain while the Roman Empire still flourished. There were three British bishops—those of Eboracum, Londinium and Lindum—present at the Council of Arles in 314; but Christianity ceased to gain headway in the following century because of the weakening of the Roman occupation and the invasion by the Anglo-Saxons who remained firmly attached to their pagan gods. On the other hand, the sister island of Eire had been converted at about the same period. What St Martin was to Gaul St Patrick was to Ireland. (Significantly, St Martin was neither a Gaul nor a Frank and St Patrick was not an Irishman; nevertheless from about the year 425 Ireland became the 'isle of Saints' as a result of Patrick's mission.)

The biography of this saint, which is largely legendary, bears witness to the fervour of the cult which grew up around his memory in Ireland at an early date:

'Saint Patrick was a prisoner of the Scots of Ireland [says Nennius in the *History of the Britons*]. His master was one Milchu, and made him a swineherd. Now in his sixteenth year he came to Britain from captivity, and by the will of God learned the Holy Scriptures and journeyed to Rome, where he stayed a long time studying in books for closer knowledge of the mysteries of God and the Holy Scriptures. Now, when he had been there seven years, Palladius was sent by Celestinus, bishop and pope of Rome (422–32) to be the first bishop among the Scots and to convert them, but God prevented him from so doing by sending many storms at sea to prove that no man can accept anything of this world unless it has been confirmed by the will of heaven. So, the said Palladius abandoned his mission to Ireland and arrived in Britain to die in the country of the Picts.

'When news came of the death of the Bishop Palladius, another envoy, Patrick, was sent to the Scots to convert them to the faith of Christ, in the consulate of Theodosius and Valentinian (425) by Pope Celestinus above-named; and an angel of God by name Victor, on the advice and counsel of Germanus, the Holy Bishop. . . . There the saint, foreknowing all that should happen to him, received the episcopal dignity from king Amatheus and took the name of Patrick, for hitherto he had been called Maun; Auxilius and Iserinus together with others of lower rank were ordained at the same time as he.

'Having received benediction and having accomplished all things in the name of the Holy Trinity, he fitted out a ship and journeyed to Britain; but did not preach there long, for having prepared all things necessary he was ordered by an angel to cross the sea to Ireland in a very fast ship with a favourable wind. The ship was laden with marvellous gifts of foreign origin as well as spiritual treasures, and when it had brought him to Ireland he baptized those who dwelt there.

'St Patrick preached the Gospel of Christ to the nations for forty years. He wrought miracles as did the Apostles, giving sight to the blind and curing the lepers, making the deaf hear and casting out evil spirits from the bodies of the possessed. He also brought back to life nine dead men, and out of his own pocket ransomed many prisoners of both sexes from the pirates. He read 365 books and more; he founded as many churches. He consecrated upwards of 365 bishops, in whom was the spirit of God. He ordained about 3,000 priests and converted 12,000 people to the faith of Christ in the province of Connaught alone, and baptized them. In one day, he baptized seven kings who were the sons of Amolgith. He fasted forty days and forty nights on the peak of the Hill of Cruachan. On that hill, which towered up into the sky, he sent up three prayers in his piety for the salvation of those who had taken the faith in Ireland.

'From this high mountain, he sent down a blessing on all the people of Ireland and if he climbed up there at all, he did it the better to pray for them and see the fruit of his labour. After that, countless bright coloured birds came to him for his blessing as a sign that all the saints of Ireland, both male and female, would come flocking to him on the Day of Judgment as if to follow their father and mother when the Judgment is given. At last, after a pious old age, he journeyed onward to heaven, where he enjoyed eternal felicity. Amen.'

The tone and the pace of this biography bear witness to the prestige which St Patrick enjoyed in Ireland. His example was catching and the fifth and sixth centuries in the country were marked by an upsurge of piety which manifested itself in an extraordinary development of monasticism. This religious impulse also found its outlet in a highly original form of mysticism, sometimes to the point of eccentricity as we see in the famous and poetic account of the voyage of St Brendan the Navigator, one of the most popular Irish saints.

His biographer tells us how the saint and fourteen of his disciples took ship in quest of the promised land in a boat which they built themselves, and in it they sailed from island to island. A shepherd, whom they met on one of the islands, mapped out their route for them:

' "This night you shall make a landfall in the next island to this and you shall stay there until the sixth hour of the day and sail then on to another neighbouring island to the west, which is called the Island of Birds. You will stay until the octave of Pentecost." Then St Brendan began again to ask him questions about the sheep which appeared everywhere in the island, asking how they had grown so big for, indeed, they were the size of oxen. And the man said: "There is nobody here to milk them in all the island and during the winter the bad weather doesn't trouble them, so they can stay day and night grazing on the pastures. And that is why they are larger than the sheep that grow in your country." After having had this speech with the man and received his blessing, Brendan and his disciples set sail in their boat for the next island which had been shown them.

'When they drew near to the shore, the boat stopped of its own accord for them to get out. So then Brendan ordered the Brothers to jump into the sea and tow the boat by the painter to the spot where he wished to moor it. And that is what they did do. Now this island was covered with rough hairs, so there wasn't so much as a blade of grass or a grain of sand on the shore. Now, when the Brothers had spent the night on the island praying and keeping watch, Brendan stayed in the boat alone, for well he knew what that island was; Almighty God, whose will all creatures obey, had caused a whale to raise his back up out of the sea to make a habitable place where his servants could spend the night on the Feast of the Resurrection. And for this reason the man of God was unwilling to tell his companions the real nature of the place where they were to pass the night, lest fear should cloud their faith.

'Morning came, the pious pastor ordered all the priests to sing Mass, which they did. However, while Brendan was celebrating Mass in his boat itself, his companions began to unload the meat and fowls which they had brought from the last island in order to salt some of them down and cook the rest on dry land. They put the cauldron on a fire which they had kindled, and no sooner had it begun to boil than the island began to quake. Seeing which, the Brothers rushed towards the boat imploring the help of their leader. Then the man of God having helped them one by one into the boat, they abandoned everything that they had left on the island and set sail once more. Meanwhile, the island began to swim away from them and they could still see the fire burning on it at a distance of two leagues. Then the holy man revealed the secret and told them what the island really was: "Brothers, do you not wonder at this island moving across the face of the ocean?" The Brothers answered him, "Indeed, we are filled with admiration and at the very sight of this island we were seized by a great fear." But he said to them: "My children, fear not, for God has revealed to me this night in a vision the mystery of this thing. The place where you landed was not an island but a fish, the greatest of all beings that swim. Continually he tries to touch his head with his tail, but is prevented from doing so by his very length. His name is Casconius."

'Later, they discovered a very delightful island full of grass and flowers and fruit trees. When they were looking for a harbour to land at, they found at the south of the island a stream of fresh water emptying into the sea, and there they moored their boat. When they had landed, St Brendan ordered the Brothers to haul the boat as far on land as they could so as not to be at the mercy of the current. Now, the width of the river was about the length of a boat. The Brothers did as the Holy Father commanded and hauled the boat right up to the spring from which the stream took its source. Thus said Brendan to the Brothers: "Behold our Saviour Jesus Christ has given us a place to stay over the Feast of his Holy Resurrection. Indeed, he is kind and compassionate. Brothers, even had we nothing else to restore us bodily, this spring would suffice to feed us and give us drink."

'There was above the spring a tree of prodigious height and covered with snow-white birds so densely that the branches could hardly be seen through it, and at this sight the man of God began to ponder to himself why there should be such a great multitude of birds assembled at that tree. And the thought caused him such unease that in his need to dispel the object of his doubt he burst into tears saying: "Oh God, thou who knowest the secret places of the heart and to whom hidden things are revealed, thou knowest the anguish of my heart. Therefore, I pray thy majesty to deign in great compassion to tell me the hidden secret of this flock of birds. Not that I boast of my dignity or merit to obtain this answer, but I only ask it humbly as a favour to be rid of this doubt which has tormented me."

'Now while this man of heavenly longings was deliberating with himself, one of the birds flew down from the tree, and the sound of his wings beating against the boat was like bells. Then, perching on the prow of the boat, it began to clap its wings together as a sign of inner joy and bent on the man of God a look full of sweetness. And he immediately perceived that God had answered his prayer, and said to the bird: "Since thou art the servant and the messenger of God, tell us where you came from and why such a great multitude of birds is assembled in this place." The bird answered: "We are they who during the great fall of the Adversary of God were not exactly his accomplices, but being partially so we have incurred our own disgrace. For God is just, being the source of truth and mercy. Therefore following his judgment he has placed us here where we have but one punishment to suffer, that of being deprived of His presence. It has sufficed for him to remove us from the society of them who have held fast in the faith. On Sundays and high days we put on bodies such as you see here and we remain here praising our Creator. Like the other spirits that roam the earth and the sea we may wander at will. But as for you and the brethren, you have now been on your travels for a whole year, and they will continue for the space of six years more. And during all the years of your pilgrimage you will keep the Feast of Easter at the same place where you are keeping it now, and not until later will you find the goal on which you have set your hearts, that is, the promised land of the saints." And so saying the bird spread his wings and flew over the prow of the ship back to his companions roosting in the tree.'

The mysticism and the spirit of independence which were characteristic of the religious life of Ireland as well as of the Cornish Christians and Welsh religious communities were retained by those who emigrated to Armorica: but they were quite foreign to the temperament of the Anglo-

Saxons, who remained faithful to their own religious traditions. So the Britons of the former Roman province never converted the invaders (with whom they were in direct, and mostly hostile, political contact), and it was not until the end of the sixth century that Pope St Gregory the Great undertook the heavy task of evangelization.

The zeal exercised by the pope in this difficult task has impressed all the historians of the English race, and, most gifted of them all, the Venerable Bede felt sure enough of his facts to record a curious anecdote, which, even if it is legendary, serves to explain and illustrate the personal interest which Gregory took in Bede's countrymen.

'We must not be silent concerning a story about the blessed Gregory which has been handed down by our forefathers and is preserved to this day. It shows us the reason why he showed so much zeal and devotion to the salvation of our people. The story goes that on a certain day after the arrival of a convoy much merchandise was exposed for sale in the market so that a large number of would-be buyers were come together, among them the said Gregory; now he had seen that among other goods there were slaves up for sale with surprisingly white skins, beautiful features and magnificent heads of hair. Having looked them up and down he asked from what country or province they had been brought, and the answer was that they came from the isle of Britain where the people all looked like them. Then he asked if the islanders were Christian or whether they were yet bound to heathen error. And the answer was that they were still heathen. Then he sighed heartily and exclaimed: "Alas, what sorrow to think that men so fair of face should be subject to the Prince of Darkness and that such graceful countenances should mask souls destitute of grace." And again he asked what was the name of their nation. On being told that they were Angles, "That is well," said he, "for they have angels' faces, and such men must partake of the inheritance of the angels in heaven; what is the name of the province from which they came?" The answer was, from that kingdom which is called Deira. "Good again," said he: "Let them be snatched away from anger [de ira] and dedicated to the mercy of Christ. But who is the king of that province?" "Alle" [Aelle] was the answer. Then, playing on the name, he exclaimed: "Alleluia! The praise of God the creator shall be sung in that country." '

(This passage of punning rhetoric, in whatever form he received it, seems to have made a great impression on Bede.)

Once elected pope of all Christendom, Gregory lost no time in turning his talents to the conversion of the Saxons of Britain. Having established the fact that British priests (no doubt that is what is meant by 'local clerics') showed little zeal in converting the invaders to whom they were still hostile, he turned for the fulfilment of this delicate task to Roman monks, and the mission which he sent to Britain was led by Augustine, prior of the convent of St Andrew on Monte Celio.

About Easter 597 the little band landed on that very island of Thanet at the mouth of the Thames where the first Anglo-Saxon invaders had landed a hundred and forty years earlier. The choice of the kingdom of Kent was a happy one, as has been emphasized, because the local king Ethelbert had married a Christian princess Bertha, the daughter of the Frankish king Caribert. Ethelbert in his turn was converted and received baptism on Whitsunday the same year at Canterbury. He gave up his 'palace' there for Augustine's use. Not long after, the latter was consecrated bishop, and the following Christmas he baptized more than ten thousand Anglo-Saxons. Thereafter he organized the young Church of England according to exact orders sent him by Pope Gregory. Before his death he consecrated Mellitus, the first bishop of London, where a church dedicated to St Paul the Apostle had been founded.

The conversion of the northern kingdoms of Northumbria by the missionary bishop Paulinus took place in the first third of the seventh century. King Edwin, who had espoused the princess Ethelburga (Tate), a Christian and the sister of the king of Kent, consented to baptism, but being more intellectually inclined than Clovis, the Frankish king, he wished for enlightenment about his new faith and he invited the pagan high priest and several nobles of his realm as well as Paulinus to a debate as to the justice of his change of faith.

Bede the Venerable, to whom we owe a full account of these deliberations, has summed up the bitter words of the high priest and the touching allegory suggested by one of the local chieftains:

'The king, having declared his intention of adopting the faith that Paulinus taught, added nevertheless that he would consult the chief men of his realm and his counsellors so that if they were of one mind with him in the matter, all would equally devote themselves to Christ as the fountain of life, and with the consent of Paulinus he was as good as his word. Having assembled the wise men of his council, he put it to each of them in turn that they should speak their minds about this hitherto unheard of doctrine, and of the new cult of the Godhead which was being preached.

'Immediately the high priest was the first to answer: "You can see for yourself, O King, the merits of that which is now being preached to us. As for me, I confess in all honesty one thing which I now learn for certain: which is, that the religion that we have all practised hitherto is entirely without virtue, or indeed use. There is no man of your following who has devoted himself with more zeal to the cult of our gods, yet nevertheless many men have received greater favours at your hands and higher dignities, while their affairs prosper more and their wealth increases. Now if the old gods had power indeed, it is me whom they would favour since I have made greater efforts to serve them. It follows then that if you have considered after due reflection that the new things which are now being preached are better and of more help, we shall hasten to adopt them without further delay."

'Another of the leading men having concurred with the opinion of the high priest and his sage comments, declared for his own part: "It seems to me, O King, that the life of all men here on earth is like the weather which none of us can forecast. When you are sitting feasting with your nobles and counsellors in the winter time and the fire is lit down the middle of the hall while without the wind rages and cold rain falls mingled with snow, a sparrow might find its way into the hall and fly down it from end to end; it comes in at one door and goes out by another. Now while he is inside the building, he is sheltered from wintry storm, but once that moment of calm is passed he passes out again into the winter night and beyond the range of your vision. Such or nearly so is the life of man. All that which came before and all that which is to come we know nothing about whatever. Therefore, if this new teaching will bring us any measure of certainty about these things, we would do well to fall in with it." '

This debate had decisive results. It was concluded by the high priest himself leaping on to a stallion and riding up to the heathen temple at which he threw a spear in sign of contempt for those very gods whose servants he had been. Then on the following Easter Day (627) King Edwin received baptism at York with all the nobles of his court and a great number of subjects. This baptism of an Anglo-Saxon king followed by that of a great mass of people seems to follow exactly the same pattern as the baptism of Clovis.

*Part VIII*

# THE RISE OF THE CAROLINGIANS
# AND CHARLEMAGNE

# 26

# THE DECLINE OF THE MERWINGS
# AND CHARLES THE HAMMER

## *Anarchy in the Palace*

THE decline of the Merovingians begins with the death of Dagobert in 639. He has been called the most brilliant of his dynasty, and the last. After him came an eclipse of the Frankish royalty, and—what was far more serious—a period of complete anarchy. The very unity of the Frankish kingdom was in jeopardy, with the aristocracy of the three great regions of the kingdom, Neustria, Austrasia and Burgundy, quarrelling for the sovereign power wielded by the mayors of the palace; and during this period the south-western region of Gaul, Aquitaine, won an independence which was still hers under the Carolingians.

Unfortunately this is one of the worst documented periods in French history. We have no day-to-day record such as Gregory of Tours provides for the sixth century, and the colourless continuation of the *History of the Franks* by the chronicler whom the sixteenth century miscalled Fredegar stops short in 640. Our curiosity has to make do with the dry bones of history supplied by writers who continued his work even less successfully than he, among them the author of the pathetic compilation known as the *Liber historiae Francorum*, written at the abbey of St Denis in 727.

Meagre and colourless as these texts are, we shall quote one or two of them to give the reader some idea of the confusion which reigned in the Frankish kingdom down to the beginning of the eighth century, and of the inadequacy of the documentation we have for the period.

When he comes to the second half of the seventh century, the monk of St Denis offers us an explanation of the evils which were to befall the kingdom:

'At that time [he tells us] Clovis, son of Dagobert, cut off the arm of the blessed Denis, at the instigation of the devil.'

And after the cause, the effect:

'And at that time the kingdom of the Franks fell into ruin after catastrophic disasters.' (*44*: p. 3.)

## Ebroin and St Leodegar

But it is no good expecting the author of the *Liber historiae Francorum* to give us a coherent account of these disasters. All he provides is a few details of the ambitions and quarrels of a succession of mayors of the palace who controlled the whole kingdom through their puppet-kings. Against this drab backcloth one figure stands out—Ebroin, mayor of the palace of Neustria, who held the stage for more than twenty years:

'At that time [says the chronicler], Erchinoald, mayor of the palace, having died, and the Franks being vacillating and uncertain, they finally decided to raise Ebroin to the dignity of mayor of the palace in the king's court.' (*44*: pp. 317–18.)

He was too brutal and despotic a man not to rouse violent hatred. A few lines further on, the author tells how the Franks rebelled against his cruelty:

'At that time [he says, without giving an exact date], the Franks plotted against Ebroin, and rose against Theuderic [the king, and the creature of the mayor of the palace] and deposed him, and forcibly cut the hair of both. They tonsured Ebroin and sent him to the monastery of Luxeuil in Burgundy.'

But the fiery Ebroin was not content to stay mouldering in the cloister. He seized his chance in one of the palace revolutions so frequent in those troubled times and left prison:

'Ebroin, letting his hair grow again, gathered his companions to his aid, and leaving the monastery at Luxeuil in warlike fashion returned to Francia [that is, Neustria] with a display of armed force. He asked the blessed Audoinus [bishop of Rouen, and an influential man] to counsel

168. Monogram of Ebroin.

him; but the saint only sent him by messengers a writing which said simply: "Remember Fredegund." Ebroin was quick-witted enough to understand this password. He rose during the night, collected an army, and coming to the River Oise killed the guards and crossed the river at St Maxence; there he slew all those of his enemies he could find. Leudesius [Erchinoald's son] fled with king Theuderic and many companions; Ebroin pursued them, and coming to the villa of Baizieux [near Corbie (Somme)] he seized the royal treasure. Then coming to Crécy (in Ponthieu) he received the king. He summoned Leudesius treacherously, having pledged him his word, and killed him. He then cleverly regained possession of the post of mayor of the palace. He ordered Leodegar to be killed by the sword, after various tortures.'

The chronicler of the *Liber Historiae Francorum* does not dwell on this murder, though it made a considerable sensation; but he was a Neustrian, and Leodegar, bishop of Autun, was a notable in the kingdom of Burgundy, where he was for some time mayor of the palace. In any case it is hard to tell whether Leodegar was a saint or simply an ambitious politician. It seems likely, though, that it was the frightful and prolonged torture he suffered at the hands of Ebroin which won him the honours accorded to a martyr. He became the patron saint of many Burgundian churches. One of his biographers gives us a detailed account of his sufferings:

'The blessed Leodegar desired to end his life with his brother [who had been stoned to death], so that together they might be found worthy to share the blessed life to come. But the tyrant Ebroin, wishing to delay his death, . . . ordered him to be made to walk through a pool in which were stones with cutting edges like sharp nails. Then in his cruelty he ordered that his lips and the hollow part of his face should be cut away and his tongue torn out with a cutting iron; so that with his eyes put out,

309

his feet pierced through, and his tongue and lips cut away, when he perceived that he was deprived of all happiness, and that all his physical faculties were denied to him, since he could not see his path with his eyes, nor follow it with his feet, nor praise his Creator with his tongue by celebrating the office before men—that when he perceived this, he should despair and fall into blasphemy, and so deprive himself of the salvation which he would have deserved from heaven in full measure by praising [God].'

But Ebroin had miscalculated, as the hagiographer goes on to show. He handed his victim over to one of his cut-throats named Waringus, who was well fitted by temperament for his butcher's work; he was to keep Leodegar in his own house:

'As his lodging was a great way off, they put the holy martyr of God on a miserable pack-horse. When he perceived that all was done, his mind seized on the verse of the psalm: "I am become as a beast before thee: and I am always with thee." And though he had neither lips nor tongue he could not cease from praising God, and his spirit echoed a hymn of devotion that came from his inmost heart. Seeing him thus bloodstained, all believed for that reason that he would give up the ghost. One of our brethren, an abbot by name Winobertus, having followed the said saint to the lodging, besought his guards to let him come to him secretly. He found him lying in straw, covered with a tattered piece of tent-cloth, his breath feeble. And even while he believed the saint to be dying, he found himself witnessing an unhoped for miracle; for as the saint spat blood, his tongue which had been cut out and no longer had lips began to speak as it had been accustomed.' (*42*: col. 361 f.)

We need not follow the author of the *Life* of the saint through all the sufferings which dragged on for two years before the torturers finally executed their victim.

The martyrdom of St Leodegar was not only a crime; it was a political mistake, for the scandal it created added to the unpopularity of Ebroin:

'Ebroin oppressed the Franks ever more cruelly [says the author of the *Liber historiae Francorum*], until at length the Frank Ermenfred secretly prepared a plot. Falling on the aforesaid Ebroin without warning by night, he killed him ruthlessly, and escaped by flight to Pepin in Austrasia.' (*44*: p. 320.)

## The Beginnings of a Dynasty

The chronicler does not give the date of this assassination, which was probably between 680 and 683. The protector to whom the murderer fled for asylum was Pepin of Herstal. We have seen in chapter 23 that at the beginning of the seventh century the Austrasian aristocracy wielded a good deal of political influence. The aristocracy continued to flourish during the century, and it was one of its members who profited from the fall of Ebroin. Pepin the Young, also called Pepin of Herstal from the name of one of his largest properties (near Liège, in Belgium), was the son of Ansegis, and Ansegis was the son of the famous bishop of Metz, St Arnulf. Pepin's mother, Begga, was the daughter of Pepin of Landen, who had been a mayor of the Austrasian palace. Pepin of Herstal had in fact illustrious forbears, and he seems himself to have been energetic and clear-headed; unfortunately our sources are so regrettably scanty that we cannot build up a picture of him.

After the death of the redoubtable Ebroin, Pepin contrived to get rid of his other rivals one by one. The last to be eliminated was the mayor of the palace of Neustria, Berthar:

'Pepin, coming up out of Austrasia and collecting a great army, marched against King Theuderic and Berthar. They met in battle at a place called Tertry [commune of Ham (Somme)], and while they fought King Theuderic, with Berthar the mayor of the palace, took to flight. Pepin was left victorious. In the days that followed, Berthar was killed by time-serving adherents of Pepin, and then at the instigation of Ansfleda [the widow of Berthar's predecessor as mayor of the palace], Pepin began to be the chief mayor of the palace to King Theuderic.'

Behind the bare bones of this brief entry we can guess at the intrigues of a court where the king was no more than a puppet, where assassination was still the usual form of government, where women still played a leading part, as in the time of Fredegund and Brunhild; this last characteristic of political life under the Merovingians faded out as the Carolingians climbed to power.

By clever political manoeuvring, Pepin the Young succeeded in restoring in his own person the unified government of the whole Frankish kingdom, though he kept the façade of kingship, illusory as this was. Unfortunately we know very little about his mayoralty, which lasted until 714. Unlike most of his predecessors, he lived to be eighty and died in his bed instead of being assassinated:

311

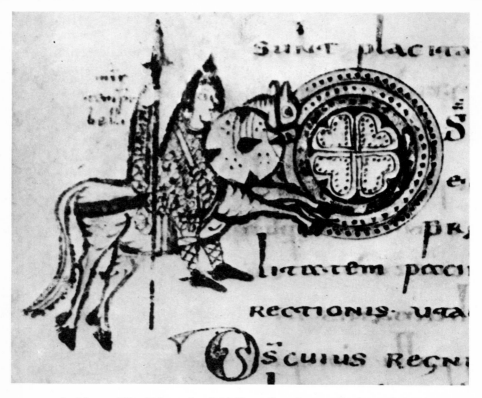

169. Mounted Frankish warrior. Initial letter from the mass for those going to war.

'At that time [writes the author of the *Liber historiae Francorum*], Pepin was seized by a violent fever and died. He had held the chief office under the aforesaid kings[1] for twenty-seven and a half years.' (*44*: p. 325.)

## The Rise of Charles the Hammer

Pepin's legitimate sons had predeceased their father, and the crisis which followed his death was resolved by his son by a concubine named Alpais. The *Liber historiae Francorum* ends with the accession to the mayoralty of this son, who was no other than Charles Martel:

'At this same time the said Charles, gathering an army, went out again against Chilperic [II, the Merovingian king] and Ragamfredus [mayor of the palace of Neustria]. They collected an army against him,

[1] The Merovingians who appear earlier in the *Liber historiae Francorum*.

312

and hastily prepared for war; but Charles sought peace with them. They refused, and joined battle with him at a place called Vinchy, at daybreak on Sunday, the twelfth day of the April Kalends [21st March 718] in Lent. After fierce fighting, Chilperic and Ragamfredus took to flight, leaving Charles victorious. Laying waste the country round and taking prisoners, he returned to Austrasia with much booty, and coming to the city of Cologne he stirred up rebellion. He entered into discussion with Plectruda [widow of Pepin the Young, and stepmother to Charles] and cleverly recovered his father's treasures, and then set up a king by name Lothar.' (*44*: pp. 326–6.)

Soon after this the position became clearer. Charles Martel, having got rid of all his rivals, was left in sole possession of the mayoralty of the palace for the whole kingdom, and became its effective ruler. The two puppet kings, Lothar IV and Chilperic II, died one after the other, and the monk of St Denis ends his book with these words, from which we can date its composition:

'The Franks set Theuderic, son of Dagobert the Young, as king over them, who had been reared in the monastery of Chelles; he is now in the sixth year of his reign [727].'

## *The First Battle of Poitiers*

Rightly or wrongly, Charles Martel, the real founder of the Carolingian royal house, has become for posterity the hero of the victory won over the Saracens at Poitiers.

A recent historian of Moslem Spain, Levi-Provençal, has given a detailed account of the Moslem expeditions into Gaul, showing that they fall within the short period between the occupation of the Iberian peninsula in 710 and the foundation of the Empire of Cordova in 756. Had the Moslems' rapid conquests fired them with the ambition to establish themselves in Gaul as they had established themselves in Spain? Levi-Provençal thinks it unlikely. More probably their raids into Gaul were inspired by cupidity, a spirit of adventure, and their eagerness to wage a holy war (*Djihad*) on the Infidel.

The first of these raids came very shortly after the conquest of Spain. It was led by Al-Samh, governor of Spain, in 721, and reached the gates of Toulouse; its consequences would have been serious if Eudo, duke of Aquitaine, had not vigorously attacked the invaders and repulsed them. A chronicle written in southern France, at Moissac, describes the campaign briefly but accurately:

'Soma, king of the Saracens, nine years after they had entered Spain besieged Narbonne and took it, and ordered the men of the city to be put to the sword; but he led the women and children captive into Spain. And in the third month of the same year, they marched to besiege Toulouse. While they were besieging it, Eudo, prince of Aquitaine, came out against them with an army of Aquitainians and Franks, and joined battle with them. And when the battle began, the army of the Saracens took to flight, and the greater part of the army perished there by the sword.' (*43*: vol. i, p. 58, n.1.)

Flushed with victory, Duke Eudo at once reported the defeat of the infidels to Pope Gregory II, and the biography of the pope in the *Liber Pontificalis* gives an account of it which was inspired by the duke and no doubt much exaggerated:

170. Moslem horseman. Shroud of St Carilefus, 7th century Syrian fabric.

'At the same time the abominable race of the sons of Agar, who had overrun the province of Spain and occupied it for ten years, attempted in the eleventh year to cross the river Rhone and occupy the Frankish lands where Eudo ruled. He mobilized the Franks against the Saracens, who were surrounded and destroyed. 375,000 (*sic*) were killed in one day, as is reported in a letter from the said Eudo duke of the Franks, to the pontiff. Only 1,500 of the Franks are said to have been killed in that battle. The duke adds that the year before he had received from the said pontiff three sponges which had been blessed for the use of the papal table; and at the moment when battle was joined the same Eudo, prince of Aquitaine, had distributed them in small pieces to his men, and not one of those who had had a piece was wounded or killed.' (*45*: vol. i, p. 401.)

Despite all this publicity, the campaign of 721 and Duke Eudo's victory were eclipsed by the 732 campaign, and the Battle of Poitiers, whose hero was Charles Martel, has become one of the great dates in French history.

It is not without interest to compare some of the contemporary accounts of this famous feat of arms. Here first of all is the second of the chroniclers who continued Fredegar, an Austrasian of Charles Martel's household:

'Duke Eudo, seeing that he was defeated and become a laughing-stock, stirred up the treacherous Saracen people against Prince Charles and the Frankish nation. Under their king, Abdirama by name, they crossed the Garonne and came to the town of Bordeaux. They burnt down the churches and slew the inhabitants, and then came to Poitiers; they burnt the church of St Hilary—grievous is it to tell—and purposed to destroy the house of the blessed Martin. But Prince Charles boldly drew up his army in battle array, and flung himself on them valiantly. With Christ's help he overthrew their tents, and hastened after them in the battle to destroy them. And when their king Abdirama had been slain, he overwhelmed their army and utterly defeated them. And so he triumphed victoriously over his enemies.' (*26*: p. 175.)

Here the chronicler has turned the limelight full on Charles Martel, and alludes caustically to the alleged treachery of the duke of Aquitaine, who had many times quarrelled with the great mayor of the palace. The author of the Moissac Chronicle says nothing of this, and in fact maintains that Eudo, in the face of the Saracen invasion which was threatening to outflank him, appealed to Charles, as a loyal vassal should, to contain it:

'In the year 732 Abderaman, king of Spain, crossing over by way of Pampeluna and the Pyrenees with a great army of Saracens, besieged the city of Bordeaux. Then Eudo, prince of Aquitaine, collected an army and came out against them and they fought by the River Garonne. But as soon as the battle began the Saracens were victorious. Eudo fled, and lost the greater part of his army; and so the Saracens straightway began to lay waste Aquitaine. But Eudo, coming to Charles the prince of the Franks, asked help of him. Then Charles gathered a great army, and went out to meet them; battle was joined, and the Saracens were vanquished by the Franks in a suburb of Poitiers; and there King Abderaman fell with his army in the battle; and those that were left of them fled back to Spain. But Charles collected the spoils and returned with great triumph and glory to Francia.' (*43*: p. 62, n.5.)

It should be noted that the chronicler of Moissac gives a number of precise and accurate details about the Saracen advance and the preliminaries to the battle which are lacking in the first account. On the other hand, he omits any mention of the burning of the basilica of St Hilary at Poitiers, and of the Saracen threat to St Martin of Tours. Possibly the devotion of southerners for these two great saints was rather less fervent than that accorded to them by Austrasians and Neustrians.

If we piece together the information we can glean from the many chronicles, both Latin and Arabic, which make mention of the Battle of Poitiers, and from archaeological evidence too, it seems probable that it was fought in October 732, not in a suburb of Poitiers, as the author of the Moissac Chronicle claims, but some $12\frac{1}{2}$ miles to north-east of the town, near a Roman road running between Chatellerault and Poitiers, and most likely at Moussais-la-Bataille, whose name may well commemorate the engagement.

# 27

# PEPIN THE SHORT

THE Battle of Poitiers was not the end of the struggle against the Saracens; but it is all too easy for posterity to over-simplify history, and a second campaign which Charles Martel undertook in 737 has been left in the shadows. Though it was perhaps less spectacular than the first, it was more decisive, for it successfully drove the Moslems from Languedoc. But even then Gaul was not entirely free of her redoubtable foemen. Clinging to the shores of the Mediterranean, the Saracens still kept their grip on Provence, and La Garde-Freinet was a haunt of Saracen pirates until the end of the tenth century.

In fact the greatest achievement of Charles Martel was that he restored unity to the Frankish kingdom by waging war on enemies within as well as without. He was a great fighter, and won decisive victories, and yet his reputation has been overshadowed by that of his immediate successors. The explanation of posterity's ingratitude lies in his treatment of the Church. He paid little attention to anything but material power, and seems to have been blind to spiritual values. The Church of his day was wealthy, and he had no scruples about confiscating her property and distributing it to his warriors. Often too the ecclesiastical offices to which this property was attached suffered the same fate, and were bestowed on ambitious and grasping laymen in no way qualified to fill them. This contributed in large measure to the destruction of ecclesiastical discipline and the spiritual degradation of the Frankish clergy.

## The Crisis in the Church

St Boniface, the apostle of Germany, has left us this picture of the Frankish Church at the death of Charles Martel. Carloman, brother of Pepin the Short, had urged the saint to restore religion within his kingdom; the difficulties of the task appalled Boniface, and in 742 he wrote to Pope Zacharias setting before him the desperate plight of the Frankish Church and appealing for his support and collaboration:

'Be it known to you, Holy Father, that Carloman, duke of the Franks, has called upon me to summon a synod in that part of the Frankish kingdom which is under his dominion, and has assured me that he wishes to correct and amend the ecclesiastical discipline which for a long time, not less than sixty or seventy years, has been trodden underfoot and scattered to the winds.' (*11*: col. 745.)

He goes on to give concrete examples of the decadence of the Church:

'The Franks, so the elders among them say, have not held a synod for more than eighty years, nor had archbishops, nor have the churches conferred canonical rights on anyone in the churches, nor removed them. But for the most part the episcopal sees in the cities have been given over to greedy laymen, or to adulterous clerks, fornicators and publicans, and used for worldly enjoyment.'

Then he goes into details, to show how urgently the pope's backing is needed for the reform that is so essential:

'If I find among those they accuse deacons living since childhood in constant debauchery, constant adultery, and in all kinds of filthiness, who have come to the diaconate with this reputation; and having four or five or even more concubines in their bed at night, even when they have become deacons, yet do not fear to read the gospel or call themselves deacons; and if, in spite of their lewdness, they attain to the order of priesthood, and still persist in these sins, adding to them still others, and perform the offices of a priest, claiming that they can intercede for the people and offer the holy sacrifice; if then, which is worse still, in spite of their evil reputation they rise from rank to rank and are ordained bishops; if I find such men among them, I ask that I may have your order and written authority, so that yours may be the decision about such men, and that they may stand convicted as sinners by your pronouncement.'

He adds that besides these bishops of notoriously immoral life there

171. Frankish prince crowned by the hand of God, between two dignitaries of the Church. Fragment from a sacramentary, second half 9th century.

172       173

are, alas, many whose sense of the dignity of the priesthood is blunted, and who are in fact no more than laymen in disguise:

'And among them are found bishops who, though they say they are not fornicators and adulterers, are drunkards and criminals, or follow the chase or fight fully armed in battle, shedding with their own hand the blood of Christian or heathen alike.'

After painting this melancholy picture, St Boniface urges on the pope the concerted action which alone could suppress these abuses. Charles Martel may not have been solely responsible for the degradation of the Church, but no one can deny that he did nothing to check it, and that his policy did indeed in large measure contribute to it.

## The Children of Charles the Hammer

Charles Martel, basing his authority on force, never troubled to give it a legal foundation, and the pope, who realized that though still mayor of the palace he was in fact the effective ruler of the whole Frankish kingdom, hardly knew what title to bestow on him, and in his letters addressed him as *subregulus* (under-king).

320

172. Head of the child Geta(?) second son of Septimus Severus, Grand, Vosges.

173. Woman's head from ruins of Gallo-Roman temple.

174. Head of veiled dancer. Stone carving from Genainville.

The honour of creating a new royal dynasty, the Carolingian house, fell to Pepin the Short, Charles Martel's eldest son; he too it was who gave a religious character to the Frankish kingship.

When Charles Martel died in 741, he left two legitimate sons, Carloman and Pepin, and a third son who was the offspring of his liaison with a Bavarian concubine called Swanhild. Carloman and Pepin lost no time in getting rid of their brother, whose name was Grifo. This family drama is the first chapter in the *Annales regni Francorum*, our most valuable source for the history of the early Carolingians:

'741. In this year died Charles, mayor of the palace, leaving three sons as his heirs, that is, Carloman, Pepin and Grifo. Grifo, who was younger than the others, had a mother by name Swanhild, the granddaughter of Odilo, duke of Bavaria. She by her evil counsel kindled in him the hope of possessing all the kingdom, so much so that without delay he occupied the city of Laon and declared war on his brothers. They quickly gathered an army and besieged Laon, received the surrender of their brother, and then applied themselves to ordering the kingdom and recovering the provinces which on the death of their father had cut themselves off from the Frankish confederacy. And so that they might leave all safe at home when they were away from their country, Carloman took Grifo and had him shut up at Neufchâtel, which is situated near the Ardennes.' (4: p. 3.)[1]

The association of the two brothers lasted no more than four years after they had eliminated Grifo. A strong religious vocation decided Carloman to enter an order, and his younger brother Pepin, who seems to have been ambitious to rule alone, far from attempting to dissuade him, gave him every encouragement. Manners were milder in Carolingian times. In the Merovingian royal household, assassination was the usual method employed to get rid of a brother or nephew who was in the way. Now less sanguinary means were beginning to be used:

'745. In this year [the author of the *Annales regni Francorum* records] Carloman made known to Pepin his brother the plan he had long had in mind, to leave the conversation of the world and serve God in a monk's habit. Wherefore the expedition for that year was abandoned, and Pepin devoted himself to accomplishing Carloman's desires and preparing his journey, for he had decided to go to Rome. (4: p. 5.)

Carloman left for Rome the next year; but he did not stay there, and settled in the monastery St Benedict had founded at Monte Cassino.

## A New Dynasty: Pepin the Short

Pepin the Short was now sole mayor of the palace of the Frankish kingdom. Wider horizons opened before him, and he began to aspire to the throne. In this ambition he found an ally in the papacy. Threatened by the Lombards who had established a kingdom in northern Italy, ill defended by the Eastern emperors, the sovereign pontiffs sought the protection of the Franks. But in an age dominated by brute force, their spiritual authority was not sufficient to make them respected; they needed temporal power and an independent state of their own. The support of Pepin the Short made it possible for them to build up a papal state. In return, the Roman pontiffs were ready to countenance Pepin's ambition to exchange his mayoralty of the palace for the royal title, and to have his usurpation recognized by the supreme authority of the Church.

[1] The original version of these annals was the work of an anonymous author, and dates from 788. His text was later reworked and expanded by Einhard.

This *quid pro quo* had lasting consequences. The Frankish kingship passed to a new royal house and was given a sacerdotal character; and the papal state thus created under the auspices of Pepin the Short in the eighth century lasted until 1870.

The *Annales regni Francorum*, faithfully recording the reigns of the early Carolingians, tell how Pepin succeeded to the throne and how as the other half of the bargain the pope's temporal power was established:

'749. Burchard, bishop of Wurzburg, and Fulrad the chaplain [who was also abbot of St Denis] were sent to Pope Zacharias, to ask him, in the matter of the kings of France, who had no royal power in those days, whether this was good or not. And Pope Zacharias sent word to Pepin that it was better that he should be called king who wielded the power, than he who remained without royal power; and so that order might not be disturbed, he ordered by virtue of his apostolic authority that Pepin should be made king.'

It need hardly be said that this answer to Pepin's request for the pope's opinion accorded so well with the ambitions of the mayor of the palace that he lost no time in acting on it.

'750. In this year [the annalist reports], according to the decree of the Roman pontiff, Pepin was hailed as king by the Franks and anointed to the dignity of this honour by a sacred unction at the hand of Boniface, archbishop and martyr of blessed memory, and raised to the royal throne according to Frankish custom, in the city of Soissons. But Childeric, who was falsely called king, was tonsured and sent to a monastery.' (4: pp. 8–9.)

175. Base of column in the Carolingian basilica begun in 749 by Fulrad, at St Denis.

Pepin had indeed handled the business with great skill. He did not abandon the traditional ceremonies which had raised his predecessors to the throne in Merovingian times, but rounded them off by a religious ceremony which was already in use among the Visigoths and Anglo-Saxons. Finally, it is worth noting how neatly he got rid of the last Merovingian king, Childeric III.

## Creation of the Papal State

Pope Zacharias' valuable services to King Pepin had earned a reward. It was the next occupant of the throne of St Peter, Stephen II, who in 753 came to claim it from the Frankish king.

'753. In the same year [the *Annales* record], Pope Stephen came to King Pepin in the villa which is called Quierzy [near Laon (Aisne)], suggesting that the king should defend him and the Roman Church from the attack of the Lombards.' (*4*: p. 11.)

The annalist adds a curious detail:

'And Carloman the king's brother, who had already become a monk, came at the behest of his abbot, to oppose the request the Roman pontiff was making to his brother; but it is thought that he did this reluctantly, because he dared not gainsay the orders of his abbot, nor the abbot the commands of the king of the Lombards.'

That monks should be compelled to make such representations in opposition to the head of the Roman Church is significant; it shows that in the eighth century freedom was as much an illusion in the Lombard kingdom as it was in other barbarian states, and we can easily understand how urgently Stephen II needed the help of the powerful king of the Franks. Pepin was ready to give it, and the annalist tells how Stephen II showed his gratitude, as his predecessor had done before him:

'754. Stephen the pope, after he had received confirmation from King Pepin that he would defend the Roman Church, consecrated him in the honour of the royal dignity by a sacred anointing, and with him his two sons Charles and Carloman; and he remained in France throughout the winter.' (*4*: p. 13.)[1]

We have a short contemporary account of the ceremony, which took

[1] Einhard's version.

324

place in the abbey of St Denis. This passage, entitled *Clausula of the anointing of Pepin* (54: pp. 465–6) deserves to be quoted, bombastic though it is, for the only parallel to the coronation of Pepin by Stephen II is that of Napoleon I by Pius VII in Notre Dame de Paris. In both cases a new dynasty was to be enthroned and legitimatized.

'The said most excellent lord Pepin, pious king, had been raised to the throne three years earlier [the author begins by reminding us], by the authority and order of Pope Zacharias of holy memory, and by anointing with holy chrism at the hand of the blessed bishops of the Gauls, and by the choice of all the Franks. Afterwards he was anointed and blessed as king and patrician,[1] in the name of the Holy Trinity, at the hands of Pope Stephen, together with his aforesaid sons Charles and Carloman, all in one and the same day, in the church of the said blessed martyrs Dionysius, Rusticus and Eleutherius, where, as is known, the venerable man Fulrad is archpriest and abbot. In the same church of the blessed martyrs and on the same day, the aforesaid venerable pontiff blessed, through the grace of the sevenfold Spirit, the most noble and devout lady Bertha, a faithful votary of the holy martyrs, wife of the said most excellent king, she being garbed in the royal robe. At the same time he confirmed the princes of the Franks, blessing them with the grace of the Holy Spirit, and bound them all by an interdiction and the threat of excommunication that they should never in future presume to choose a king sprung from the loins of any save of those whom the divine piety has deigned to exalt and has purposed to confirm and consecrate, on the intercession of the holy apostles, at the hands of their vicar the most blessed pontiff.'

After these signal favours it was incumbent on Pepin to provide something more than fair promises, and to furnish the pope with military as well as moral support. This he did in 755, when in person he escorted Stephen II back to Rome:

'755. Pepin the king, on the invitation and suggestion of the aforesaid Roman pontiff, marched into Italy with a strong army, to exact from the king of the Lombards the justice due to the blessed apostle Peter. The Lombards resisted, and defended the approaches to Italy, and there was very fierce fighting in the mountain passes; but the

[1] 'The illustrious title of patrician of the Romans, whose practical significance we do not know, together with the consecration itself, was the price which the Sovereign Pontiff was prepared to pay for the formal pact he hoped to extract from the Frankish king'. (*Louis Halphen, Charlemagne et l'Empire carolingien*, p. 33.)

Lombards fell back and the Frankish forces made their way up the somewhat difficult road without much trouble.

'But the king of the Lombards, Aistulf, who had not dared to come to close quarters, was besieged in the city of Pavia by King Pepin; and he did not raise the siege until he had received forty hostages as guarantee that justice would be done to the holy Roman Church.' (4: p. 13.)

On his return to his own kingdom, Pepin left the pope in Rome in the charge of his chaplain Fulrad and a strong force of Franks; but he made a mistake in relying on the good faith of the Lombard king, and another campaign was needed to induce him to fulfil his engagements. This was in 756:

'756. Aistulf, king of the Lombards, although he had given hostages the year before, performed nothing of what he had promised. Therefore King Pepin marched into Italy again with an army, and besieged Aistulf who had shut himself into the city of Pavia, and forced him to fulfil his promises. And when Ravenna and Pentapolis and all the Exarchate belonging to Ravenna had been restored to him, he delivered them up to St Peter. Having done this, he returned to Gaul.'

Yet once more, according to the authors of the *Annales*, Aistulf thought to evade the performance of his promises; but in the course of that year he was thrown from his horse while hunting, and died of his injuries.

Such were the changing fortunes which marked the beginnings of the papal state. Henceforward the pope was the effective ruler of the Duchy of Rome and the Exarchate of Ravenna. But in fact the territories Pepin had presented to him were no more his to give than they were the Lombard king's. They were part of the dominions of the Eastern emperors. But by now the sovereignty of the Eastern Empire was purely theoretical, and Constantine V, the reigning emperor of Constantinople, cannot have borne the king of the Franks any ill-will for what he had done, since we are told that in 759 he presented Pepin with magnificent gifts. The most impressive of these was an organ; the anonymous annalist seems to have been surprised that it arrived safely in France: *Misit . . . organum qui in Franciam usque pervenit.* (4: pp. 14–15.)

# 28

# THE PRIVATE LIFE OF
# CHARLEMAGNE

CHARLEMAGNE is not only one of the great figures of history; legend too has made him her own, transformed and idealized him, taking an active if somewhat corpulent German, no doubt moustached, who had established his capital at Aix-la-Chapelle and spent much of his reign in subduing the Saxons and extending his kingdoms eastward, and turning him into a noble old man with a long white beard, a kind of crusader warring against the Saracens. And to hang beside this sentimentalized portrait legend has painted the picture of 'la douce France', sweet France, the Île-de-France of the first Capetians.

Fortunately legend has not entirely succeeded in blurring the lines of history. The historical Charlemagne has been preserved for us by some of his contemporaries; and through the *Life of Charlemagne* written by one of them, Einhard, we can discover something of the intimate life of the great emperor.

When Pepin the Short died of dropsy on 24th September 768, he left two legitimate sons, Charles and Carloman, who ruled the kingdom together for three years. Then Carloman fell ill and died in December 771, and Charles, who was champing at the bit, was recognized by the Franks as their sole king.

Einhard, educated at the abbey of Fulda in Germany, who entered the court of Charlemagne in 791 and subsequently became an important person in the palace, has left us a biography of the great emperor which he modelled on the life of Augustus in the *Lives of the Caesars*

176. Charlemagne. Detail of an equestrian statue in bronze of the Carolingian period, from the treasury of Metz cathedral.

by Suetonius; he must have written it about 828, after his retirement
to Seligenstadt.

He describes Charlemagne's appearance with a wealth of minute
detail:

'The person of Karl was large and robust, and of commanding
stature, though not exceeding good proportions, for it appears that he
measured seven feet in height [probably a mistake for five feet]. The
top of his head was round, his eyes large and animated, his nose somewhat long, his hair white and his face bright and pleasant; so that,
whether standing or sitting, he showed very great presence and dignity.
Although his neck was thick and rather short and his belly too promi-
nent, still the fair proportions of his limbs concealed these defects.
His walk was firm, and the whole carriage of his body was manly. His
voice was clear, but not so strong as his frame would have led one to
expect. His health was good until the last four years of his life, when
he was attacked by frequent fevers and latterly walked lame on one
foot. Even in illness he leaned more on his own judgment than on the
advice of physicians, whom he greatly disliked, because they used to
recommend him to leave off roasted meats, which he preferred, and
to accustom himself to boiled.'

Einhard also gives us details of Charlemagne's usual costume:

'He wore the dress of his native country—that is, the Frankish; on
his body a linen shirt and linen drawers; then a tunic with a silver
border, and stockings. He bound his legs with garters and wore shoes
on his feet. In the winter he protected his shoulders and chest with a
vest made of the skins of otters and sable. He wore a blue cloak, and
was always girt with his sword, the hilt and belt being of gold and
silver.'

Charlemagne was attached to the Frankish style of dress; he cared
little for Roman costume, and submitted to wearing it only to please
the sovereign pontiff, and in exceptional circumstances:

'He thoroughly disliked the dress of foreigners, however fine, and
he never put it on except at Rome—once at the request of Pope Adrian,
and again a second time, to please his successor, Pope Leo. He then
wore a long tunic, chlamys and shoes made after the Roman fashion.'

We know too how Charlemagne lived, thanks to Einhard, who was
one of his intimates and has described how he spent the day when he
was in residence in his palace:

177. 'As if sitting in court . . .' Utrecht psalter, 9th century.

'The daily service of his table was furnished with only four dishes, in addition to the roast meat, which the hunters used to bring in on spits, and of which he partook more freely than of any other food. While he was dining he listened to music or reading. History and the deeds of men of old used to be read. He derived much pleasure from the works of St Augustine, especially from his book called *City of God*. He took very sparingly of wine and other drinks, rarely taking at meals more than three or four draughts. In summer, after the midday repast, he would take some fruit and one draught, and then, throwing aside his clothes and shoes as if at night, he would repose for two or three hours. He slept at night so lightly that he would break his rest four or five times, not merely by awakening, but even getting up.

'While he was dressing and binding on his sandals he would receive

178. 'He not only invited his sons to bathe with him, but also his chief men and friends.'
Utrecht psalter, 9th century.

his friends; and also, if the count of the palace announced that there
was any case which could be settled only by his decree, the suitors
were immediately ordered into his presence, and, as if sitting in court,
he heard the case and gave judgment. And this was not the only business
that used to be arranged at that time, for orders were then given for
whatever had to be done on that day by any officer or servant.'

Charlemagne was a keen sportsman, an enthusiastic huntsman,
horseman and swimmer:

'He took constant exercise in riding and hunting, which was natural
for a Frank, since scarcely any nation can be found to equal them in
these pursuits. He also delighted in the natural warm baths, frequently

exercising himself by swimming, in which he was very skilful, no one being able to outstrip him. It was on account of the warm baths there that he built the palace at Aachen, living there constantly during the last years of his life and until his death. He not only invited his sons to bathe with him, but also his chief men and friends, and occasionally even a crowd of his attendants and guards, so that at times one hundred men or more would be bathing together.' (*21*: pp. 73–6.)

Charlemagne was no ascetic. Einhard's biography is an honest and unprudish work, and leaves us with no illusions on this point; and it is clear from what he tells us that the king was a robust man who kept his vigour to the end of his life:

'It was by the desire of his mother that he took for his wife a daughter of Dedier, king of the Lombards; but at the end of a year he divorced her, for what reason is uncertain. He then married Hildegard, a Swabian lady of noble birth; by her he had three sons, Karl, Pippin and Ludwig, and three daughters, Hruodrud, Berthrad and Gisla. He had also three other daughters, Theoderada and Hiltrud by his wife Fastrada, a German of the Eastern Franks, and Ruodhaid by a concubine whose name I do not remember. On the death of Fastrada he married Liudgard, of the Alemanni nation. She bore him no children. After her death he had four concubines.' (*21*: pp. 65–6.)

Einhard had no difficulty in remembering the names of these women; he records them carefully. Each of them gave Charlemagne at least one child, and he makes a point of noting the births for posterity. In striking contrast, only one legitimate heir remained to the emperor at his death in 814: the weak Louis the Pious, who inherited the whole of his father's estate.

Charlemagne was an excellent family man, and loved to have his children round him:

'He was so careful in the bringing up of his sons and daughters [says Einhard] that when at home he never dined without them, and they always accompanied him on his journeys, his sons riding by his side, and his daughters following close behind.'

But we may note that Charlemagne's deep, and perhaps even excessive, fondness for his family sometimes had awkward consequences, at least where his daughters were concerned; Einhard discreetly implies as much:

'His daughters were very fair, and he loved them passionately. Strange to say, he would never consent to give them in marriage, either to any of his own nation or to foreigners; but he kept them all at home and near his person at all times until his death, for he used to say that he could not deprive himself of their society. On account of this, although happy in all else, he here experienced the malignity of fortune; but he concealed his vexation, and conducted himself as if they had never given rise to injurious suggestions, and as if no reports had ever gone abroad concerning them.' (*21*: pp. 70–1.)

Charlemagne may have behaved as though he had no suspicions, but posterity is better informed. We know in fact that one of them, Hruodrud, was the mistress of the count of Le Maine Rorgon and had by him a son Louis, who became abbot of St Denis; and that another, Berthrad, had several children by the court poet Angilbert, one of them being the historian Nithard.

No portrait of Charlemagne would be complete without a mention of one of his most original characteristics, his eagerness to improve his mind and to encourage intellectual interests in his court. This is what particularly marks him out from his predecessors; to call the intellectual life of his times the 'Carolingian renaissance' is perhaps to exaggerate, but at least it can be said that after several centuries of almost complete stagnation in all forms of culture the Carolingian period saw the awakening of intellectual activity, particularly in the monasteries, and a renewal of interest in classical antiquity which had the happy result of preserving many literary works for us.

Einhard expatiates on Charlemagne's eloquence and his linguistic talents:

'He was ready and fluent in speaking [he says], and able to express himself with great clearness. He did not confine himself to his native tongue, but took pains to learn foreign languages, acquiring such knowledge of Latin that he used to repeat his prayers in that language as well as in his own. Greek he could better understand than pronounce.'

Though he was an eloquent speaker, sometimes to the point of prolixity (*Adeo quidem facundus erat ut etiam dicaculus appareret*, says Einhard), Charlemagne found great difficulty in learning to write. Einhard tells us as much with a touching naivety:

'Karl also tried to write, and used to keep his tablets and writing book under the pillow of his couch, that when he had leisure he might practise his hand in forming letters; but he made little progress in a task too long deferred and begun too late in life.'

Charlemagne's curiosity was all-embracing, and he surrounded himself with tutors of the highest qualifications to complete his education:

'He was an ardent admirer of the liberal arts [says Einhard], and greatly revered their professors, whom he promoted to high honours. In order to learn grammar, he attended the lectures of the aged Peter of Pisa, a deacon; and for other instruction he chose as preceptor Alcuin, also a deacon—a Saxon by race, from Britain—the most learned man of the day, with whom the king spent much time in learning rhetoric and logic, and most especially astronomy.' (21: pp. 77–8.)

As we shall see, Alcuin was more than just an excellent pedagogue, and he showed Charlemagne more things than the stars and the heavens. He was a shrewd adviser in political matters, and when Charlemagne rose to be emperor he owed his dazzling success at least in part to his astronomy master.

# 29

# THE WARS OF CHARLEMAGNE

## *The Conquering King*

Charlemagne was a great soldier, and every year of his reign, at least until he was crowned emperor in 800, saw a military expedition which lasted several months. In early spring a great assembly was summoned, which was an ecclesiastical synod and a military review combined. Charlemagne would then take the field with the forces thus to hand, returning in late autumn to take up his winter quarters in one of his palaces, usually Aix-la-Chapelle.

This uniform rhythm of Charlemagne's life is illustrated in the *Annales regni Francorum*, whose authors carefully follow every one of the king's movements. Here, for example, is the entry for the year 794:

'794. Easter was celebrated in Frankfurt; and there a great synod was assembled of bishops of Gaul and those of the Germans and Italians, in the presence of the aforesaid prince [Charlemagne] and of the envoys of the apostolic lord Hadrian . . . Then the army began its march into Saxon territories in two bands; in one was the Lord Charles, the most glorious king; in the other he sent Lord Charles, his son, who went by way of Cologne. . . . [When the campaign was over,] the king returned to his palace which is called Aix and there celebrated the Nativity of the Lord and Easter.' (*4*: p. 94.)

179. 'Iron' crown of the Lombard kings. Treasury of Monza cathedral. Stone and enamel settings.

## The Campaign in Lombardy

Charlemagne began his career of conquest by annexing the kingdom of Lombardy. Pepin the Short, his father, had stopped half way, creating the Papal States for the benefit of the pope but leaving the Lombard kingdom still in existence. Charlemagne had no use for half measures. Although, as we have seen, he had on his mother's advice married the daughter of the king of the Lombards (though he quickly repudiated her), he at once answered Pope Hadrian's appeal for help against King Dedier. This is how Einhard summarizes the conquest of the Lombard kingdom in his reworking of the *Annales regni Francorum*:

'773. Pope Hadrian, when he could no longer endure the insolence of king Dedier and oppression by the Lombards, determined to send an embassy to Charles, king of the Franks, and ask him to aid him, with the Romans, against the Lombards. And because it was not possible to make the journey by land across Italy, he caused his legate, by name Peter, to take ship at Rome and go by sea as far as Marseilles, whence he journeyed overland to France. The king diligently and carefully investigated the matters at issue between Romans and Lombards, and decided to make war on the Lombards in defence of the Romans. He came with his whole army to Geneva, a city of Burgundy situated on the Rhone; and there, deliberating on the war he was about to undertake, he divided the forces he had brought with him, and ordered one part, under his uncle Bernard, to go by way of the Mount of Jupiter [Great St Bernard]. He himself, at the head of the other, hastened into Italy by Mt Cenis. Crossing the col of the Alps, he put King Dedier to flight, who vainly tried to withstand him, without coming to blows, and besieged him in Pavia where he had taken refuge; Charlemagne spent the whole winter in this siege, because it was difficult and required much exertion.' (*4*: p. 35.)[1]

It was not until the following year that Charlemagne achieved his purpose:

'774. The king, leaving his army to continue the blockading and storming of Pavia, set out for Rome to pray there; and when he had accomplished his vows and had returned to the army, he forced the city, which was exhausted by the long siege, to surrender to him. All the other cities followed suit and submitted to the authority of the king and the Franks; and the king, now that he had subdued Italy and for the time being reduced her to order, returned to Francia, bringing King Dedier back in captivity.' (*4*: p. 39.)

So ended the conquest of the kingdom of Lombardy, and from 5th June 774 onwards Charlemagne styled himself, in his official acts, 'king of the Franks and the Lombards'.

[1] Einhard's version.

180. Agilulf, king of the Lombards, in majesty. Plaque of gilded copper forming the centre piece of a helmet, 7th century.

DANES

FRISIA

Verde

SAX

Meuse

Aix-la-Chapelle

Frank

St-Riquier

Corbie

F R A N C I A

AU

Soissons

Laon

Verdun

Seine

BRITTANY

NEUSTRIA

ALA

Loire

S

Tours

BURGUNDY

Poitiers

AQUITAINIA

Lyons

Geneva

Bordeaux

Rhone

Garonne

PROVENCE

Gellone

GASCONY

Toulouse

Narbonne

Roncevaux

SEPTIMANIA

Pampeluna

NAVARRE

SPANISH
MARCH

Gerona

SARACENS

Barcelona

*ABOTRITES*

*WILZI*

*Oder*

S L A V S

*Elbe*

*THURINGIA*

*SORBS*

*Fulda*

**BOHEMIA**

*Vistula*

MAP 7
CHARLEMAGNE'S
EMPIRE

*SIA*

**BAVARIA**

*NNIA*

CARINTHIA

*Theiss*

*AVARS*

LIBURNIA

P A N N O N I A

*Danube*

**LOMBARDY**

ISTRIA

DALMATIA

*Save*

Pavia

*Po*

Ravenna

**PAPAL**

PENTAPOLIS

DUCHY
OF
SPOLETO

**STATES**

Rome

DUCHY
OF
BENEVENTO

**CORSICA**

**SARDINIA**

0    100   200   300   400 km

181

## Thirty-three Years of Saxon Wars

The toughest of his wars ended in the conquest of Saxony, the vast plain that stretched between the Low Countries and the Elbe, and between the Harz Mountains and the North Sea, or even the Baltic. This war was begun in 772, and ended only in 804.

Einhard describes the often deceptive nature of the struggle against a still pagan enemy, a struggle not unlike some of the colonial wars of our own times:

'No war undertaken by the Franks [he says in his *Life of Charlemagne*] was so protracted or so fierce, and so full of toil and hardship, since the Saxons, like most of the nations inhabiting Germany, were naturally brave, and, being addicted to heathenism, were hostile to our religion, and thought it no disgrace to dishonour divine laws or violate human ones.' (*21*: p. 39.)

340

182

183

Frontier incidents had long since antagonized Franks and Saxons; their hostility broke out into full-scale war only when Charlemagne came on the scene, perhaps because he was the first Frankish king to have at the back of his mind the possibility of annexing Saxony:

'War was therefore declared [says Einhard], and was carried on continuously during thirty-three years, with much bitterness on both sides, but with greater loss to the Saxons than to the Franks. It was the bad faith of the Saxons which prevented a more speedy termination. It is hard to say how often they were beaten, and humbly surrendered to the king, promising to obey his orders, giving up at once the hostages he asked, and acknowledging the ambassadors sent to them; how sometimes they were so tamed and compliant as even to promise to give up their idolatry, declaring they wished to embrace Christianity. But ready as they were at times to undertake all these things, they were always far readier to renounce them.'

## Bloody Reprisals

Einhard goes on to praise Charlemagne's magnanimity, but without denying that he inflicted 'just penalties' on the rebel Saxons. On occasion his repressive measures were merciless. The *Annales regni Francorum* tells of what amounted to a real massacre ordered by Charlemagne in 782.

A Frankish army, sent to deal with the Slav peoples of Swabia, had been surprised by the Saxons and cut to pieces on the east bank of the Weser. Two generals were killed in the ambush, and twenty nobles:

'When the king received news of this, he decided that it was no time to delay, and gathering an army in haste he set off for Saxony; and summoning all the chief men of the Saxons he questioned them about the authors of this defection. They all declared that Widukind was the author of the crime, but that they could not hand him over, because after he had perpetrated his treacherous act he had betaken himself to the Northmen; and so up to 4,500 other Saxons were delivered up, who had had a part in this great crime, and fallen in with his proposals. By the king's order they were all beheaded in a single day on the banks of the River Aller, in a place which is called Verden. When he had thus wreaked his vengeance, the king went into winter quarters at Diedenhofen.' (4: p. 63.)[1]

[1] Einhard's version.

342

184. Charlemagne mourning the dead. Detail of the Charlemagne reliquary. Treasury of the cathedral of Aix-la-Chapelle.

Widukind was one of the most valiant of the Saxon leaders, and the only one named in history text-books. He made his submission three years later, after the fierce campaign of 785:

'Widukind and Abbi, another Saxon chieftain, were led to the Lord King Charles; and there the aforesaid Widukind and Abbi were baptized with all their companions; and then all Saxony was sub-jugated,' says the chronicler of the *Annales regni Francorum.* (4: p. 70.)

His statement is over-optimistic; Einhard, who later reworked his text, had to admit that the truce lasted only a few years after the conversion of the two chieftains.

343

185. Little bronze hare from Sausay.

## Charlemagne and the Making of Europe

Charlemagne's ambitious plans for extending the Frankish kingdom eastward did not stop at Italy and Saxony, and the author of the *Life of Charlemagne*, who took pride in the conquests of the 'most potent prince', enumerates them for us.

After describing the annexations which followed the campaigns in Italy and Saxony, he adds:

'[He conquered] both Pannonias, and Dacia which lies on the other bank of the Danube; also Istria, Liburnia and Dalmatia, with the exception of the maritime towns, which for friendship's sake, and on account of a treaty, he allowed the Constantinopolitan emperor to hold; lastly, all the wild and barbarous nations which inhabit Germany between the Rhine and the Vistula, the ocean and the Danube, who speak a similar language, but are widely different in manners and dress. Chief among these were the Welatabi, Sorabi, Abodriti and Baemanni.' (*21*: p. 58.)

Today we might be tempted to describe Charlemagne as a great European; but the legend which grew up round his name between the tenth and twelfth centuries, at a time when all eyes were turned to the Holy Land, saw the great emperor rather as the indefatigable champion of Christianity, whose whole life was spent in warring against the Saracens.

## The Spanish Expedition and the Fight at Roncevaux

But a grain of truth lies at the heart of every legend. Charlemagne was too shrewd and realistic a politician to disregard his frontier in the Pyrenees. So he was ready to listen to the proposals of Ibn al-Arabi,

344

a governor of Barcelona in revolt against his emir, who in 777 arrived with his son Youssef and his son-in-law at the general assembly in session at Paderborn, and made a number of more or less sincere promises; in 778 Charlemagne launched a Spanish expedition, which met with little success. The anonymous author of the *Annales regni Francorum*, writing during the lifetime of Charlemagne, glossed over the disaster; but Einhard's recension is more explicit:

'778. Then, being persuaded by the aforesaid Saracen, and conceiving the hope of seizing certain cities in Spain to some purpose, he collected an army and set out; he crossed the range of the Pyrenees in the territory of the Gascons and, attacking Pampeluna, a town of the Navarri, he received its surrender. Then he forded the river Ebro, and came to Saragossa, the chief city of those parts, and accepting the hostages which Ibn al-Arabi, Abuthaur and certain other Saracens offered him, he returned to Pampeluna. He razed its walls to the ground, to prevent any insurrection, and deciding to return, he entered the pass of the Pyrenees. At the highest point the Gascons, who had laid ambushes, fell on the rearguard, and threw the whole army into confusion by their sudden attack. And although the Franks showed themselves superior to the Gascons both in weapons and in courage, yet by reason of the unfavourable terrain and the unequal nature of the battle they were overmatched. In this battle were slain many of the paladins to whom the king had given command of the troops, the baggage was plundered, and the enemy melted away in every direction, thanks to their knowledge of the locality. Grief for this wound inflicted on him overshadowed in the king's heart a great part of his successes in Spain.' (*4*: p. 51.)

186. Wooden hen for use as a jewel-box.

In his life of Charlemagne Einhard returned to this defeat which seems to have weighed upon him, and recorded the names of the most illustrious of the dead:

'There were killed in this fight, Eggihard, the king's Sewer; Anselm, the Pfalsgraf; Roland, count of the British [Breton] March, and many others.' (*21*: p. 46.)

This dramatic episode was the historical seed—and the only seed—from which sprang the *Song of Roland*.

# 30

# CHARLEMAGNE AS EMPEROR

THE tragic ambush in which the Frankish army lost a tenth of its number as it returned from an expedition into Spain would not in itself have been enough to create an epic legend, or to inspire the author of the *Song of Roland*, if Charlemagne had not in the year 800 revived the Western Empire. In the eyes of posterity he will always be the great emperor 'with the snow-white beard'.

That a king of the Franks should have succeeded in restoring the empire which had ceased to exist in 476 must be attributed chiefly to the extraordinarily forceful personality of Charlemagne; it cannot be denied that he was one of the great figures of history. All the same, this unexpected revival of the empire was made possible only by the concomitance of a number of favourable circumstances.

## An Exacting Protector

One of these was the insolvency of the Eastern Empire, which was at that time ruled by a woman, the Empress Irene, who had not only dethroned her son Constantine II, but had had his eyes put out (799). But more important were the weakness of the papacy and the mediocrity of the pope who found himself head of the Roman Church at the end of the eighth century. Even after the creation of the papal states, popes were not safe from sudden attack, and their personal position was still precarious. This was the case with Leo III, who has been the subject

187. Decoration on a great silver dish, Gallo-Roman.

of much discussion. He had been elected pope unexpectedly in 795. His enemies accused him of adultery and perjury, and they conspired against him with the intention of blinding him and cutting out his tongue.

If the pope were to withstand his powerful enemies, he needed a powerful protector. Charlemagne was at hand, ready to be cast for the role and to make himself responsible not only for the defence of the papacy, but also for the spiritual direction of the Church, her head being thus discredited, and of Christendom. He accepted the part without hesitation, as we can see from the instructions he gave Angilbert, lay abbot of St Riquier, the Homer of the palace academy, and his ambassador to the pope, for transmission to Leo III. Their tone is startlingly dictatorial; no head of state nowadays, even those with the slenderest links with Catholicism, would think of treating the sovereign pontiff in so cavalier a fashion.

'The mercy of God having directed thy journey [Charlemagne writes to Angilbert], and led thee prosperously to the apostolic Lord, our father, thou shalt diligently admonish him about the respectability of his behaviour, and especially about observing the holy canons and piously governing the Holy Church of God; and this thou shalt do according to the opportunities of conference between you and the disposition of his mind. And thou shalt impress upon him that the honour which he now possesses is for a few years, but that the reward given to those who toil in this world is everlasting and for all time; and thou shalt most diligently exhort him to suppress the Simoniac heresy which defiles the holy body of the Church in many places.' (2: pp. 135–6.)

348

And Charlemagne ends his letter:

'May the Lord God guide thee and bring thee back prosperously. May the Lord God rule and direct his heart [Leo III] in all goodness, so that in all his actions he may accomplish what is profitable to Holy Church, and that he may be for us a pious father and the chief of our intercessors.'

## Pressure from Alcuin

Charlemagne would perhaps not have taken it on himself to adopt this haughty attitude towards the head of the Church if he had not been encouraged by his entourage, in particular by his tutor and intimate

CAROLINGIAN MANUSCRIPTS:
188. Christ in majesty. Manuscript written by Godescalc between 781 and 783, at the order of Charlemagne and his wife Hildegard, for their personal use.
189. Illuminated Canons of the Gospels, produced at Tours in the time of Alcuin, *c.* 800.

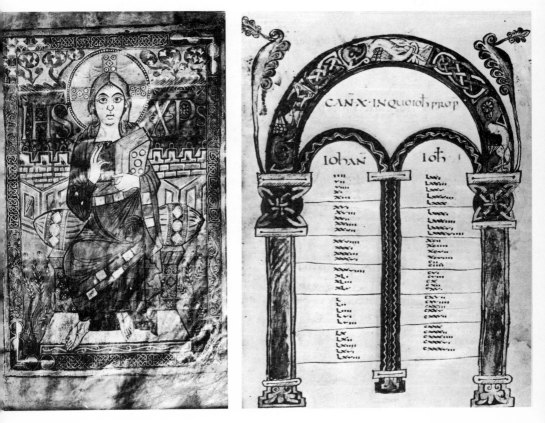

190. Binding of an Evangelistary for use in the church at Metz, 1st half of 9th century. Ivory plaque with border of copper ornamented with repoussé work, stones and enamel cloisonné of oriental style.

adviser Alcuin. It was Alcuin who urged him to it with the argument that this was a matter not merely of a right, but of a duty laid on him by Jesus Christ himself.

Here are some lines from a letter which Alcuin wrote to the king in June 799:

'I would recommend many things to your worshipful dignity at present, if you had opportunity to hear me and I had eloquence to speak. For the charity within my heart often inspired my pen to write of hidden thoughts about your prosperity and about the stability of the kingdom given you by God, and the increase of Christ's Holy Church which has been thwarted in a thousand ways by the wickedness of scoundrels and sullied by the audacious crimes of bad men, directed not merely against obscure people, but against the greatest and most exalted.

'Until now there have been three men of the highest rank in the world. The first is the apostolic sublimity, governing from the throne of the blessed Peter, prince of the apostles, as his vicar; what has been done to him who sat in that throne [Leo III] you have in your kindness advised me. The second is the imperial dignity and imperial power of the other Rome [Constantinople]; it is rumoured abroad far and wide how the ruler of that empire [Constantine VI] has been impiously deposed not by strangers but by his own people and fellow citizens. The third is the royal dignity which by the dispensation of our Lord Jesus Christ is conferred on you as governor of the Christian people; and this is more excellent than the other dignities in power, more shining in wisdom, more sublime in rank. Now on you alone rests the tottering safety of the churches of Christ. It is for you to avenge crimes, to guide the erring, to console the sorrowing and to raise up the good.' (2: p. 288.)

## The King of the Franks Becomes 'Emperor and Augustus'

An invitation at once so urgent and so flattering called for a swift decision, and Charlemagne unhesitatingly took it, for it chimed in with his own ambitions. But an appropriate title was needed to set the seal on the supreme authority, spiritual as well as secular, that the king of the Franks was taking to himself. The pope, who himself recognized this authority, sanctified it by crowning Charlemagne emperor on 25th December 800. The *Annales regni Francorum* record the ceremony in unwonted detail:

'800 . . . and at the beginning of the month of August the king came to Mainz and thence journeyed into Italy. . . .

'The day before he arrived in Rome, Pope Leo and the Romans

351

191. Denarius of the emperor
Charlemagne (reverse); temple
type; silver.

with him met him at Nomentum [Mentana], twelve miles from the
town, and received him very humbly and with much honour; and when
they had eaten together in that place the pope returned to the town in
advance of him. And the next day the pope stood on the steps of the
basilica of blessed Peter the Apostle, while the standards of the town
of Rome were carried to meet Charlemagne, and crowds both of pilgrims and townspeople were ranged and disposed in suitable places to
acclaim the visitor. The pope himself, with his clergy and bishops,
received the king as he dismounted and climbed the steps. After
delivering an oration he led him into the basilica of blessed Peter the
apostle amid the chants of all who were there. These events took place
on the eighth day of the Kalends of December [24th November].

'A week later the king called an assembly, and made it known why
he had come to Rome, and then every day he devoted himself to
performing what he had come to do. The most important and difficult
of these matters, and the one with which he began, was to sift the
accusations which had been made against the pope. But when no one
would come forward to prove the truth of the accusations, the pope,
carrying the gospels, went up into the ambo in the presence of all the
people in the basilica of St Peter the apostle, and calling on the name
of the Holy Trinity he purged himself by oath of the accusations
brought against him.' (4: pp. 110–12.)

A few lines further on the annalist adds:

[Charlemagne] 'celebrated the Nativity of the Lord in Rome, and
the date of the year changed to 801. On the most holy day of the
Nativity of the Lord, as the king rose from prayer to hear mass before
the confession of blessed Peter the apostle, Leo the pope placed a

352

crown on his head, and he was acclaimed by all the people of the Romans with the cry: "Long life and victory to Charles, Augustus, crowned by God, the great and peace-loving emperor of the Romans." And after the acclamations, Charles was worshipped by the pope in the fashion of the emperors of old, and the title of patrician was abolished and he was hailed as Emperor and Augustus.'

As is often the case in official or semi-official reports, the author of the *Annales* has failed to bring out some important details. If we are to believe Einhard, Charlemagne was crowned on the initiative of the pope, and the preparations for the coronation were made without Charlemagne's knowledge.

192. Interior of the Constantinian basilica of St Peter in Rome, from a 16th century fresco. In the foreground the 'pigna', an ancient bronze piece in the form of a fir-cone.

'It was at this time [says Einhard] that he received the title of Emperor and Augustus, to which at first he was so averse that he remarked that had he known the intention of the pope, he would not have entered the church on that day, great festival though it was.' (*21*: pp. 82–3.)

Einhard's statement has been much discussed. Why should Charlemagne have been so averse to receiving the imperial title? First of all, because he feared to arouse the resentment of the Eastern emperor and his court by thus suddenly assuming it. That is the motive which Einhard puts forward. But perhaps too Charlemagne's vanity was stung. Was it perhaps a little humiliating for a man like him to be crowned emperor by Leo III, who had cut a poor enough figure up till then? A thousand years later Napoleon I felt much the same, even though Pius VII was a much worthier pope than Leo III. Napoleon was more unmannerly than Charlemagne; he snatched the imperial crown from the pope's hands and crowned himself.

## The Effects of Prestige

Whatever Charlemagne's first reactions to his new dignity, his pride finally, and no doubt fairly promptly, accepted it with gratification. It brought him increased prestige among his contemporaries, and Einhard, who was in close contact with him, implies that such prestige was not lightly regarded by the emperor. We may note in particular the close relations he maintained with the caliph of Baghdad, Haroun al-Raschid:

'Haroun, king of the Persians [says Einhard], who, with the exception of India, ruled over nearly all the East, was held by the king in such hearty friendship, that he valued Karl's esteem above that of all other kings and princes of the world, and thought that he alone was worthy to be honoured by his regard and munificence. When the officers sent by Karl with offerings to the most sacred sepulchre and place of the resurrection of our Lord and Saviour came to Haroun and announced the pleasure of their master, he not only gave them permission to do as he desired, but granted that that revered and sacred spot should be considered as belonging to King Karl. When the ambassadors set out on their return, he sent with them his own envoys, who conveyed to the king strange and curious gifts, with garments and spices and other rich products of the East, just as he had sent him a few years before, upon his request, the only elephant he then possessed.' (*21*: pp. 59–61.)

354

Certainly the revival of the Western Empire served Charlemagne well, and helped to make the magic of the legend surrounding him. But we may add that it was an artificial creation, improvised to meet the needs of the moment, and that its only justification was Charlemagne's own force of personality. His creation might have vanished with him, without perceptibly changing the course of history; this is proved by the emergence of national states at the end of the ninth century. But human vanity takes pleasure in preserving organisms which pander to it, particularly titles, however useless they may be.

193. Charlemagne's Evangelistary, written in gold on purple; said to have been given to Angilbert, abbot of St Riquier by Charlemagne himself.

13

194. The 'Fountain of Life', Gospel of St Médard-de-Soissons, which was the property of Charlemagne; beginning 9th century.

The Empire founded for Charlemagne in 800 had a surprisingly long life, and ended only on 6th August 1806 when, as a modern sociologist has shrewdly remarked, 'a Habsburg laid his crown aside without meeting any opposition more serious than the sentimental regrets of the Romantics who clung to its outworn grandeur'.

## The Carolingian Renaissance

But in the judgment of posterity another aspect of Charlemagne's reign is worthy of note: the intellectual renaissance which he fostered, and whose most spectacular manifestation was the academy of the palace, which he founded. Many abbeys became centres of culture in his time. They were responsible for copying collections of property titles and monastic charters, and drawing up cartularies such as the famous polypitch of St Germain-des-Prés, documents of the greatest value for modern scholarship, and our best source of information on the Carolingian economy. But their most important activity was copying the works of pagan antiquity, as well as the Bible and the writings of the Fathers of the Church.

The *scriptoria* of the monasteries, of which the most famous was St Martin of Tours, might almost be called factories for copying manuscripts. Here, from the end of the eighth century onwards, the beautiful Carolingian miniscule took the place of the Merovingian script with the ligatures which make it awkward, if not extremely difficult, to decipher. This renaissance of literature, which was accompanied by a renaissance of art, has been given the name of Charlemagne, who encouraged it with unflagging enthusiasm.

## The Purple Shroud

Charlemagne lived for a little over thirteen years after being crowned emperor. He died on 28th January 814. His biographer Einhard gives a detailed account of his last moments and his burial:

'Towards the close of his life, when bowed down by disease and old age, he summoned to him his son Ludwig, the king of Aquitain, who alone survived of the sons of Hildegard, and in a solemn assembly of the chief men of the whole realm of the Franks, and with their unanimous consent, appointed Ludwig his partner in the whole kingdom and

357

heir with the imperial title. He then placed the royal crown on his head and bade that he be saluted as Emperor and Augustus.

'This proposal was received by all who were present with great approbation. It seemed to them as if Heaven inspired the king in advancing the prosperity of the kingdom, for this arrangement increased his own dignity and struck foreign nations with no slight awe.

'The king then dismissed his son into Aquitain, and, although weakened by age, went on his usual hunting expedition in the neighbourhood of the palace at Aachen. In this pursuit he passed the remainder of the autumn, and returned to Aachen early in November. During the winter, in the month of January, he was confined to his bed by a sharp attack of fever. He at once prescribed for himself a lowering diet, which was his usual treatment of fever, thinking that by this means he could throw off the disease, or at least control it; but inflammation of the side, which the Greeks call pleurisy, supervened. He still continued to starve himself, only keeping himself up by occasionally taking liquids; and on the seventh day after he had been confined to his bed he received the Holy Communion, and died soon after, at nine o'clock, on the 28th January, in the seventy-third year of his age and forty-seventh of his reign.

'His body was reverently washed and tended, and then carried into the church and buried, to the great grief of all his people. There was some doubt at first where was the most proper place for his burial, for during his life he had given no orders on this matter. At last it was agreed by all that he could be buried in no more fitting place than in the church which he had built at his own cost at Aachen, out of love to God and our Lord Christ, and to the honour of the ever blessed Virgin, His Mother. So he was buried there on the same day that he died. Above his tomb was erected a gilded monument, with his effigy and title upon it. His dignity was thus described:

UNDER THIS TOMB IS PLACED THE BODY OF KARL, THE GREAT AND ORTHODOX EMPEROR, WHO GLORIOUSLY ENLARGED THE REALM OF THE FRANKS, AND SUCCESSFULLY REIGNED DURING FORTY-SEVEN YEARS. HE DIED IN THE SEVENTY-THIRD YEAR OF HIS AGE,
JAN$^Y$ XXVIII, ANNO DOMINI DCCCXIIII
INDITION VII' (*21*: pp. 85–6.)

## *The Balance Sheet of Charlemagne's Reign*

So one of the most forceful personalities in French history leaves the stage. Too many historians have already analysed Charlemagne's character, and, as we well know, many more are still analysing it; and his reign raises too many problems for any definitive judgment to be possible. We will do no more here than suggest one or two subjects for reflection. Doubts have been cast on his military talents because in all his campaigns he never won a pitched battle; but he succeeded in extending his dominion patiently and methodically, without the loss of an inch of ground. There was nothing original about his legislative measures, and his capitularies (of which a definitive text has still to be established) are for the most part disconnected and hastily written,

195. St Matthew. Gospels written 751-4 by Gundohinus, at 'Vosevio' (not identified).

obviously dictated as need arose. But these measures, improvisations by a man of action, gradually reduced the chaos in the Frankish kingdom to order. The administration remained rudimentary and few changes were introduced, except that the institution of the *missi Dominici*, which Charlemagne greatly developed even if he did not originate it, made the work of righting abuses very much easier; it is obvious that under the strong hand of Charlemagne his states were freed of the swarm of corrupt and often bloodthirsty officials who had disgraced the administration of the Merovingians.

There is no indication, either, of any financial reforms in Charlemagne's reign. The Carolingian state had no budget. This insolvency is surprising, for nowadays we expect the state to provide a host of services that were not demanded of it in the ninth century. At that time the only important charge on it was the army; and as Ferdinand Lot has observed, this cost nothing at all, because all free men bore the cost of their arms and provisions themselves. The largest part of public expenditure—in particular the upkeep of the court and high officials— was met from the revenues of the royal domain. Charlemagne, who was essentially a practical man, seems to have taken a close interest in the administration of his many domains, and the cartulary *De villis imperialibis*, drawn up under his direction, shows him managing his properties as a family man should. We can see his practical mind at work again in his monetary policy. The silver standard was made general—and indeed excluded any other—the manufacture and circulation of money were carefully supervised, the palace mint was given the monopoly of striking coins, though in fact this was not entirely successful. All these were energetic measures well suited to an almost exclusively agricultural economy which had no external markets.

In short, the most obvious conclusion to be drawn from a study of the various aspects of Charlemagne's reign is that though he was not a great general like Napoleon, or a systematic lawgiver like Justinian, or a reformer like Augustus, he was nevertheless a shrewd politician, well balanced, sincere and honest. His surest claim to glory is perhaps his achievement in restoring the kingdom to a healthy state, and indeed one of his chief virtues was a robust common sense. This is a quality often regrettably absent in even the most gifted and eminent of statesmen. Though Charlemagne was surrounded by flatterers, his sense of his own greatness never seems to have degenerated into megalomania.

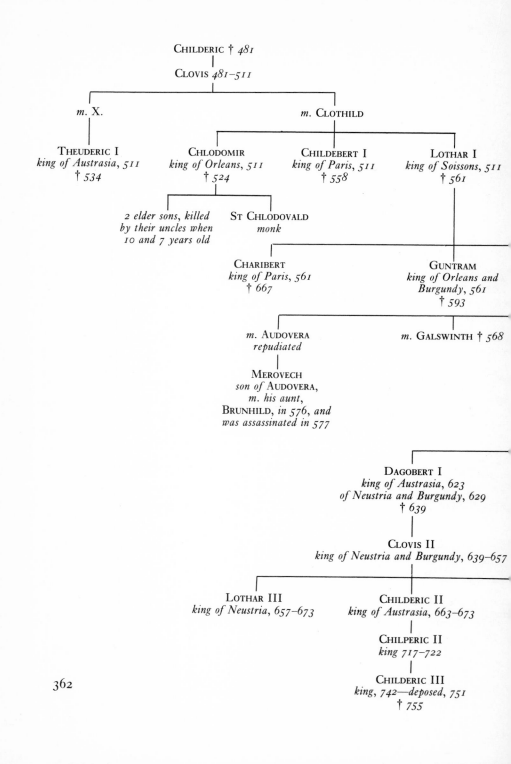

CHILDERIC † *481*

CLOVIS *481–511*

m. X.                                                m. CLOTHILD

THEUDERIC I                CHLODOMIR              CHILDEBERT I               LOTHAR I
*king of Austrasia, 511*   *king of Orleans, 511*   *king of Paris, 511*       *king of Soissons, 511*
*† 534*                    *† 524*                  *† 558*                    *† 561*

              *2 elder sons, killed*      ST CHLODOVALD
              *by their uncles when*         *monk*
              *10 and 7 years old*

                         CHARIBERT                              GUNTRAM
                      *king of Paris, 561*                *king of Orleans and*
                           *† 667*                          *Burgundy, 561*
                                                               *† 593*

              m. AUDOVERA                                   m. GALSWINTH † *568*
              *repudiated*

              MEROVECH
              *son of* AUDOVERA,
              *m. his aunt,*
              BRUNHILD, *in 576, and*
              *was assassinated in 577*

                                                      DAGOBERT I
                                                 *king of Austrasia, 623*
                                              *of Neustria and Burgundy, 629*
                                                        *† 639*

                                                      CLOVIS II
                                           *king of Neustria and Burgundy, 639–657*

              LOTHAR III                              CHILDERIC II
         *king of Neustria, 657–673*            *king of Austrasia, 663–673*

                                                      CHILPERIC II
                                                       *king 717–722*

                                                      CHILDERIC III
                                                 *king, 742—deposed, 751*
                                                        *† 755*

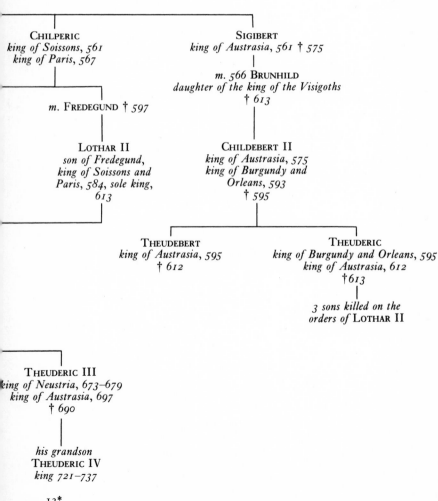

CHILPERIC
*king of Soissons, 561*
*king of Paris, 567*

SIGIBERT
*king of Austrasia, 561 † 575*

*m. 566* BRUNHILD
*daughter of the king of the Visigoths*
*† 613*

*m.* FREDEGUND *† 597*

LOTHAR II
*son of Fredegund,*
*king of Soissons and*
*Paris, 584, sole king,*
*613*

CHILDEBERT II
*king of Austrasia, 575*
*king of Burgundy and*
*Orleans, 593*
*† 595*

THEUDEBERT
*king of Austrasia, 595*
*† 612*

THEUDERIC
*king of Burgundy and Orleans, 595*
*king of Austrasia, 612*
*†613*

*3 sons killed on the*
*orders of* LOTHAR II

THEUDERIC III
*king of Neustria, 673–679*
*king of Austrasia, 697*
*† 690*

*his grandson*
THEUDERIC IV
*king 721–737*

363

13*

# GENEALOGICAL TABLE OF
# THE CAROLINGIANS

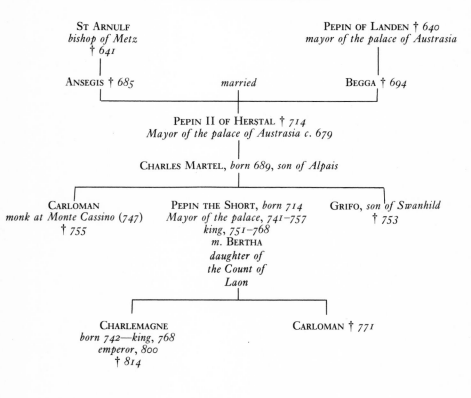

ST ARNULF
*bishop of Metz*
† *641*

PEPIN OF LANDEN † *640*
*mayor of the palace of Austrasia*

ANSEGIS † *685*          *married*          BEGGA † *694*

PEPIN II OF HERSTAL † *714*
*Mayor of the palace of Austrasia c. 679*

CHARLES MARTEL, *born 689, son of Alpais*

CARLOMAN
*monk at Monte Cassino (747)*
† *755*

PEPIN THE SHORT, *born 714*
*Mayor of the palace, 741–757*
*king, 751–768*
*m.* BERTHA
*daughter of*
*the Count of*
*Laon*

GRIFO, *son of Swanhild*
† *753*

CHARLEMAGNE
*born 742—king, 768*
*emperor, 800*
† *814*

CARLOMAN † *771*

# INDEX

Noyon, 290
— bishop of, 265
Numidia, 71–2
Numisius, 57

Octavianus, Emperor, 95
Octha, 206
Odilo, Duke of Bavaria, 321
Oghgul, isle of, 205
Oise, River, 309
'On his little Patrimony', 115
Orange, 29
— triumphal arch, 39
Order of Famous Cities, The, 99, 102
Orleans, 244–5, 294
— siege of, 177
Orosius, Paulus, 162
Otho, 55

Paderborn, 345
Palais des Arts, 50
— the, 100
Palestine, 162
Palladius, 297
Palmyra, princess of, 80
Pampeluna, 316, 345
Pannonia, 89, 139, 152, 172, 174, 212, 344
Pannonias, the, 219
Panthéon, the, 233
Papal States, creation of the, 336, 347
Papianilla, 181
Parentalia, 109
Paris, xxvii, 5, 30, 99, 127, 174–6, 233,
236–7, 239, 244, 255, 263
Parisii, the, 30, 211
Paul, 128
— (bishop of Verdun), 265
Paulinus, Bishop, 302
— Suetonius, 44–5
— Tiberious Claudius, 72–4
Paulus, Bishop of Narbonne, 127
Pavatius, the deacon, 129
Pavia, 326, 337
Pax Romana, 58, 62, 77

Pectorius, 125
Pelagius, 203
Peloponnese, the, 286
Pentapolis, 326
Pepin, 310, 312
— coronation of, 325
— house of, 269
— of Herstal, 267, 311
— — Landen, 267, 311
— the Short, 259, 268, 321–6, 336
— — — death of, 327
Pergamos, 121
Périgueux, 26
Persians, 78
— king of the, 354
Persicus, 51
Peter of Pisa, 334
— the Apostle, basilica of, 352
Petrocorii, the, 26
Pflaum, H. G., 70, 77
Pharsalia, 18
Phocaens, the, 23, 25
Phoebicius, 111
Phrygia, 70
Phrygians, 216
Picts, the, 46, 202–4, 297
Pippin, son of Charlemagne, 332
Piraeus, the, 217
Pius, 72, 85
— Antoninus, 70
— VII, 325, 354
Placidia, Princess, 162
Plautius, Aulus, 44
Plectruda, 313
Pliny the Elder, 20, 167
Plutarch, 12
Plutarch's Lives, 12
Po, 52
Poëte, Marcel, 99, 174
Poictiers, 111
Poitiers, 5, 93, 133, 140, 146–7, 229, 231,
247, 285, 288, 290, 313, 315–16
— Battle of, 315–17
— bishop of, 231, 256
— churches of, 145
Poitou, 260